Quilts from El's Attic

Eleanor Burns

For Patty
My Friend,
My Sister Forever.

First Edition
May, 2016
Published by Quilt in a Day®, Inc.
1955 Diamond Street, San Marcos, CA 92078

ISBN 1-945171-14-6

Art Director: Merritt Voigtlander

Contents

Introduction

For nearly 40 years I have been passionately collecting antique quilts. Recently, while adding a new acquisition to my cherished collection, I noticed a pattern I hadn't thought about in years, Dresden Plate. It struck me how much I enjoyed this pattern and how pretty it looked in vintage feedsack fabrics. It peaked my inspiration to look at countless other charming patterns that have been forgotten, Goose in the Pond, English Flower Garden, Ocean Waves, Spider Web, and more. I realized it would be fun to make a sampler quilt of these lovely old patterns, using a variety of modern techniques. I chose twelve of my favorite or unusual antique quilts to recreate. What a great time I had researching original patterns and designers. I was even inspired to finish pieces and parts of quilts left behind years ago.

Please join me as I "reinvent" these delightful patterns from a bygone era. On our journey, we'll learn different techniques, make "new" blocks, delight in their history, and finish with skills and a sampler quilt or a repeat pattern quilt worth bragging about.

Dig in your trunk and have a great time recreating quilts from the past.

Eleanor Burns

Antique Sampler Quilt *64" x 80"*
Pieced and Quilted by Unknown

While there is no positive proof, this quilt was in all likelihood made from patterns printed in weekly newspapers. The Kansas City Star began publishing patterns in September, 1928. Ruby Short McKim is credited with the idea of including a weekly pattern to increase women's readership. Quilting was gaining in popularity at the time and the patterns were a huge success. During the years of World War II, the patterns ran intermittently. The feature ended in 1961.

Fabric Selection

The fabric line featured in the Sampler Quilt on the right is *Forever Love* by Eleanor Burns and Benartex. Yardage and cutting chart is on next page. Cut all pieces for Sampler quilt at one time and bag individually, or cut one block at a time.

Hue

Begin by finding a Designer Fabric Collection which has already been coordinated for you. Start with one multi-colored piece which combines two or three of your main color families. By combining warm and cool colors, excitement is created as colors visually bounce off one another. Examples include red and blue, red and green, or blue and yellow. From your selected collection, choose twenty different fabrics.

Value

To create depth and contrast, choose a full range of values within each color family. Include light to light medium, medium, dark medium, and dark.

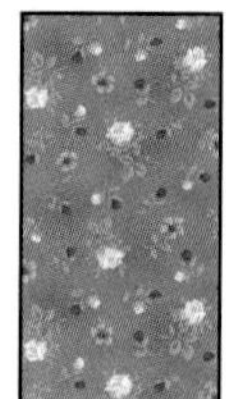

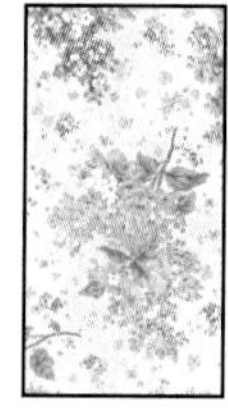

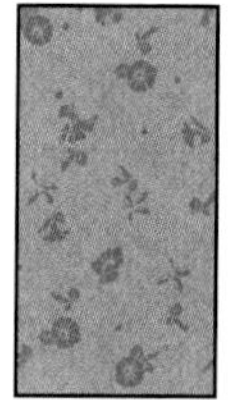

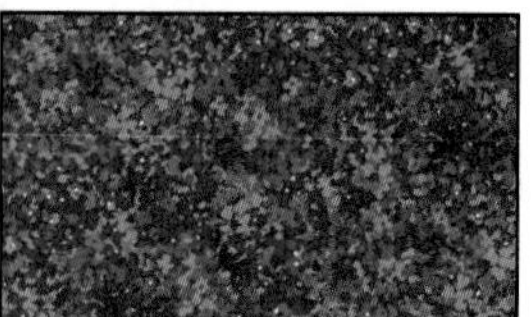

Intensity

Combine colors with the same degree of brightness or dullness. A small accent of a brighter color can make other colors pop.

Scale

To add richness and interest, look for variety in textures, and scales of prints. Select some fabrics that appear solid from a distance, and others with smaller scales. Large scale designs could be fussy cut as the Crows Nest or Fan Quarter Circles.

Balance

Create balance when planning the layout of your blocks. Place blocks with dominate colors or contrasting colors equally spaced throughout the design.

Pieced by Teresa Varnes
Quilted by Merry Jo Rembold

59" x 73"

Yardage and Cutting Chart for a Sampler 59" x 73"

Background	4½ yds
Border	(7) 7½" strips
	(1) 17" strip cut into
English Flower Garden	(1) 17" square
Dresden Plate	(1) 17" square
	(1) 9½" strips cut into
Spacers/Arrow & Crow's Nest	(3) 9½" x 7½"
Posey	(2) 9" squares
	(2) 8½" strips cut into
Scalloped Fan	(4) 8½" squares
Solid Squares	(2) 8½" squares
Spacers/Fan Baskets	(2) 5½" x 8½"
Fan Basket	(1) 6½" x 12½"
	(1) 7½" strip cut into
Posey	(4) 7½" squares
	(1) 5½" strip cut into
Fan Basket	(2) 5½" x 9½"
Fan Basket	(2) 5½" squares
Fan Basket	(1) 4" square
	(1) 5" strip cut int
Ocean Waves	(4) 5" squares
Arrow	(4) 4½" squares
	(1) 4" strip cut into
Goose in the Pond	(3) 4" x 8"
Crow's Nest	(1) 4" x 8"
	(2) 3¾" strips cut into
Spider Web	(3) 3¾" x 21"
	(1) 3½" strip cut into
Goose in the Pond	(5) 3½" squares
Arrow	(2) 3½" squares

	(1) 3" strip cut into
Dividers/ Arrow & Crow's Nest	(2) 3" x 16½"
Framing Two Posey	(4) 3" strips
	(2) 1¾" strips cut into
Spider Web	(3) 1¾" x 21"
Goose in the Pond	(2) 1½" strips
Crow's Nest	(1) 1½" x 21"
Arrow	(1) 1½" x 21"
Framing Goose in the Pond	(2) 1¼" strips

Light Weight Non-Woven Fusible Interfacing	**1½ yds**
Dresden Plate	(1) 15½" square
Dresden Plate	(1) 4½" x 8½"
English Flower Garden	(1) 4½" x 7½"
English Flower Garden	(1) 4½" x 6½"
Posey	(2) 8½" square
Posey	(2) 3" x 10"
Posey	(2) 3" x 12"
Fan Basket	(2) 3½" x 9"
Fan Basket	(2) 2" x 5½"

¾" Rick-Rack (Optional)	**4 yds**
Binding	**1 yd**
Backing	**5 yds**
Batting	**70" x 86"**

20 Fat Quarters from the *Forever Love* Fabric Line

1014103B

Ocean Wave	(1) 3" x 6"
Dresden Plate	(1) 3" x 5"
Scalloped Fan	(4) 2¾" x 6"
Ocean Wave	(1) 3" square

1014110B

Spider Web	(1) 3¾" x 21"
Spider Web	(1) 1¾" x 21"
Spider Web	(2) 3½"squares
Ocean Waves	(1) 3" x 6"
Dresden Plate	(1) 3" x 5"

1014122B

Posey	(2) 8½" squares
Ocean Waves	(1) 3" x 6"
Dresden Plate	(1) 3 x 5"

1014150B

English Flwr Grdn	(1) 4½" square
Ocean Waves	(1) 3" x 6"
Dresden Plate	(1) 3" x 5"
Ocean Waves	(1) 3" square

1014202B

Ocean Waves	(1) 3" x 6"
Dresden Plate	(1) 3" x 5"
Ocean Waves	(1) 3" square
Scalloped Fan	(4) 2¾" x 6"

1014210B

Ocean Waves	(1) 3" x 6"
Ocean Waves	(1) 3" square

1014222B

Scalloped Fan	(4) 2¾" x 6"
English Flwr Grdn	(1) 4½" square
Ocean Waves	(1) 3" x 6"
Dresden Plate	(1) 3" x 5"
Spider Web	(2) 3½" squares
Spider Web	(1) 3¾" x 21"
Spider Web	(1) 1¾" x 21"

1014223B

Goose in the Pond	(3) 1½" x 21"
Ocean Waves	(1) 3" x 6"
Dresden Plate	(1) 3" x 5"

1014727B

Fan Basket	(1) 3¾" x 12"
Ocean Waves	(1) 3" x 6"

1014722B

Ocean Waves	(1) 3" x 6"
Dresden Plate	(1) 3" x 5"
Ocean Waves	(1) 3" square

1014327B

Ocean Wave	(1) 3" x 6"
Dresden Plate	(1) 3" x 5"
Scalloped Fan	(4) 2¾" x 6"
English Flwr Grdn	(1) 4½" square

1014750B

Ocean Waves	(1) 3" x 6"
Dresden Plate	(1) 3" x 5"

1014248B

Posey	(2) 3" x 12"
Ocean Waves	(1) 3" x 6"
Dresden Plate	(1) 3" x 5"
Posey	(2) 1"x 11" Bias

1014255B

Crow's Nest	(2) 1½" x 21"
Crow's Nest	(1) 4" x 8"
Scalloped Fan	(4) 2¾" x 6"
Ocean Waves	(1) 3" x 6"
Dresden Plate	(1) 3" x 5"
Crow's Nest	(1) 3½" square
Ocean Waves	(1) 3" square

1014310B

Arrow	(4) 1½"x 21"
Arrow	(4) 4½" square
Scalloped Fan	(4) 2¾" x 6"
Ocean Waves	(1) 3" x 6"
Dresden Plate	(1) 3" x 5"
Ocean Waves	(1) 3" square

1014548B

Spider Web	(1) 3¾" x 21"
Spider Web	(1) 1¾" x 21"
Spider Web	(2) 3½" squares
Ocean Waves	(1) 3" x 6"

1014522B

Posey	(2) 3" x 10"
Ocean Waves	(1) 3" x 6"
Dresden Plate	(1) 3" x 5"

1014510B

Dresden Plate	(1) 6" x 10"
Dresden Plate	(1) 4½" x 8½"
English Flwr Grdn	(1) 4½" x 6½"
English Flwr Grdn	(1) 4½" square
Fan Basket	(2) 1⅜" x 10"
Fan Basket	(2) 1⅜" x 11½"
Fan Basket	(1) 4" Square
Scalloped Fan	(4) 4" Squares
Ocean Waves	(1) 3" x 6"

1014548B

English Flwr Grdn	(1) 4½" x 7½"
Ocean Waves	(1) 3" x 6"
Dresden Plate	(1) 3" x 5"
English Flwr Grdn	(2) 1" x 11" Bias

1014555B

Goose in the Pond	(3) 4" x 8"
English Flwr Grdn	(2) 4½" squares
Fan Basket	(1) 3¾" x 12"
Ocean Waves	(1) 3" x 6"
Dresden Plate	(1) 3" x 5"
Ocean Waves	(1) 3" square

Supplies

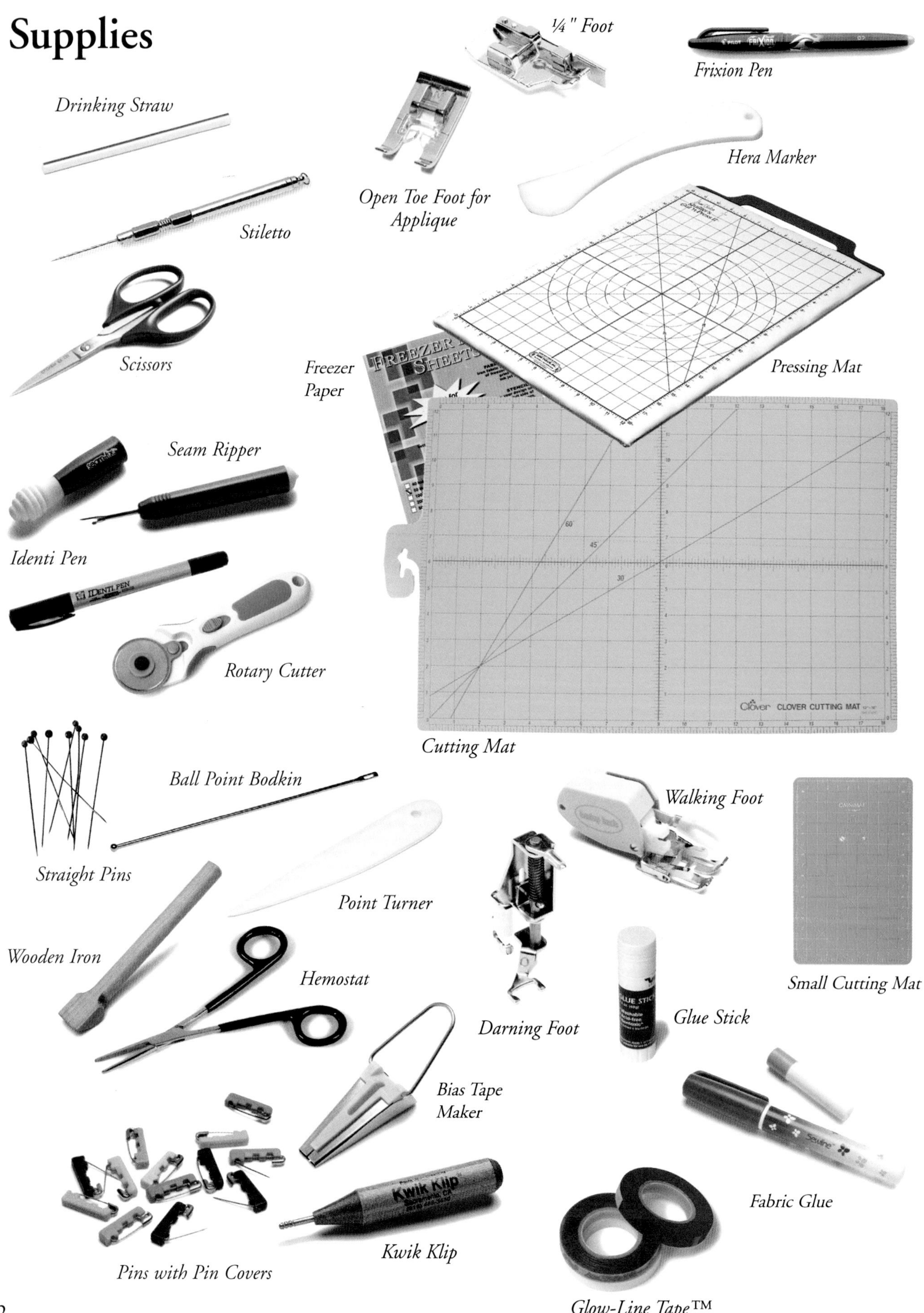

Drinking Straw
Stiletto
Scissors
Seam Ripper
Identi Pen
Rotary Cutter
Straight Pins
Ball Point Bodkin
Point Turner
Wooden Iron
Hemostat
Pins with Pin Covers
Kwik Klip
Bias Tape Maker
¼" Foot
Open Toe Foot for Applique
Frixion Pen
Hera Marker
Freezer Paper
Pressing Mat
Cutting Mat
CLOVER CUTTING MAT
Walking Foot
Darning Foot
Glue Stick
Small Cutting Mat
Fabric Glue
Glow-Line Tape™

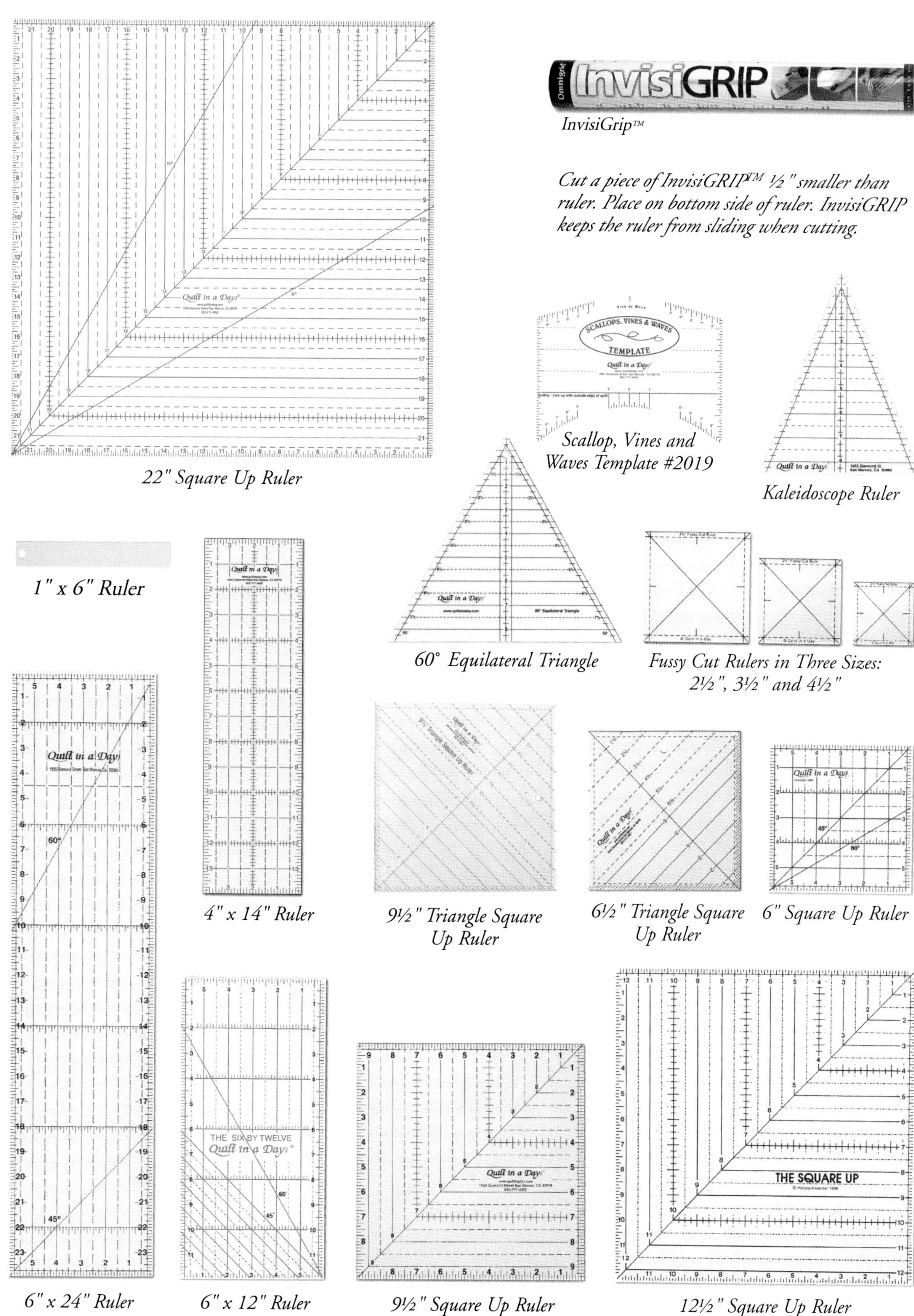

22" Square Up Ruler

InvisiGrip™

Cut a piece of InvisiGRIP™ ½" smaller than ruler. Place on bottom side of ruler. InvisiGRIP keeps the ruler from sliding when cutting.

Scallop, Vines and Waves Template #2019

Kaleidoscope Ruler

1" x 6" Ruler

60° Equilateral Triangle

Fussy Cut Rulers in Three Sizes: 2½", 3½" and 4½"

4" x 14" Ruler

9½" Triangle Square Up Ruler

6½" Triangle Square Up Ruler

6" Square Up Ruler

6" x 24" Ruler

6" x 12" Ruler

9½" Square Up Ruler

12½" Square Up Ruler

Optional: Shape Cut Plus

Quilt Show

Flower and Vine Border Sampler *58" x 58"*
Pieced by Teresa Varnes
Quilted by Amie Potter

For her stunning composition, Teresa chose to feature a Dresden Plate as her center medallion. She surrounded it with Ocean Waves and Spider Web blocks. To complete her center, she added Traditional Fan blocks to each corner. The addition of a flower and vine appliqued border add just the right finishing touch.

Shadow Play *52" x 68"*
Pieced and quilted by Linda Woll

The use of black, gray and white with just a hint of color are perfect in Linda's shadow play quilt. This alluring quilt has bold, contemporary flair with a pieced binding to frame the quilt to perfection.

Whimsical Garden 48" x 48"

Pieced and Quilted by Marilyn Belt

Her use of bright, joyful color on white background resulted in a contemporary quilt worthy of notice. Her white arrows really stand out and add to the whimsy of Marilyn's quilt.

Sunny Side Up *59" x 65"*
Pieced and Quilted by Laurie Thomas

Bright yellow and turquoise fabrics are highlighted against the crisp, white background in Laurie's Sampler. She framed her blocks with a scrappy border to continue her color play and balance her quilt.

Flower Show 41" x 45"
Pieced by Patricia Knoechel
Quilted by Amie Potter

For her dainty flower display, Patricia chose Eleanor's newest fabric collection "Forever Love". from Benartex.The blocks are appliqued with dimension added in the ribbon bows, crocheted doily, and yo yo flowers.

Dresden Plate Panache *64" x 76"*
Pieced and quilted by Linda Carlson

With bright shades of pink and lime green on a cream background, Linda's Dresden Plates really stand out! She chose to add abbreviated Arrow blocks between the plates for added appeal.

Dresden Plate Quilt

Published in 1933, this McCall Pattern contained transfer designs and a printed tissue paper pattern for quilting blocks and border. The instructions required the quilter to stamp the transfer for the pattern pieces on cardboard using carbon paper, then cut the required number of fabric pieces from the cardboard templates. The pattern envelope contained two quilt designs, Dresden Plate and Fan Quilt. Including complete directions for making each quilt and quilting.

Vintage Dresden Plate Quilt *60" x 60"*
Pieced by Teresa Varnes
Hand Quilted by Arleen Meyer

This quilt started as a diamond in the rough. Its original owner cut the fabric shapes from templates by McCall Pattern Company, dated Feb. 10, 1940. The pattern cost 35 cents. She used a variety of feed sacks, probably from the 1930's or 1940's. She tucked all the pieces away and never stitched the top together. Fast forward to 2015 when the pieces were acquired by Quilt in a Day, and stitched into this lovely, vibrant quilt by Teresa Varnes and hand quilted by Arleen Meyer from Alma, Kansas. Truly a treasure that took over 50 years from start to finish!

Dresden Plate

Fabric Selection

Select solid fabric or one that reads solid for Background. Prints should contrast with Background. Make dominant print the darkest print for Pointed Templates and Ovals. Select sixteen different medium prints for Curved Templates. Mix values and scales of prints.

Cutting Chart for One Block

Finished Size 16" Square

Background	
	(1) 17" square
Non-Woven Fusible Interfacing	
Plate	(1) 16½" square
Ovals	(1) 4½" x 8½"
Dominant Fabric	
Four Pointed Templates	(1) 6" x 10"
Four Ovals	(1) 4½" x 8½"
Sixteen Curved Templates	(1) 3" x 5" of sixteen different Prints

Supplies

Marking pen
Glue Stick
Template Plastic
28mm Rotary Cutter (Optional)
Small Scissors
Wooden Iron
Point Turner
Ball Point Bodkin
Drinking Straw
Stiletto
4" x 14" Ruler
Open Toe Foot

Making Patterns

1. Photo copy patterns found in back of book.
2. Rough cut around patterns.
3. Glue patterns to template plastic.

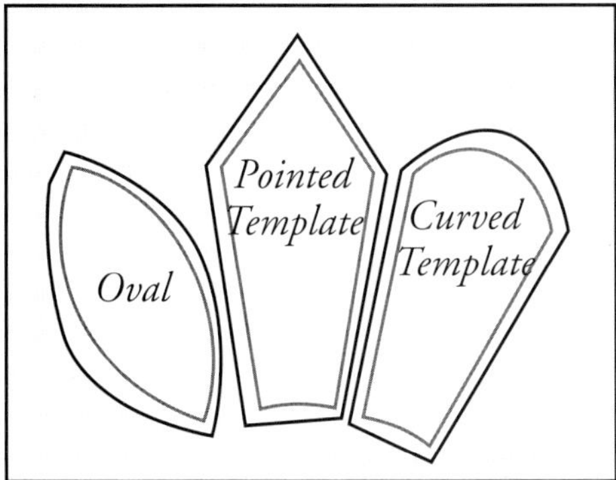

4. Cut on lines.

Making Four Pointed Templates

1. Trace four Pointed Templates on wrong side of 6" x 10" focus fabric with marker.

2. Cut straight lines and points with 4" x 14" ruler.

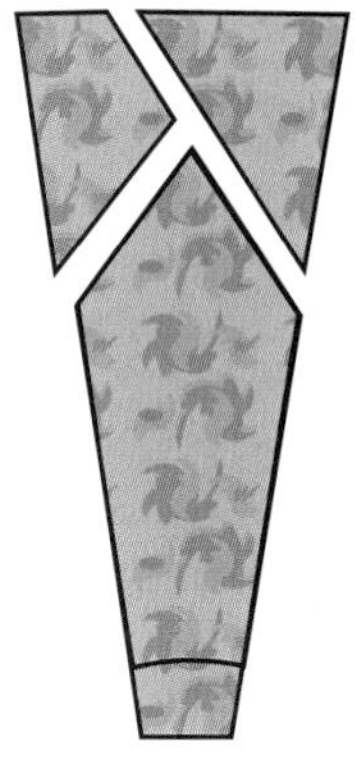

3. Cut bottom curve with 28mm rotary cutter or small scissors.

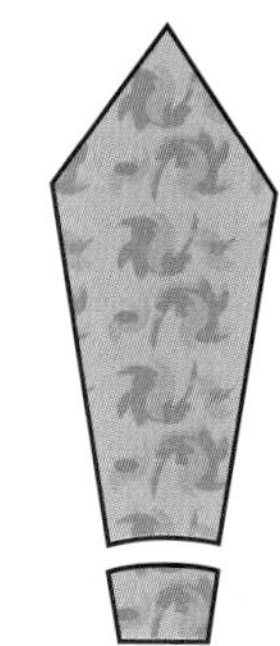

Making Sixteen Curved Templates

1. Make four stacks of sixteen different prints with wrong side up.
2. Trace one Curved Template on top fabric in each stack.

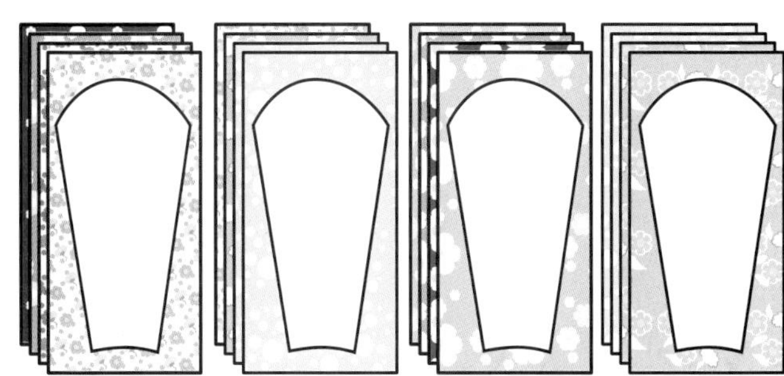

3. Layer cut straight lines with 4" x 14" ruler.

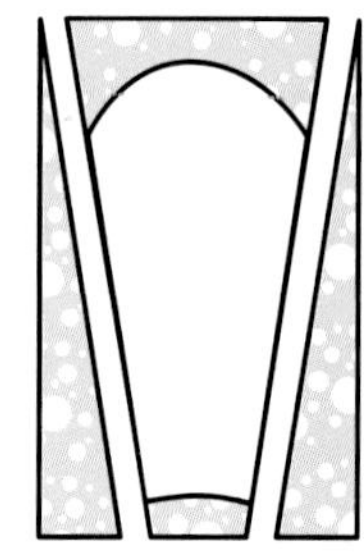
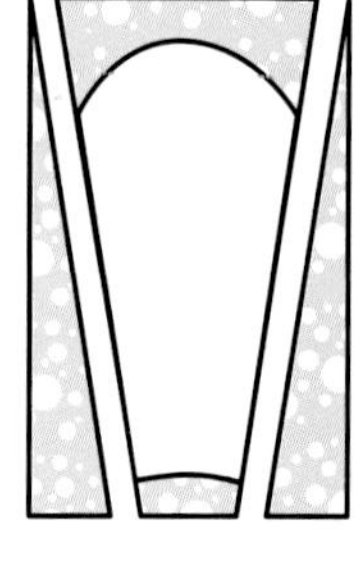

4. Layer cut top and bottom curve with 28mm rotary cutter or small scissors.

Sewing Plate Together

1. Lay out circle with four dark Pointed Templates in position, and four Curved Templates between each one.

2. Work on group of four **Curved Templates** at a time.
3. Flip pairs right sides together.
4. Assembly-line sew with accurate ¼" seam. Clip apart.

Do not use a scant ¼" seam.

5. Open. Do not press seams. Seams are pressed after circle is completed.
6. Sew pairs together.

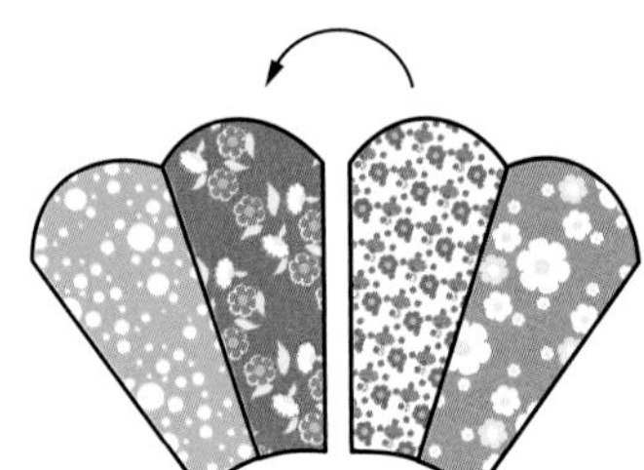

7. Place back in circle. Complete three remaining groups of four.

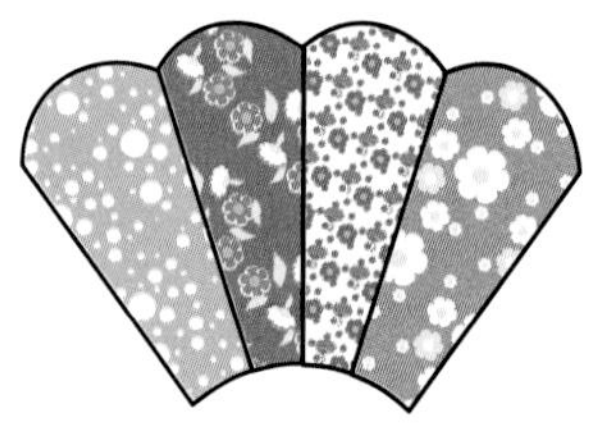

8. Lay out each group of four Curved Templates with Pointed Templates.

9. Flip Pointed Template right sides together to group of four Curved Templates. Sew.

10. Sew second set of Curved Templates to Pointed Template.

11. Continue sewing Plate together.

Finishing Dresden Plate

1. From wrong side, press seams open. *It's easier to open seams with fingernails before pressing with an iron.*
2. Place 16½" square of interfacing with bumpy fusible side up. Center circle on fusible interfacing with wrong side up. Pin each Template to interfacing.
3. Lighten presser foot pressure. Sew around outside edge with ⅛" seam and sew with 20 stitches to the inch. Pivot with needle down on seams.

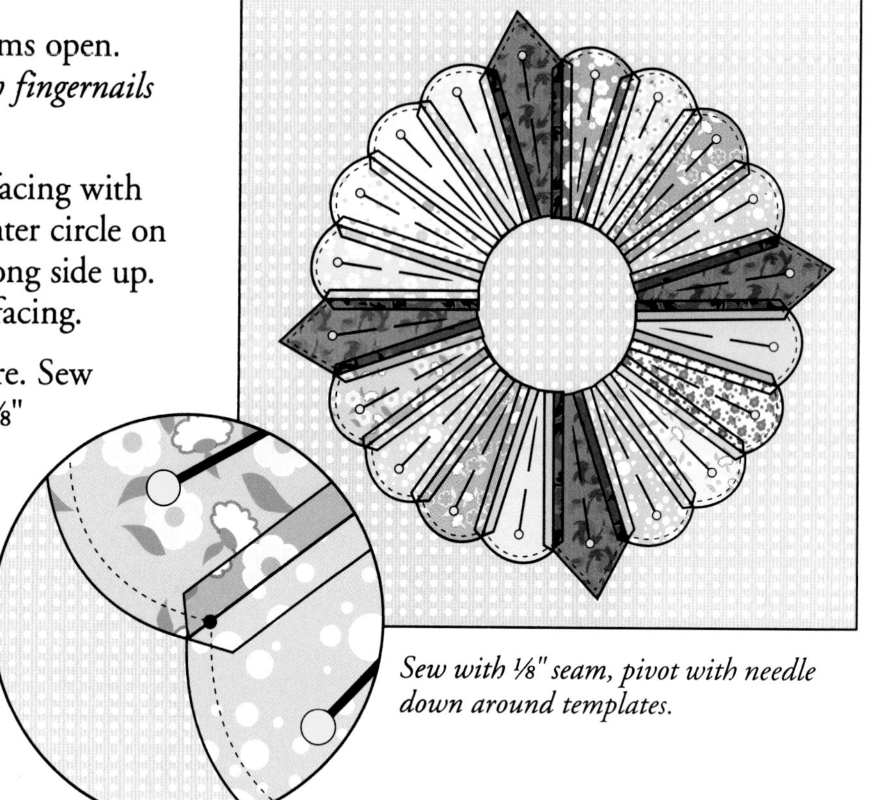

Sew with ⅛" seam, pivot with needle down around templates.

4. Trim fusible interfacing around outside edge of Circle. Carefully clip at each seam so Plate easily turns right side out.
5. Cut out circle from middle of interfacing.

6. Turn right side out through hole in middle.
7. From inside, push out curved edges with Point Turner. Gently push out points with pointed end of Point Turner.

8. From right side, gently pick out points with stiletto.

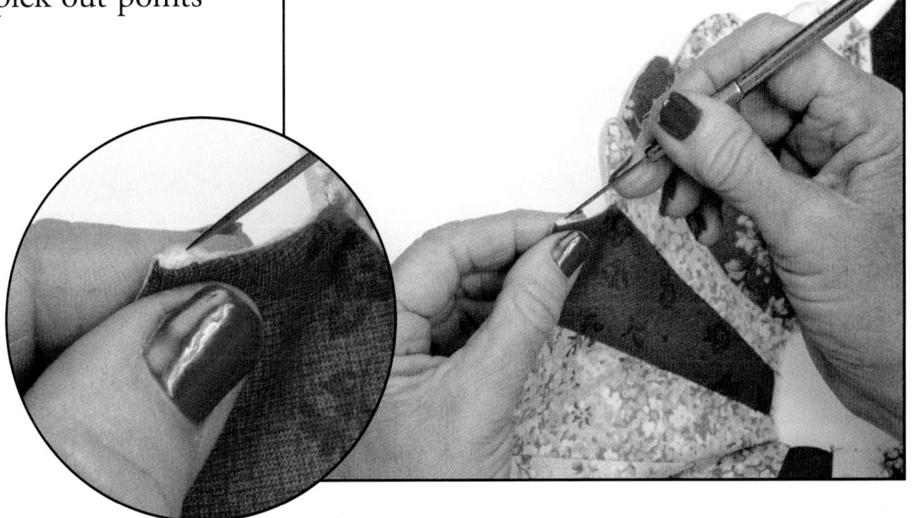

9. Smooth Plate so it lays flat.

Making Four Pointed Ovals

1. Place 4½" x 8½" **fusible interfacing smooth side up** on top of paper to protect table surface from markings.
2. Trace four Ovals with marker. Leave ½" space between each Oval.

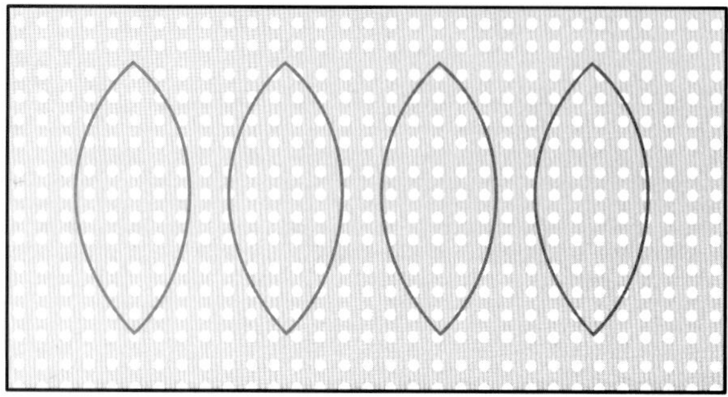

3. Place Oval fabric right side up.
4. Place fusible side of interfacing against right side of fabric. Pin.
5. Sew on lines with 20 stitches per inch. Overlap beginning and ending stitches.

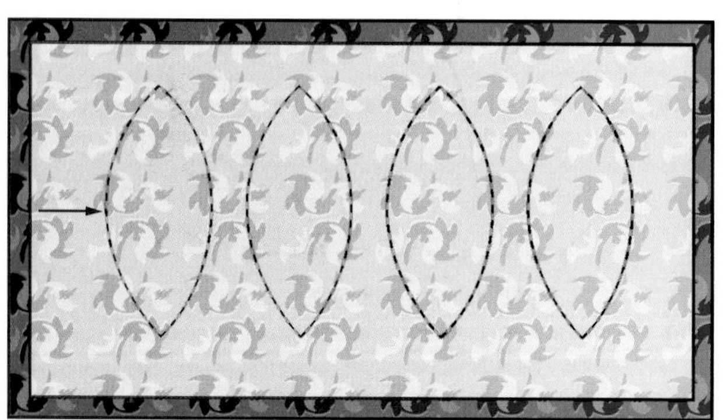

Start sewing on side of Oval.

6. From interfacing side, trim ⅛" away from stitches.

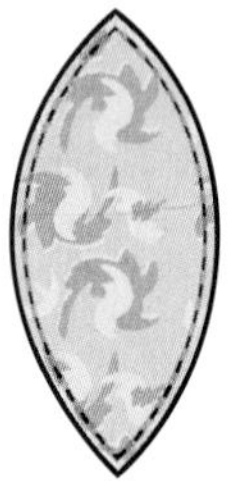
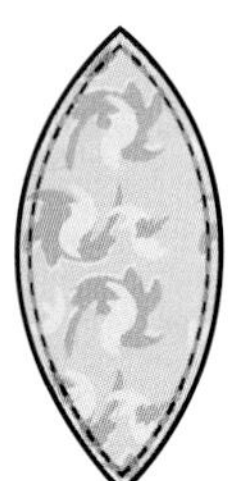
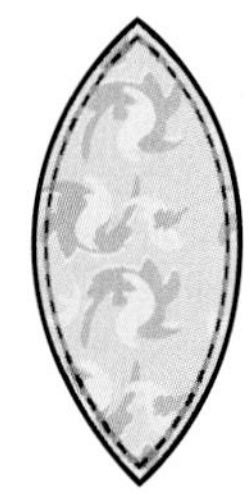
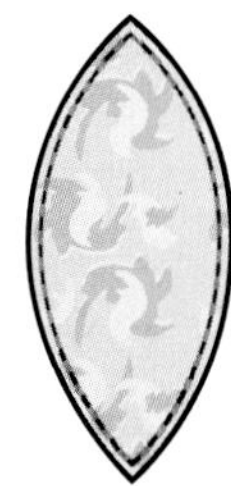

7. Cut a small slit in interfacing.

8. Insert drinking straw into one point.

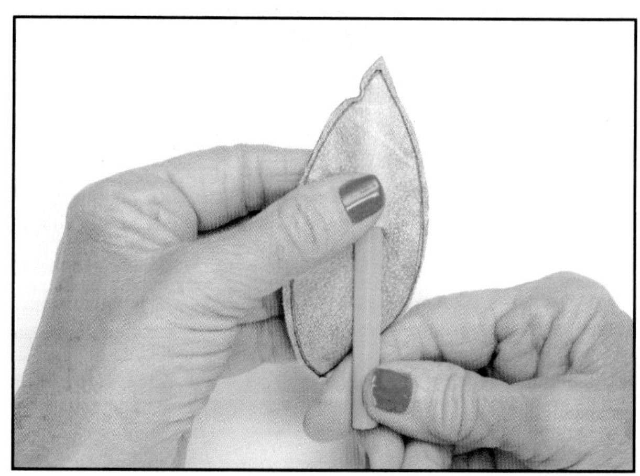

9. Stretch fabric over end of straw.
10. Place ball of bodkin on stretched fabric.

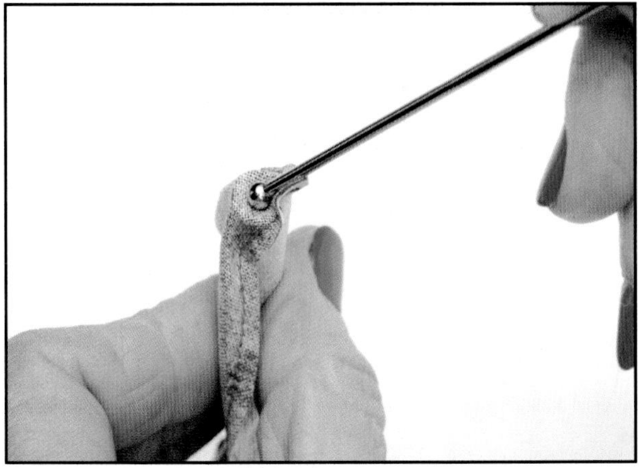

11. Gently push fabric into straw about 1" with bodkin. This technique begins to turn the oval.

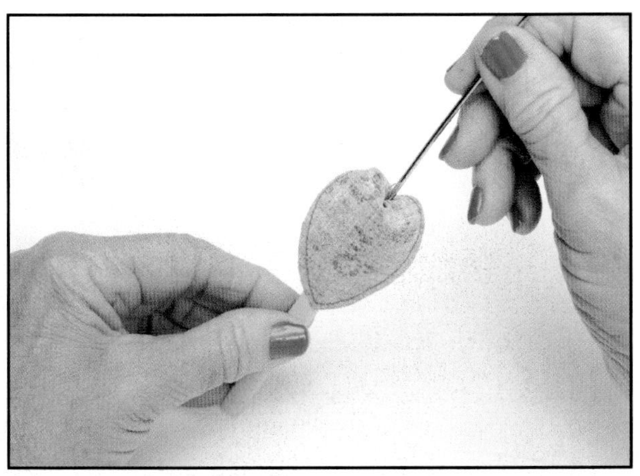

12. Remove straw and bodkin. Repeat turning other point.
13. Finish turning with fingers.

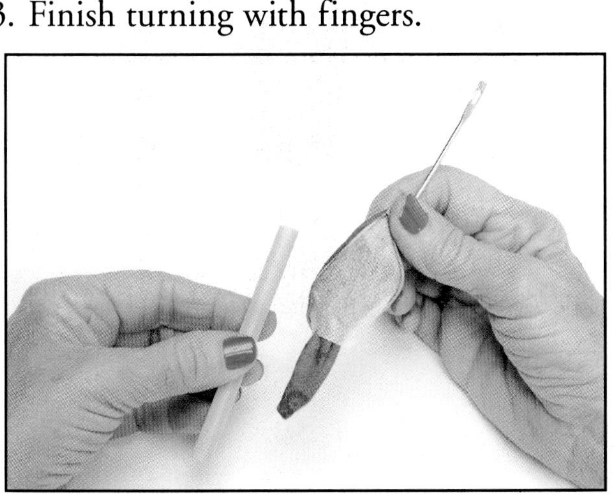

14. Carefully push out edges by running bodkin around inside.

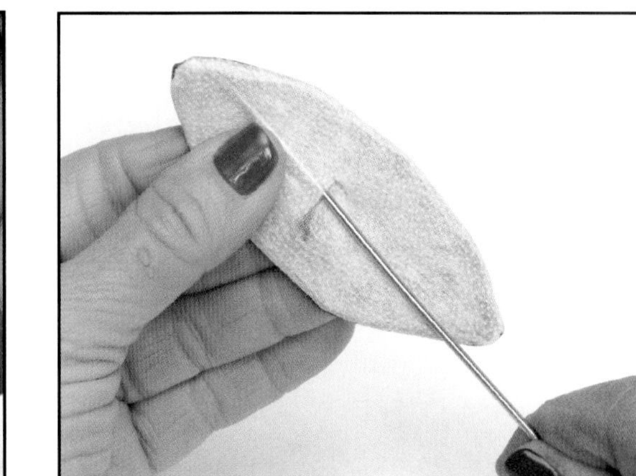

15. Pick out points with stiletto or pin.

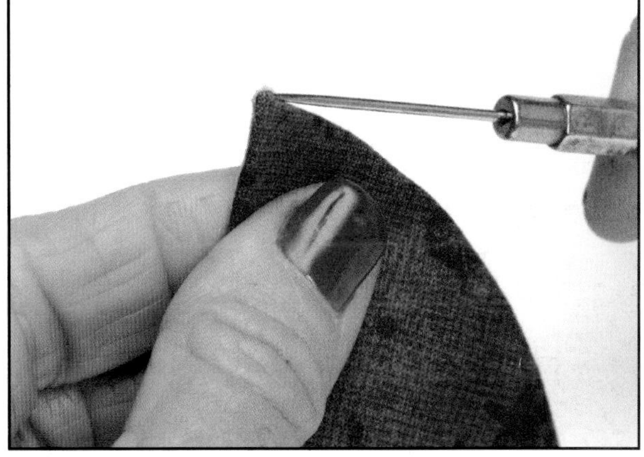

16. Press edges with wooden iron, or press on appliqué pressing sheet.

Adding Plate to Background

1. Fold 17" square Background in half and crease edges. Fold in half opposite way and crease edges. Open flat on pressing mat.
2. Carefully center Plate on Background square, lining up Points with folds.

3. Position two Ovals right side up from Pointed Template to Pointed Template. Cover raw edges.

If edges of Plate show under Points, trim out with scissors.

4. Repeat with last two Ovals. Steam press in place from right side. Steam press from wrong side.

5. Use matching thread for top and bobbin. Set machine for a blind hem stitch or blanket stitch, adjusting for a narrow bite.
6. Sew on inside edge of Ovals. Stitch around outside edge of Ovals, sewing a circle.
7. With thread matching Background, stitch around outside edges of plate, pivoting at points with needle down.

Option: Sew around Plate and Ovals by hand with hidden appliqué stitch.

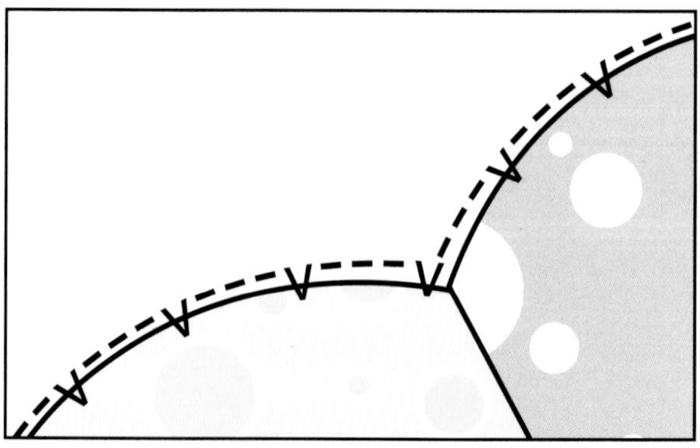

Straight stitches go in the Background, and the bite goes in the Ovals and Templates.

Antique Dresden Plate Table Runner

Pieced and Quilted
by Ruth Watts
25" x 55"

While browsing through old family photo albums, Sue Bouchard noticed a picture of this Dresden Plate Table Runner and realized her mother had given the actual Runner to her years before. The Table Runner was made by Ruth Watts, Sue's maternal grandmother who lived on a farm in Mt. Pleasant, Iowa. The Table Runner is made of feed sacks and is hand quilted with fine, even stitches.

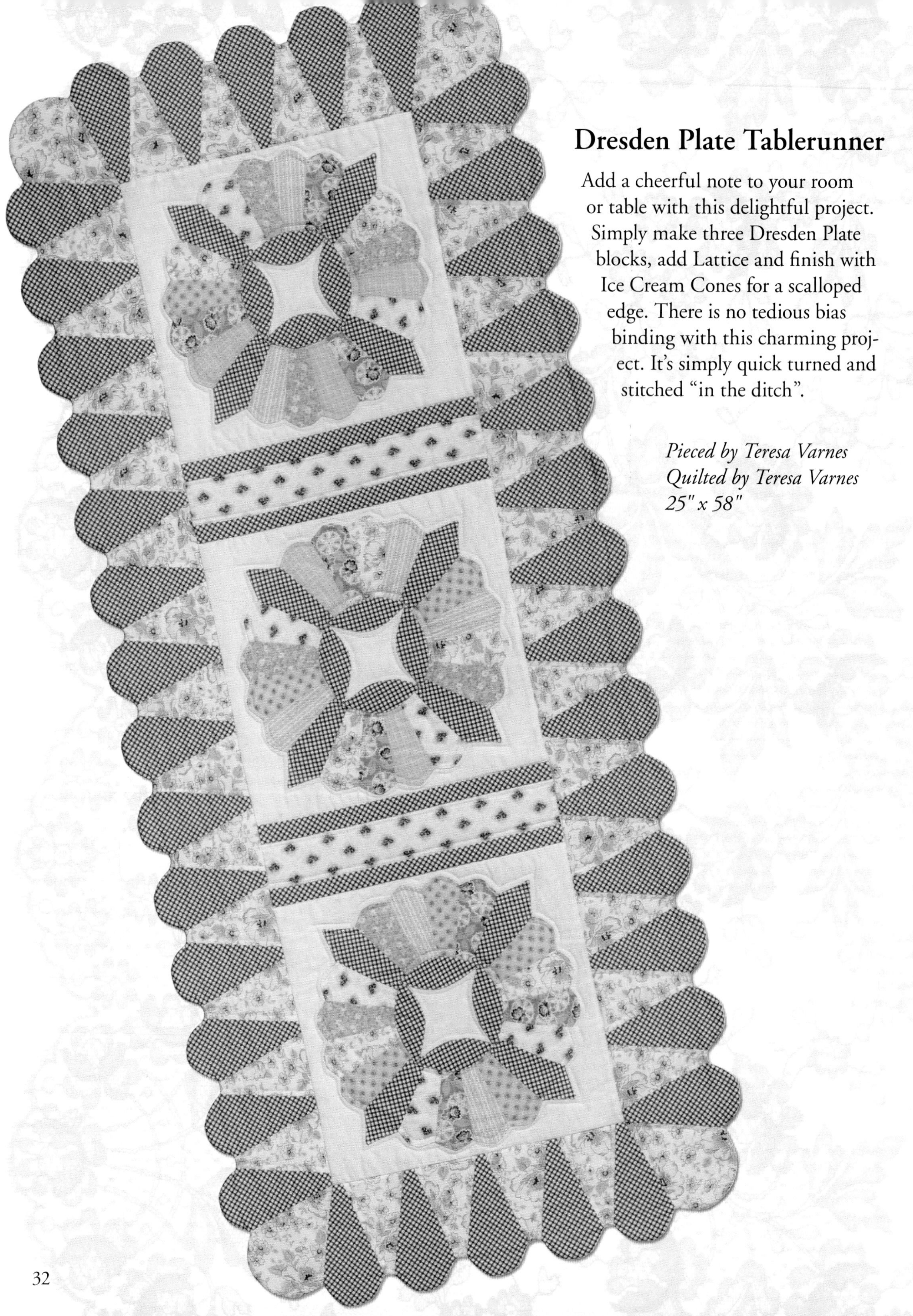

Dresden Plate Tablerunner

Add a cheerful note to your room or table with this delightful project. Simply make three Dresden Plate blocks, add Lattice and finish with Ice Cream Cones for a scalloped edge. There is no tedious bias binding with this charming project. It's simply quick turned and stitched "in the ditch".

Pieced by Teresa Varnes
Quilted by Teresa Varnes
25" x 58"

Dresden Plate Table Runner

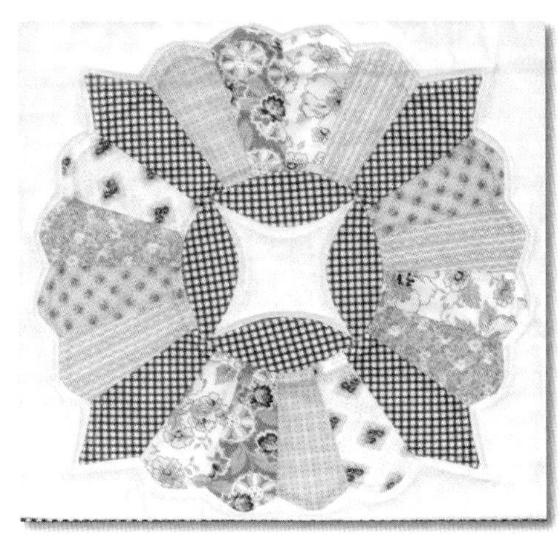

Fabric Selection

Select solid fabric or one that reads solid for Background. It should contrast with prints. Make dominant print the darkest print for Pointed Templates, Ovals and Lattice. Select sixteen different medium prints for Curved Templates. Mix values and scales of prints. Notice the orientation of the Pointed Templates.

Yardage and Cutting Chart for Table Runner

	Finished Size 25" x 58"
Background	**1 yd** (3) 14½" x 15½"
Non-Woven Fusible Interfacing	**1⅓ yds**
Plate	(3) 16½" squares
Ovals	(3) 4½" x 8½"
Focus Print	**½ yd**
Twelve Pointed Wedges	(1) 6½" strip
Twelve Ovals	(1) 4½" strip
Lattice	(2) 1⅛" strips
Forty-eight Curved Wedges	**⅛ yd of Sixteen Prints** (1) 3" x 15" from each
Dark Ice Cream Cone Border	**⅔ yd**
Rounded Cone	(3) 6½" strips cut into (38) Rounded Cones
Lattice	**¼ yd** (1) 1¾" strip
Light Ice Cream Cone Border	**½ yd**
Flat Cone	(2) 5" strips cut into (34) Flat Cones
Corner Cones	(1) 7" x 16" cut into (4) Corner Cones
Backing	**2 yds**
Batting	**32" x 66"**

Ice Cream Cone Border

1. Make three Dresden Plates using instructions from pages 22 – 30.
2. Carefully center Plates on 14½" x 15½" Background fabric. Pointed Wedges are pointing toward corners.

Cutting Thirty-four Flat Cones

1. Open two 5" print strips wrong side up, layer, and press.
2. Place template on strip, lining up top and bottom. Trace straight lines, alternating direction of template each time.

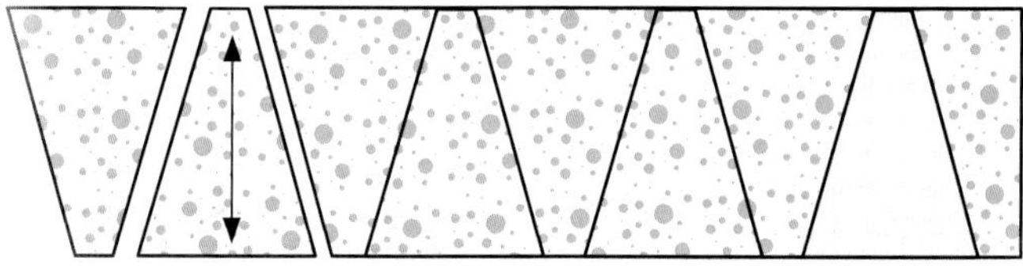

3. Layer cut on lines with ruler and rotary cutter.
4. Stack right side up.

Cutting Four Corner Cones

1. Trace four Corner Cones on wrong side of 7" x 16" print fabric, alternating direction of template each time.

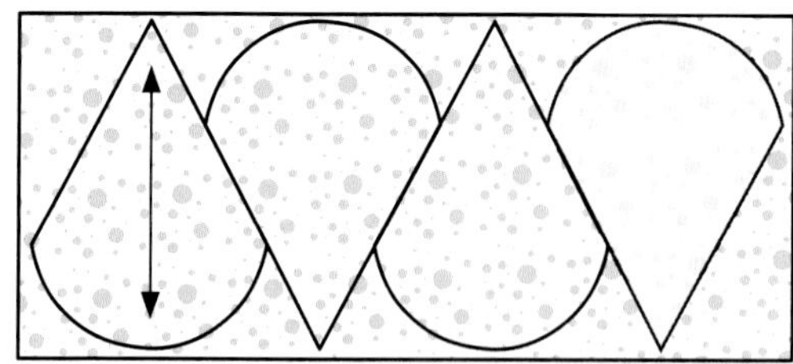

2. Cut on straight lines with 4" x 14" ruler and rotary cutter.

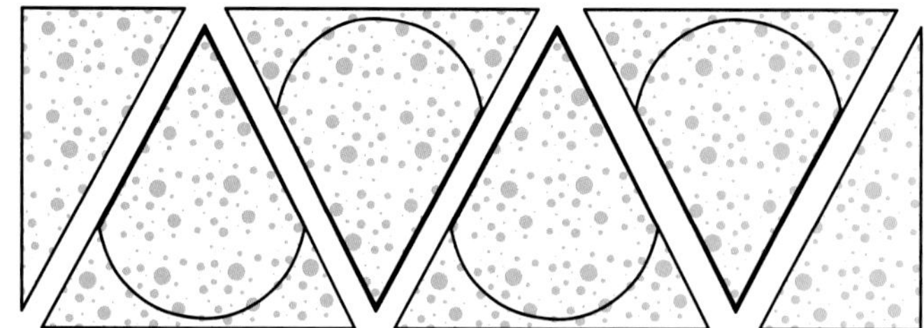

3. Cut curves with scissors.

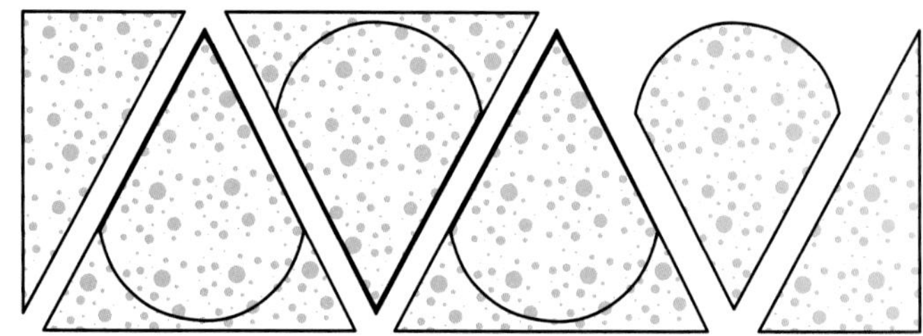

4. Stack four right side up.

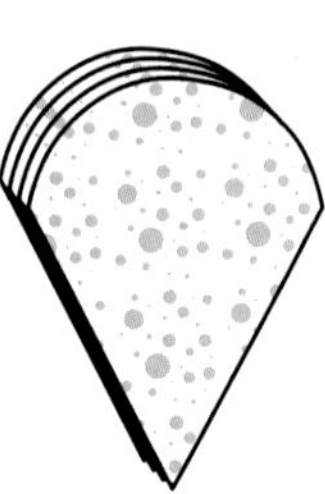

Cutting Thirty-eight Rounded Cones

1. Fold 6½" print strips in half right sides together, layer, and press.
2. Place template on strip, following grain line. Trace lines, alternating direction of template each time.

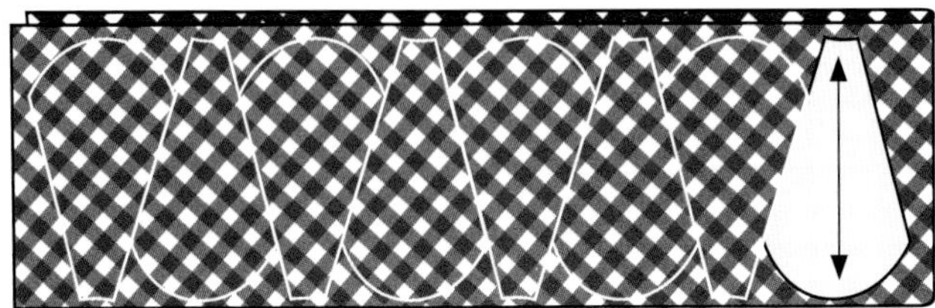

3. Layer cut on straight lines with ruler and rotary cutter.

4. Layer cut curves with scissors. Trim bottom.
5. Stack right side up.

Sewing Two Ends

1. Make two stacks right side up, with eight in each stack.

Place eight in each stack.

2. Flip Flat Cone right sides together to Rounded Cone, and center.

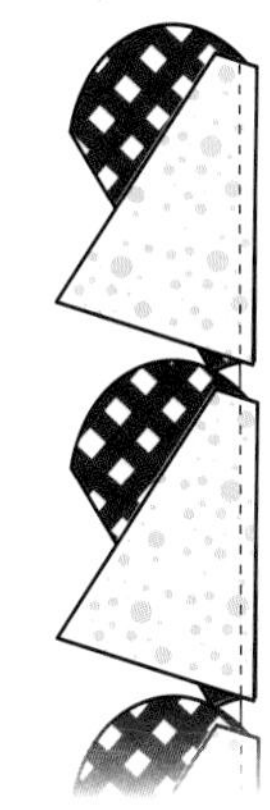

3. Assembly-line sew into pairs, using ¼" seam allowance.
4. Finger press seams open. Press seams with iron.

5. Place stacks of two pairs, with four in each stack. Flip right sides together.

Place four in each stack

6. Assembly-line sew pairs.

7. Sew into two groups of four. Press seams open.
8. Sew Rounded Cone to right end of each. Press seams open.

Sewing Four Corners

1. Place Corner Cones on both ends.
2. Flip right sides together.

3. Line up top edges.
4. Let ¼" tip hang out on bottom edge.

5. Sew Corner Cones to both ends.

Sewing Two Sides

1. Make two stacks right side up, with twenty-six in each stack.
2. Flip Flat Cone right sides together to Rounded Cone, and center.

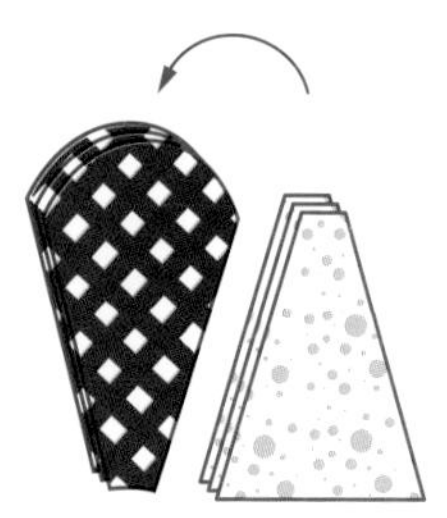

Place 26 in each stack.

3. Assembly-line sew into pairs.

4. Press seams open.

5. Assembly-line sew into two groups of thirteen. Press seams open.
6. Sew Round Cone to right end.

7. Press seams open.

Make two groups of fourteen Rounded Cones.

Sewing Lattice Together

1. Place 1¼" Red strips with 1¾" light strips.
2. Sew with ¼" seam.

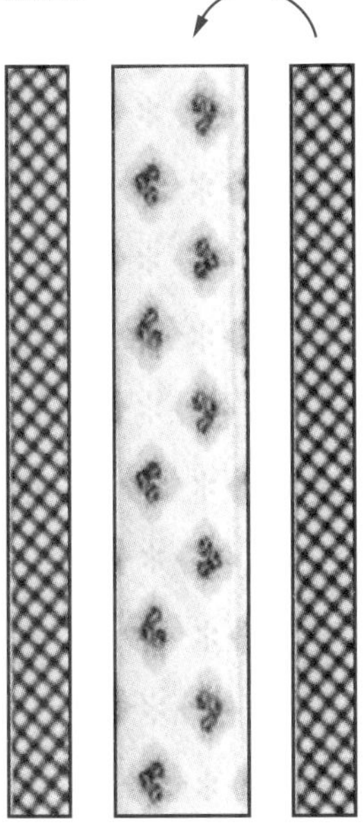

3. Set seams with Focus fabric on top. Open, and press seams toward Focus fabric.

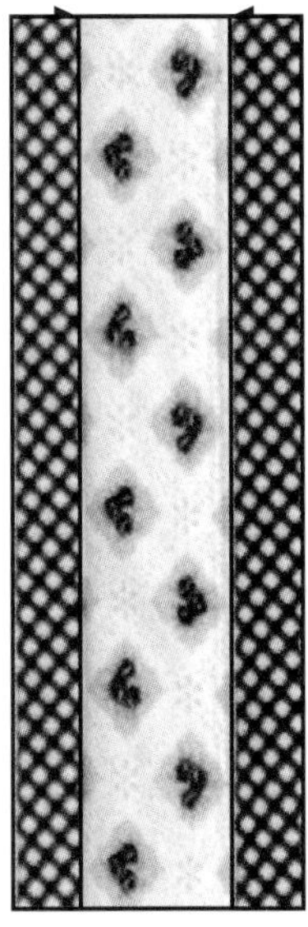

4. Cut Lattice into two 15½" strips, or width of block.
5. Flip Lattice right sides together to block. Sew and press seams towards Lattice.

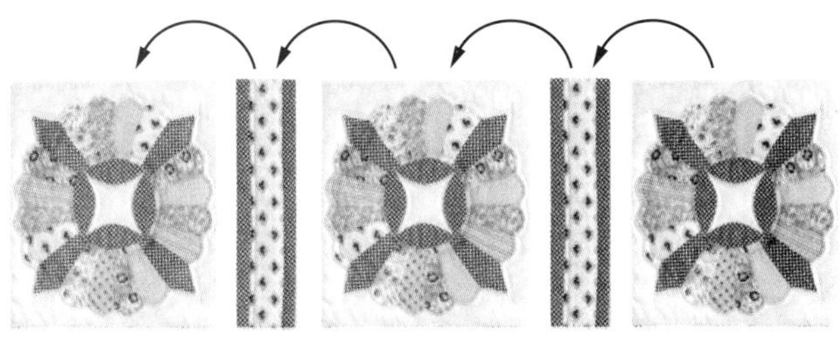

Sewing Top Together

1. Lay out Center right side up.
2. Turn Sides, Top, and Bottom wrong side up.

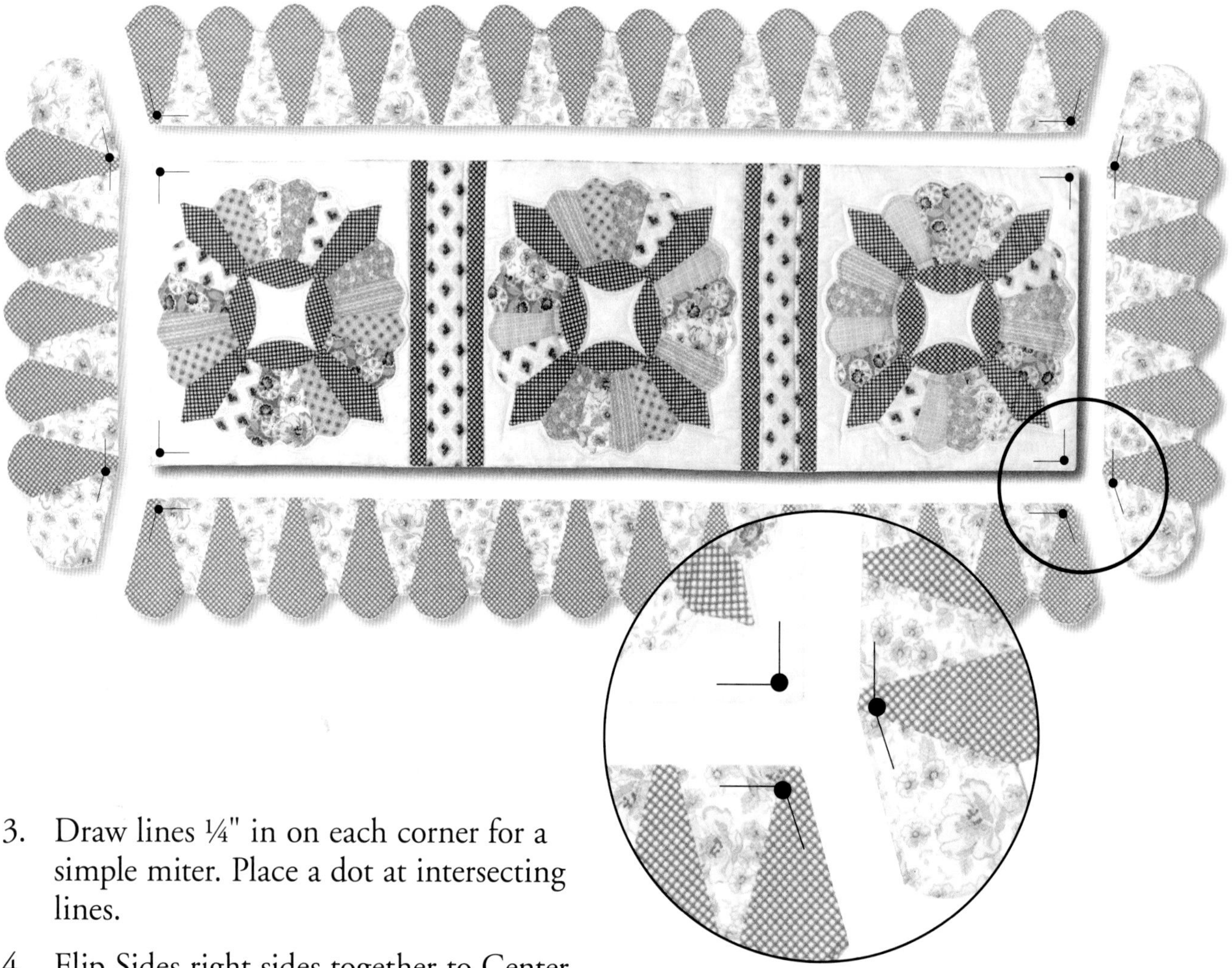

3. Draw lines ¼" in on each corner for a simple miter. Place a dot at intersecting lines.
4. Flip Sides right sides together to Center.
5. Pin to fit end to end.
6. Sew, stopping at dot ¼" in from each end.
7. Set seams with Center on top. Open, and press seams toward Center.
8. Repeat pinning and sewing Top and Bottom, stopping at dot ¼" in from each end.
9. Set seams with Center on top. Open, and press seams toward Center.

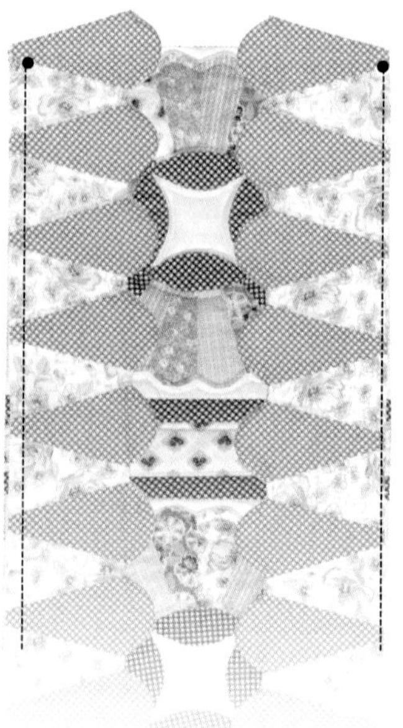

10. At each corner, fold Rounded Cone right sides together to Corner Cone. Match and pin dots. Sew from dot to outside edge.

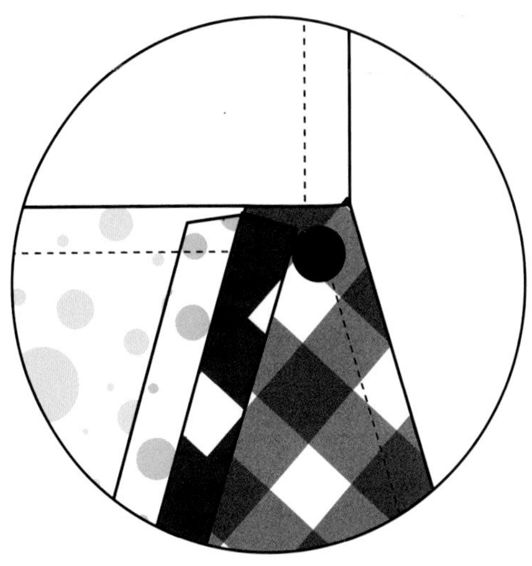

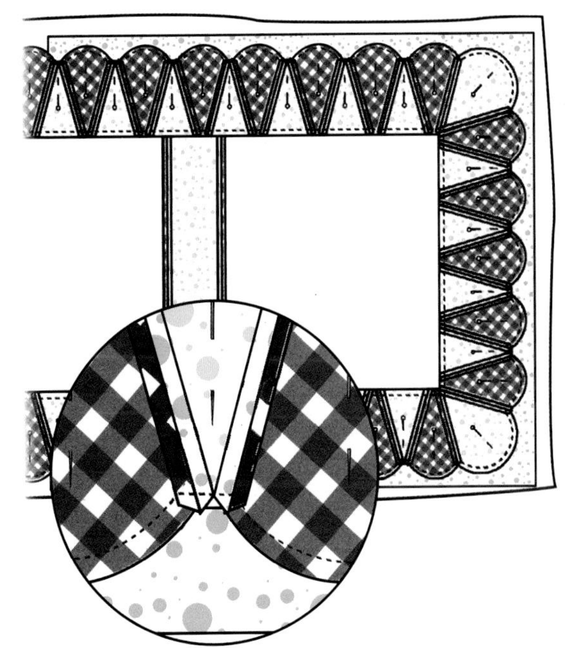

Leave open.

Quick Turning Table Runner

1. Piece Backing together.
2. Spread batting on large table. Spread backing on batting right side up. Smooth layers, tape or clamp to table.
3. Center Table Runner, right side down.
4. Pin layers together.
5. Sew around outside edge with ¼" seam.
6. Leave an opening of Three Rounded Cones in the center of one side.
7. Trim batting and backing along edge of Rounded Cones. Do not clip.
8. Turn right side out through opening. Smooth layers together.
9. Use curved edge of point turner to push out curves. Pull out edge of Flat Cone.

Turning In Seam on Opening

1. Topstitch ¼" in on raw edge of opening with a long stitch, or 3.0.
2. Repeat ¼" topstitching on batting/backing side.
3. Turn in raw edges on topstitches.
4. Slip stitch opening shut.

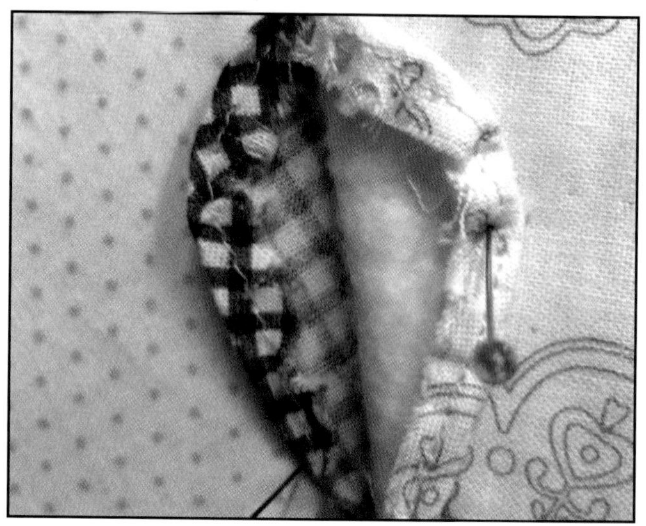

Machine Quilting

1. Place walking foot on sewing machine. Set stitch length to 4.0.
2. Quilt ¼" away, in the ditch, or stipple.

Antique Dresden Plate Quilt
Pieced and Quilted by Unknown
72" x 88"

This antique Dresden Plate quilt was pieced from 1930's feedsacks on white background. The quilter used green for her pointed wedges and framing border to make a dashing statement. The ice cream cone scalloped edges add to the charm of this quilt.

Dresden Plate Quilt
Pieced by Rose Rhoads
Quilted by Mildred Young
60" x 60"

Rose had her mind set on spring with her choice of creamy peach fabrics complimented by sage green accents for her lovely Dresden Plate quilt. She added the pretty ice cream cone border to accomplish her scalloped finished.

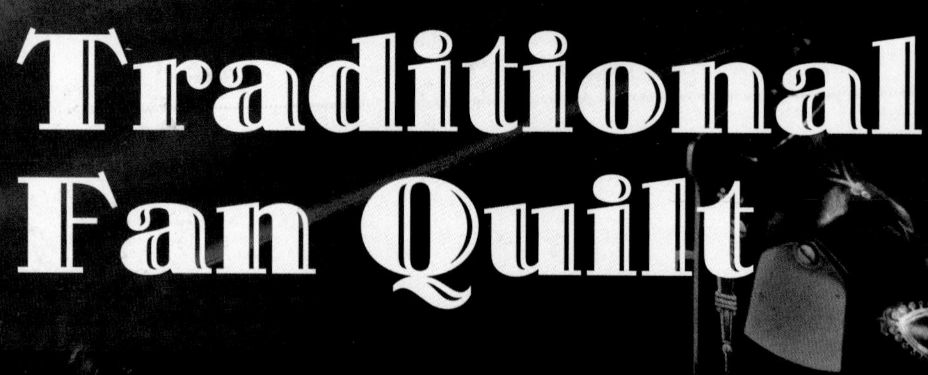

Traditional Fan Quilt

The Traditional Fan Quilt was a popular pattern and appeared in numerous newspapers and pattern ads in the 1930's and 1940's. One such was Laura Wheeler, a pseudonym used by Needlecraft Service, Inc. of New York City. They were a mail order pattern company that published ads in various newspapers. This ad appeared in the Spartanburg Herald. The pattern cost was 10 cents. Another company, John C. Michael Company in Chicago, IL offered pre-cut quilt patches for various popular quilt patterns of that era. This ad was for a pre-cut kit of 20 stamped squares for $2.50.

Vintage Traditional Fan Quilt *66" x 76"*
Made by Unknown Quilt Maker

This 1930's Depression era fan quilt is bright with Bubble Gum pink solid squares. Each 9" eight wedge fan block is created with only two fabrics, many of them stripes, and no quarter circles. Note the appropriate "Baptist fan" quilting, which are curves as far as a quilter sitting at a frame could reach.

Traditional Fan

Fabric Selection

Select six different prints in a variety of values and scales. Select contrasting fabrics for Background and Quarter Circle.

Cutting Chart for One

	Finished Size 8" Square
Background	(1) 8½" square
Six Different Fabrics	(1) 2¾" x 6" of each
Quarter Circle	(1) 3½" square
Rick Rack	1 yd of ½" or ⅝" wide for one Fan

Supplies

Template plastic

Cutting Wedges and Quarter Circle

1. Make templates.

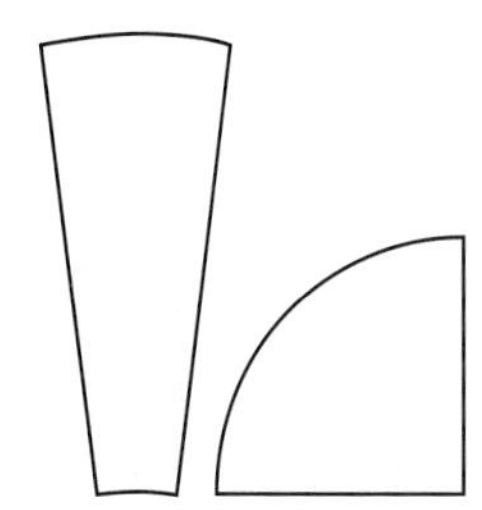

2. Plan placement of six Fan fabrics.
3. Flip right sides together in pairs.

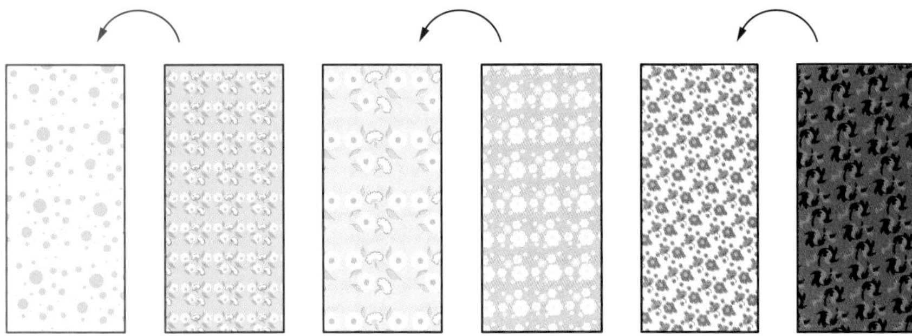

4. Stack pairs.
5. Trace Fan with template on top layer.
6. Cut straight sides with ruler and rotary cutter.
7. Trim top and bottom edges with scissors.

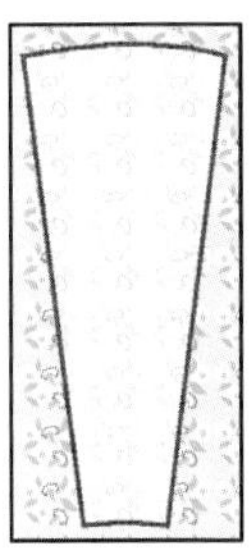

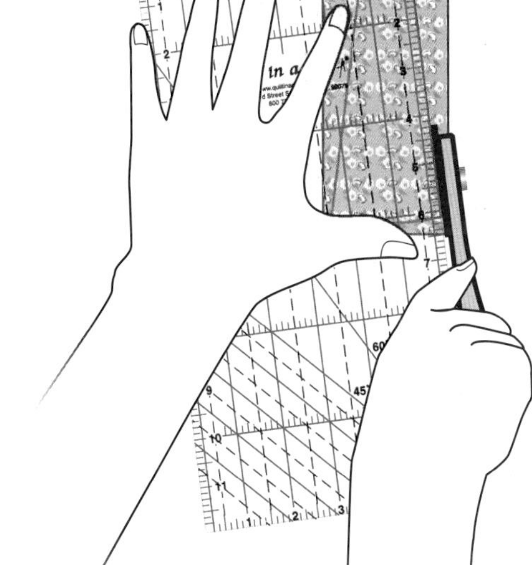

8. Place Quarter Circle on 3½" square.

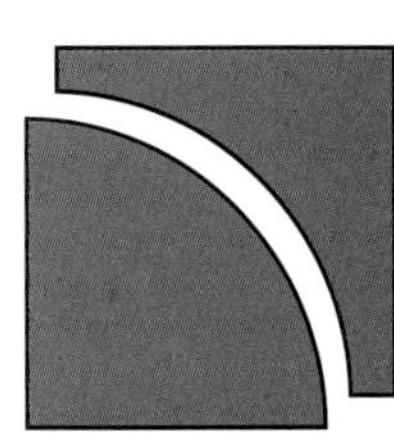

9. Trace around curve.
10. Cut with scissors.

Sewing Wedges

1. Assembly-line sew pairs together.

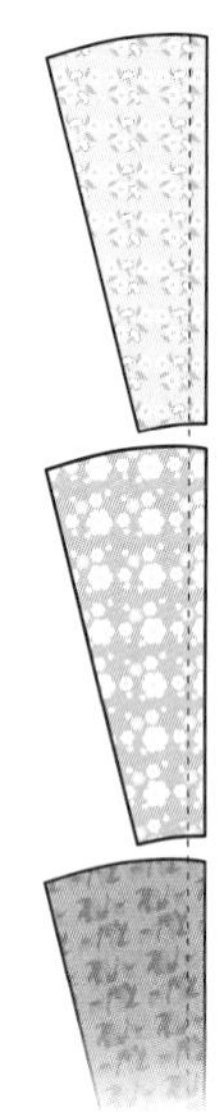

2. Press seams open.

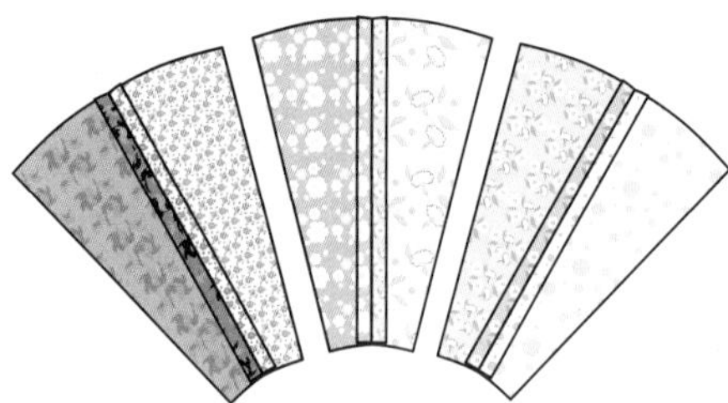

3. Sew pairs together into one Fan.

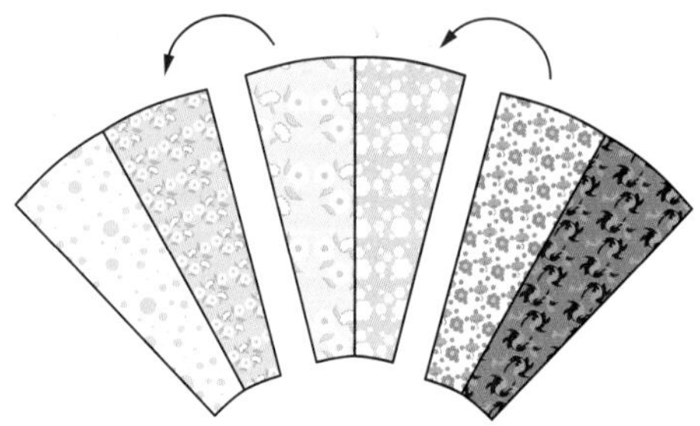

4. Press seams open.

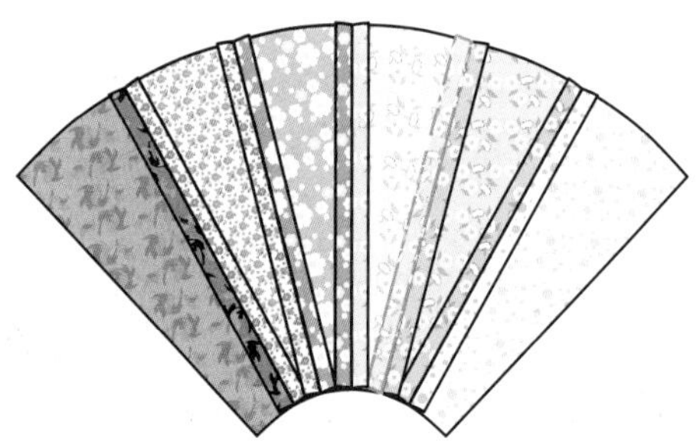

Adding Rick Rack

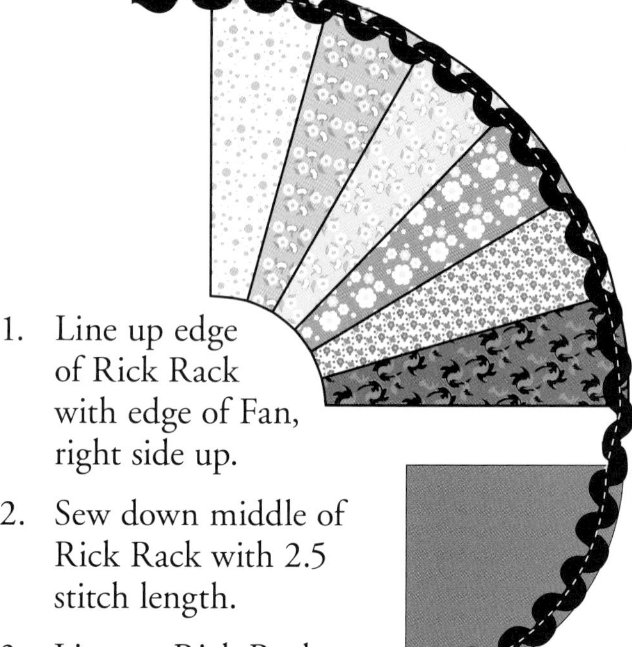

1. Line up edge of Rick Rack with edge of Fan, right side up.
2. Sew down middle of Rick Rack with 2.5 stitch length.
3. Line up Rick Rack with curved edge of Quarter Circle. Stitch down middle of Rick Rack.

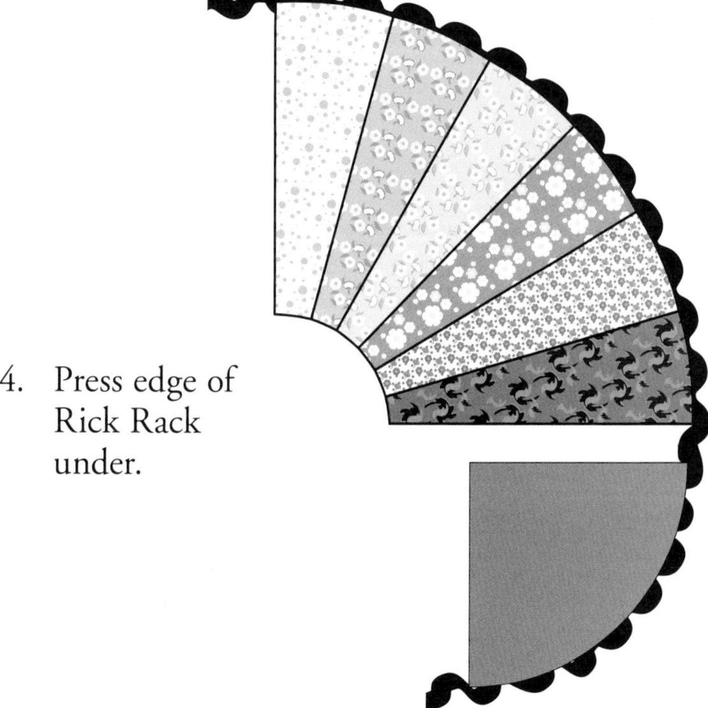

4. Press edge of Rick Rack under.

Finishing Block

1. Place Fan on corner of 8½" Background square. Pin in place.

2. Place Corner Square on top. Pin in place. Trim Rick Rack.

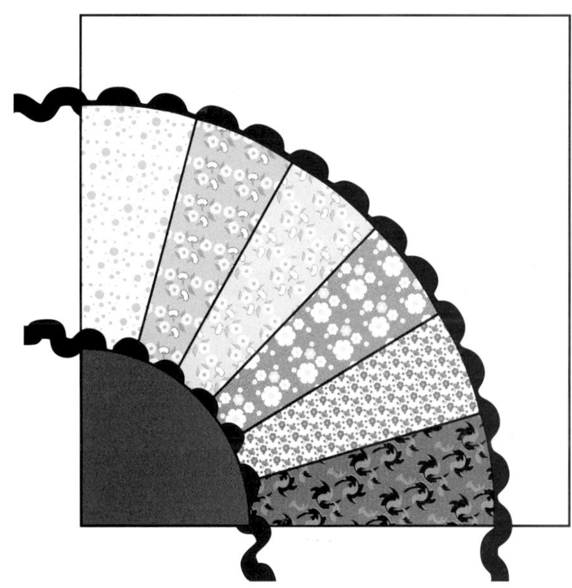

3. "Stitch in the Ditch" or ⅛" away from seam on both Fan and Quarter Circle.

Christmas Sampler *64" x 64"*
Pieced by Patty Wood
Quilted by Amie Potter

Patty made her Sampler a Christmas quilt, using fussy cut Poinsettias for her Posies, Fan Baskets, English Flower Garden, and the center of her Goose in the Pond block. She chose a tan background and added a special border with Fans in the corners to complete her holiday quilt.

Antique Fan Blocks in New Setting

59" x 73"

A box of sixty antique Fan wedges arrived at Quilt in Day, much to the excitement of the Bucket List Quilt Club. Since the objective of this group is to complete quilts, they set about adding Rick Rack and sewing the Fans to Background squares. Teresa Varnes sewed the top together, referring to Patricia Knoechel's design in *Fans and Flutterbys*, page 21. Judy Jackson did the long arm quilting, completing a lovely work of art.

Scalloped Fan Quilt

Over the years, quilt patterns have been known by a multitude of names. In addition to Scalloped Edge Fan, this pattern was known as Grandmother's Fan, Dresden Fan, and Calico Fan. In a 1931 issue of the Denver Post, the pattern was the 21st block in a series of beautiful patchwork designs. It was often pieced with silks and woolens. A similar pattern, offered by Needlecraft Services, under the pseudonyms of Laura Wheeler and Alice Brooks appeared in 1933 in various publications.

Antique Scalloped Edge Fan Quilt *64" x 64"*
Hand Pieced by Unknown Quilt Maker
Top completed by Teresa Varnes
Machine Quilted by Judy Jackson

This Scalloped Fan quilt was completed after eighty years. It was started using the Grandmother's Fan pattern by fictitious designers Laura Wheeler and Alice Brooks from Needlecraft Service, Inc, which sold for 10 cents. Eleanor purchased the nearly completed top in an antique store years ago. Teresa Varnes, her sewing assistant, completed it recently and Judy Jackson long arm quilted it.

Scalloped Fan

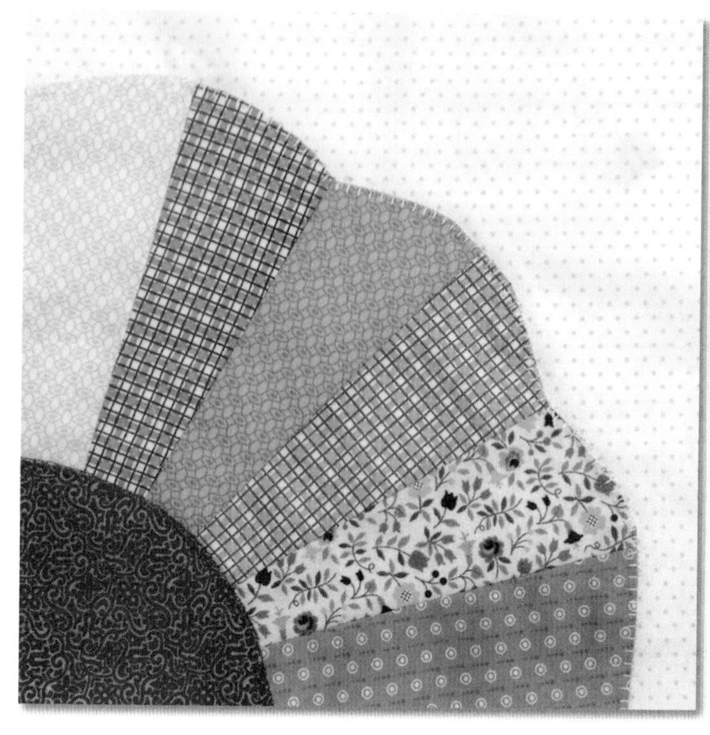

Fabric Selection

Select six different prints in a variety of values and scales. Select contrasting fabrics for Background and Quarter Circle.

Suggestion: If you make a quilt from this pattern, the template fits on 2½" jelly roll strips and is perfect for a scrappy look.

Cutting Chart for One

	Finished Size 8" Square
Background	(1) 8½" square
Six Different Fabrics	(1) 2¾" x 6" of each
Quarter Circle	(1) 4" square

Supplies

Template plastic

Cutting Curved Wedges and Quarter Circle

1. Make templates.

2. Plan placement of six Fan fabrics.
3. Flip right sides together in pairs.

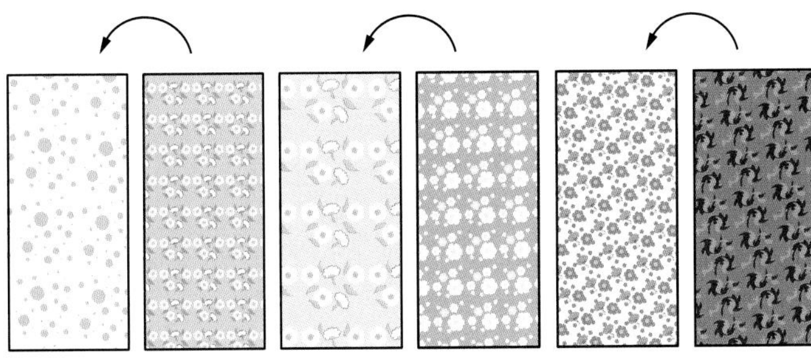

For a quilt, cut and sew strips together. Cut strips into 6" pieces.

4. Assembly line sew pairs together.

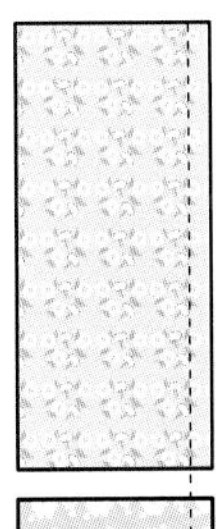

5. Stack three pairs.

   For a quilt, only stack three pairs at a time.

6. Trace Scalloped Fan template on top layer.

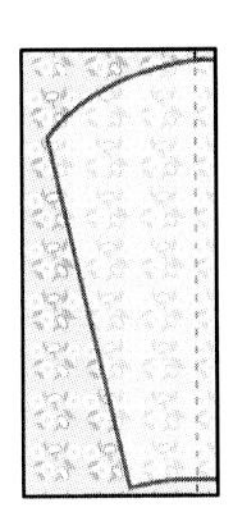

7. Cut straight side with ruler and rotary cutter.

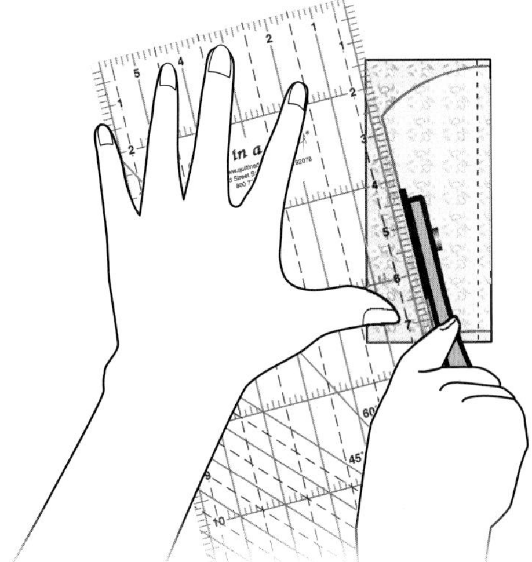

8. Trim top and bottom edges with scissors.
9. Press seams open.

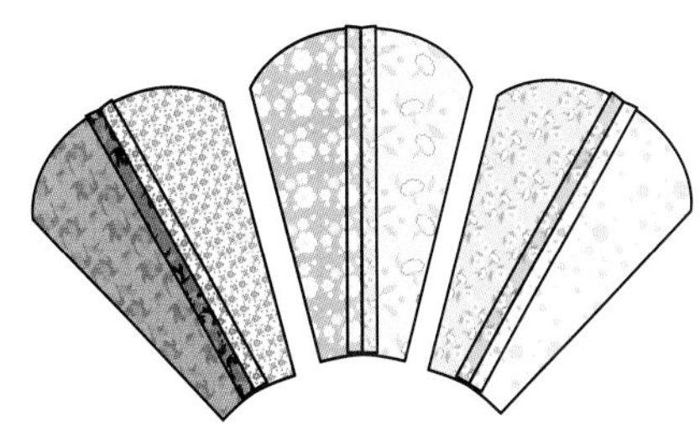

10. Place Quarter Circle on 3½" square.

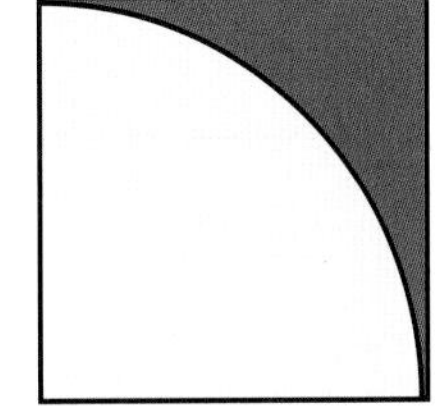

11. Trace around curve.
12. Cut with scissors.

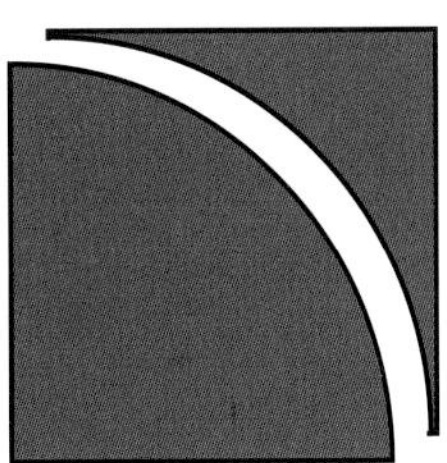

Turning Under Raw Edge

1. Set stitch length to 12 stitches per inch, or #3 setting.
2. Stay stitch ¼" seam along curved edge of Fan and Quarter circle.
3. Turn under raw edge on ¼" line. Crease line with fingernail.

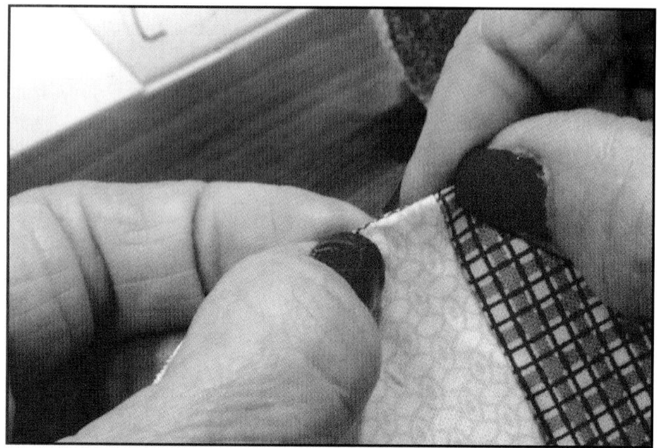

4. Steam press edges.

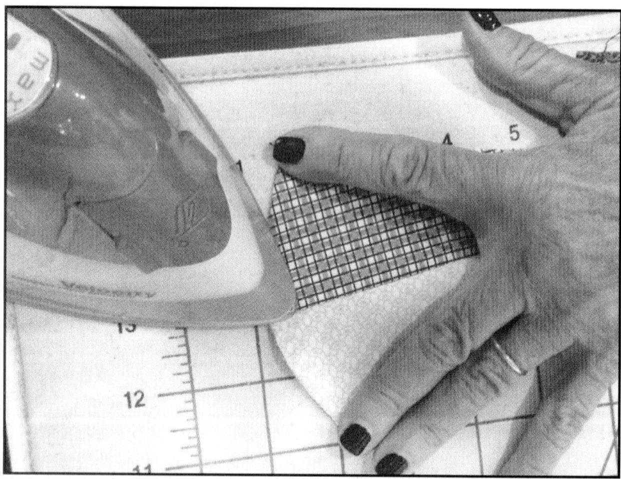

5. Pin corners of pairs together.

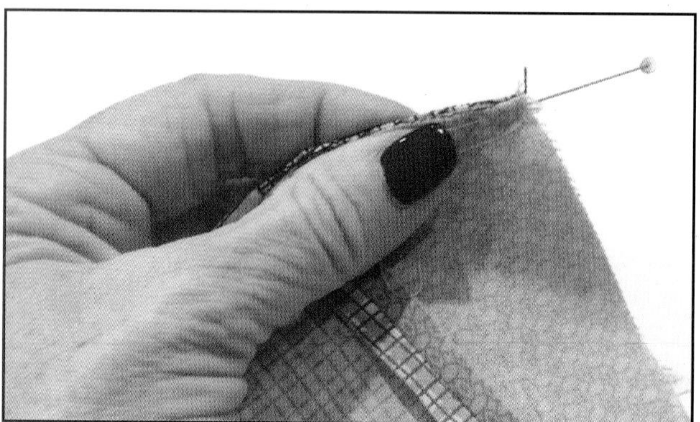

6. Sew pairs together into one Fan.
7. Press seams open.

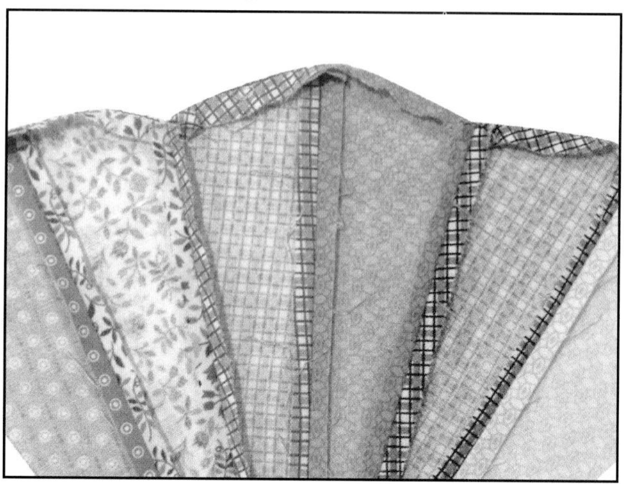

Finishing Block

1. Place Fan on corner of 8½" Background square. Place Quarter Circle on top. Pin in place.

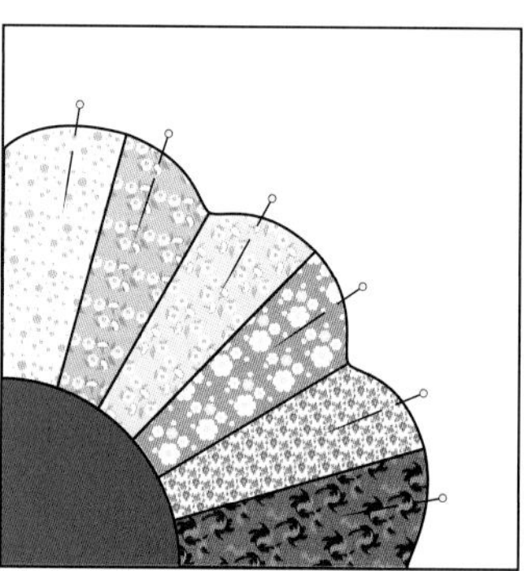

2. Sew around outside edge with blanket stitch, or stitch of your choice.

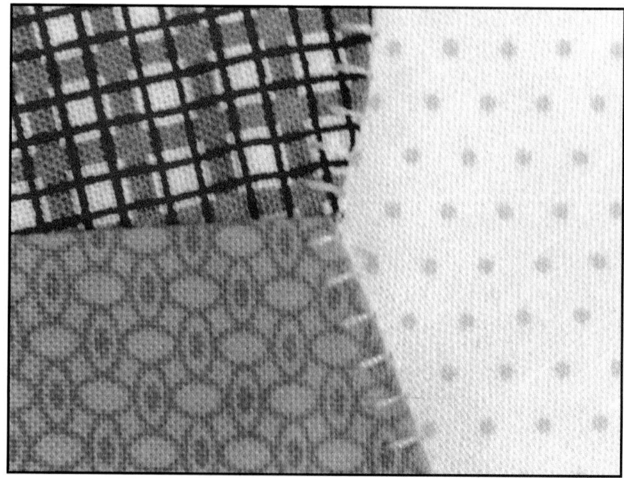

55" x 55"

In with the New
Pieced by Gail Yakos
Quilted by Amie Potter

Gail gathered up Sunny Days scraps from the Benartex reproduction line and created a masterpiece of colorful Scalloped Fans. There are forty-five charming whole blocks and ten half blocks in the quilt top with a curved edge, and three straight edges. Wow!

My Favorite Fans *55" x 60"*
Pieced by Gail Yakos
Quilted by Amie Potter

Shades of pink with bold brown quarter circles really stand out on Gail's quilt. She duplicated the use of brown in her framing border and binding to add a stunning finishing touch to her quilt.

Prism of Fans *66" x 82"*
Pieced by Patricia Knoechel
Quilted by Merry Jo Rembold

Patrica used Scalloped Fans, turned this way and that to make her stunning quilt. Her use of a dark background fabric made her Fans the strong focal point of her quilt.

Fan Basket Quilt

This antique Fan Basket Quilt was from a pattern designed by fictitious women, Laura Wheeler and Alice Brooks, for Needlecraft Service, a mail-order needlework company out of Old Chelsea Station, New York. The company was so popular that orders would arrive at the company without a street address.

Antique Goose in the Pond

Blocks Pieced by Unknown Maker *57" x 74"*
Top Pieced by Teresa Varnes
Hand Quilted by Arleen Meyer

This beautiful Goose in the Pond Quilt passed through many caring hands until completion. A quilter in Paducah, Kentucky labored over the bright fabrics and produced twelve blocks. Sue Bouchard was fortunate enough to discover them tucked away in an antique store. She passed them on to Teresa Varnes, who sewed the top together with 1½" Lattice and 3½" Nine-Patch Cornerstones. Hand quilter Arleen Meyer added the grand finishing touches to a traditional heirloom.

Goose in the Pond

Fabric Selection

Select Background that reads solid, one medium like a plaid, and one dark small scale print.

Cutting Chart for One Block

	Finished Size 15" Square
Background	
Pieced Squares	(1) 4" strip cut into (3) 4" x 8"
Squares	(1) 3½" x 20" strip cut into (5) 3½" squares
Stripes and Nine-Patches	(2) 1½" strips Cut in half
Dark	
Pieced Squares	(1) 4" strip cut into (3) 4" x 8"
Medium	
Stripes and Nine-Patches	(2) 1½" strips Cut in half

Supplies

6½" Triangle Square Up Ruler
Glow-Line™ Tape
Applique Pressing Sheet

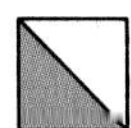 Making Twelve Pieced Squares

1. Place three medium 4" x 8" right side up.

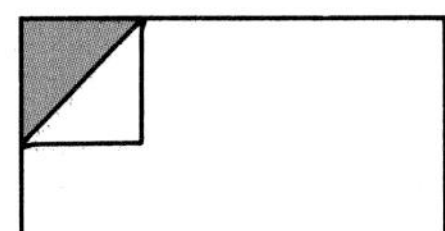

2. Place three Background 4" x 8" right sides together.
3. On wrong side of Background, draw a line at 4".

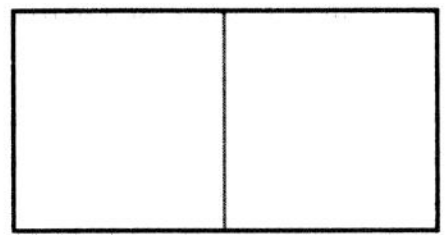

4. Draw diagonal lines with 6½" Triangle Square Up Ruler. Repeat on all pairs.

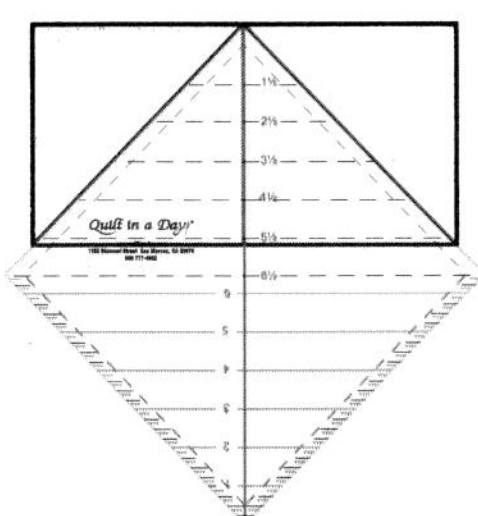

5. Assembly-line sew ¼" away from diagonal lines.

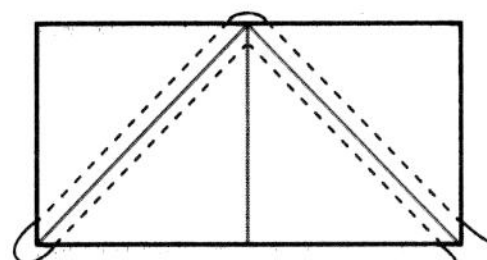

6. Cut on diagonal lines. Cut on straight line.

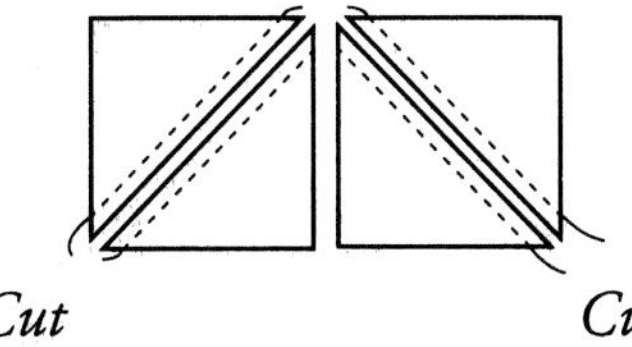

7. Select 4½" or 6½" Triangle Square Up Ruler. Put Glow Line tape under 3½" line.
8. Center ruler on patch. Line up 3½" line with stitches.

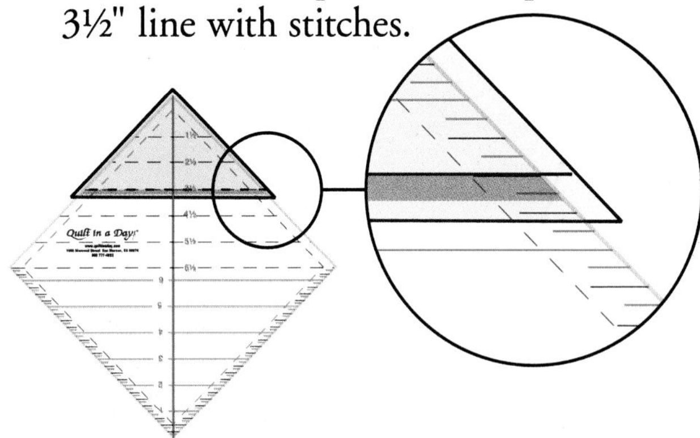

9. Trim patches to 3½" with Triangle Square Up Ruler.

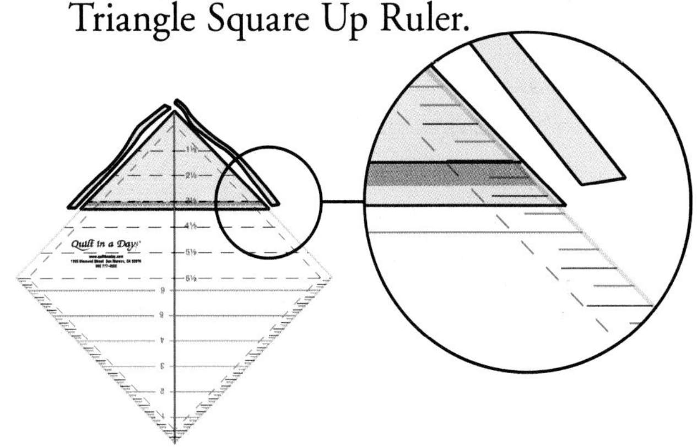

10. Set seams with dark on top. Open, and press toward dark. Trim tips.

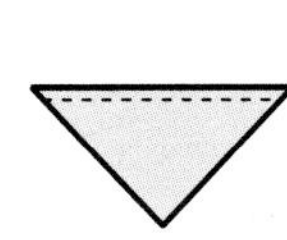
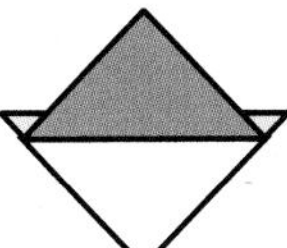
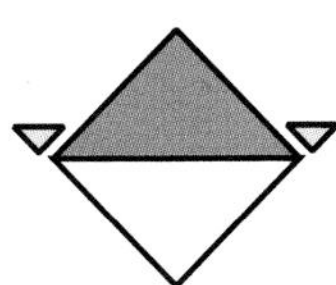

¼" Seam Test

You may need to sew with a scant ¼" seam so Nine-Patches measure 3½" to match Pieced Squares.

Test your ¼" seam allowance by sewing three 1½" x 6" pieces together and pressing seams in one direction. Size should measure 3½" from edge to edge.

Sewing Strips Together

1. Place two sets of 1½" half strips.
2. Flip middle strip right sides together with left strip.
3. Sew with ¼" seam.

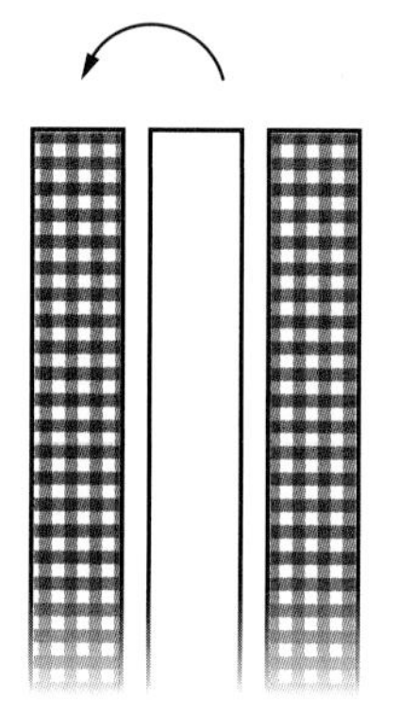

Med Bkgnd Med

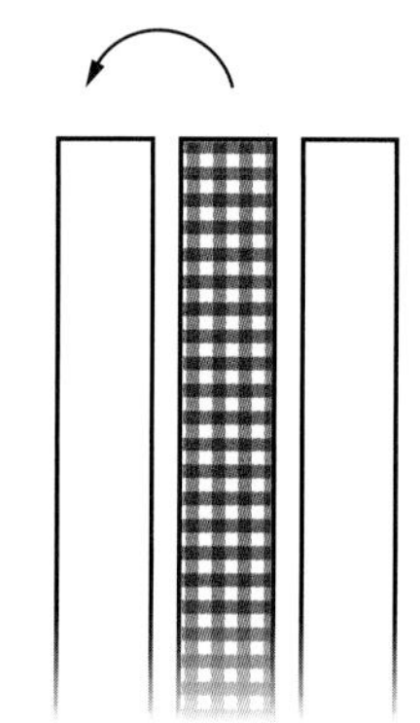

Bkgnd Med Bkgnd

4. Set seam with medium on top. Open, and press seam toward medium.
5. Assembly-line sew right strip.

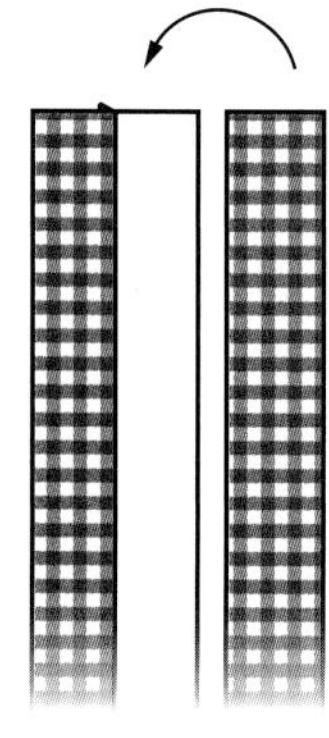

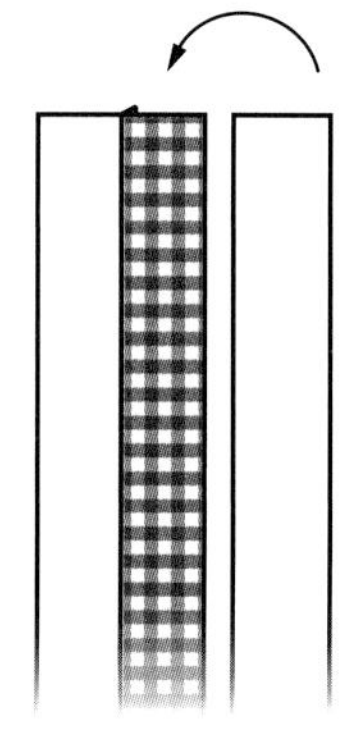

6. Set seam with medium on top. Open, and press seam toward medium.
7. Measure width of strips. Strips should be 3½" wide. Resew if necessary.

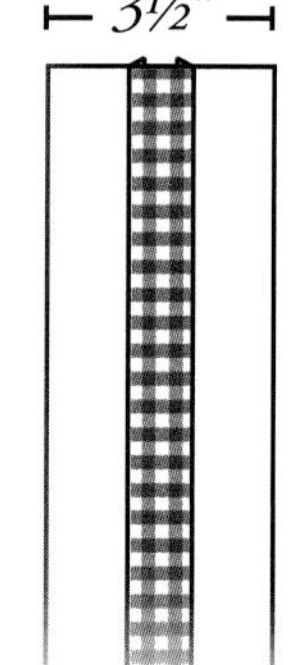

Cutting Stripes

1. Place Medium/Background/Medium strip set on cutting mat.
2. Straighten end. Cut four 3½" squares.

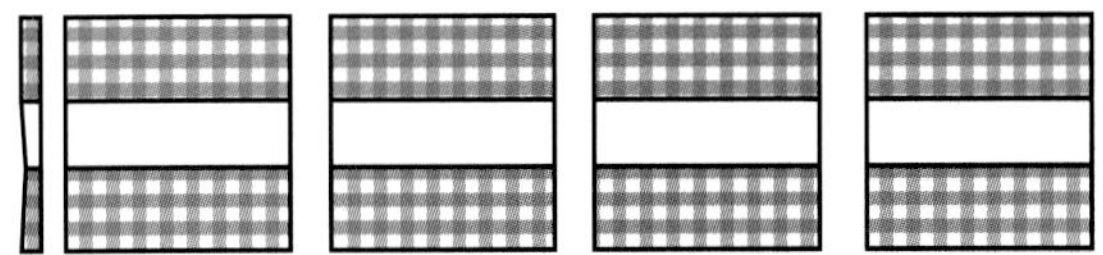

Sewing Nine-Patches

1. Place Background/Medium/Background strip set on cutting mat right side up.
2. Place reminder of Medium/Background/ Medium strip right sides together to it. Lock seams.

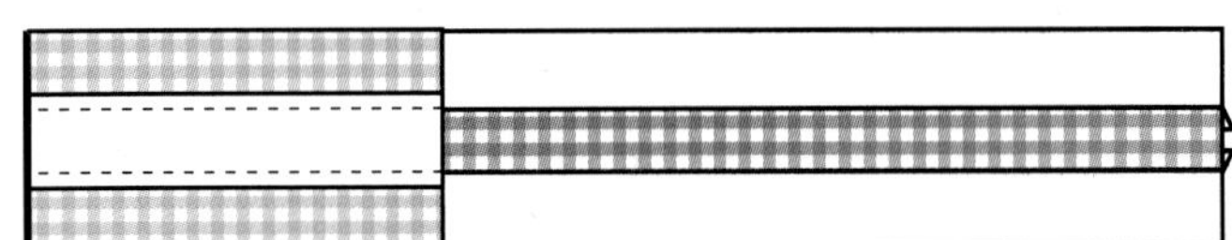

3. Layer cut four 1½" pairs. Do not open.
4. Continue to cut four 1½" single layers.

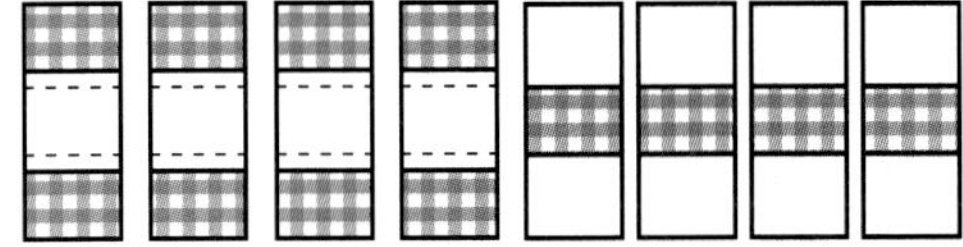

5. Assembly-line sew four pairs.
6. Open. Stack four 1½" pieces.
7. Flip right sides together, lock seams, and assembly-line sew.

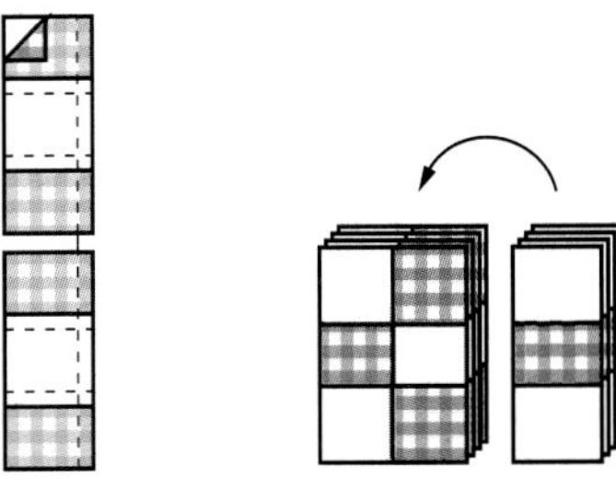

8. From wrong side, press seams **toward middle.**
9. Measure. Patch should measure 3½". Trim if necessary.

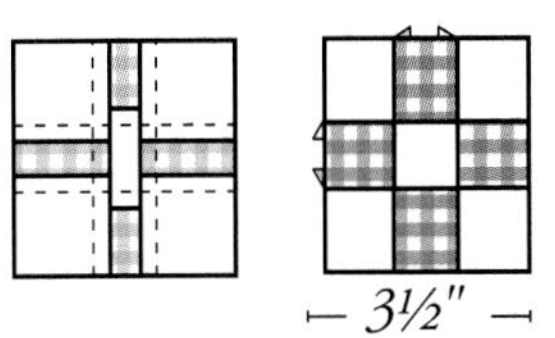

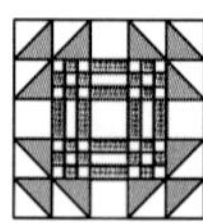

Sewing Block Together

All pieces lock together.

1. Lay out pieces. Flip second vertical row right sides together to first vertical row.

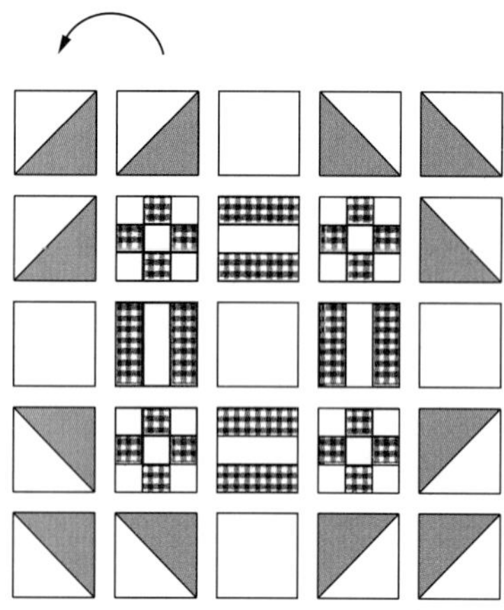

2. Stack pairs, keeping top blocks on top.

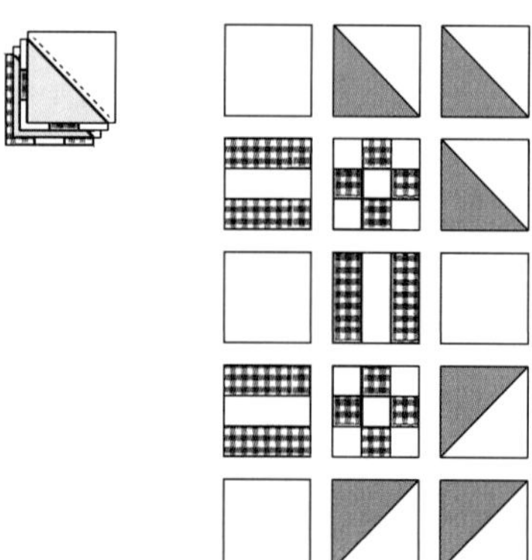

3. Stack remaining vertical rows, keeping top blocks on top.

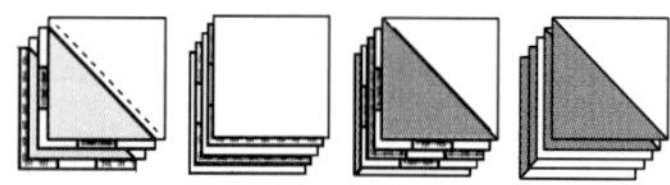

4. Assembly-line sew first two vertical rows.

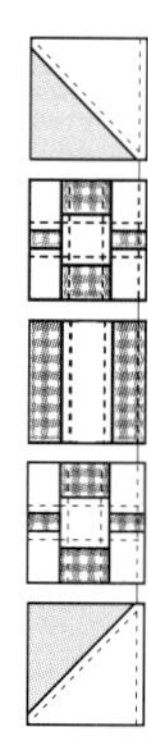

5. Open. Assembly-line sew remaining vertical rows.

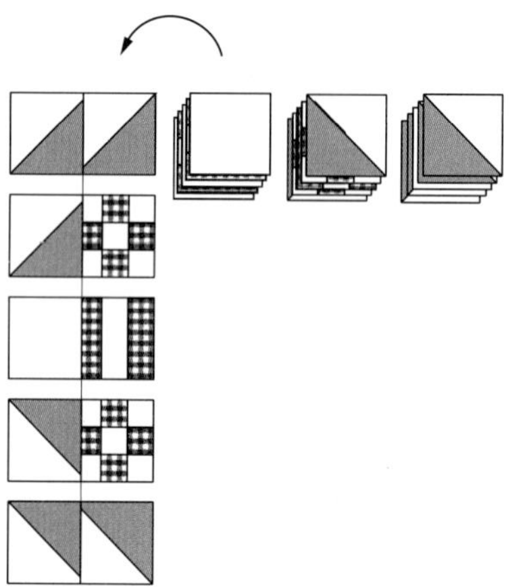

6. Do not clip apart.
7. From wrong side, press each row in opposite directions. *Cover pressed rows with appliqué pressing sheet to prevent twisted seams.*

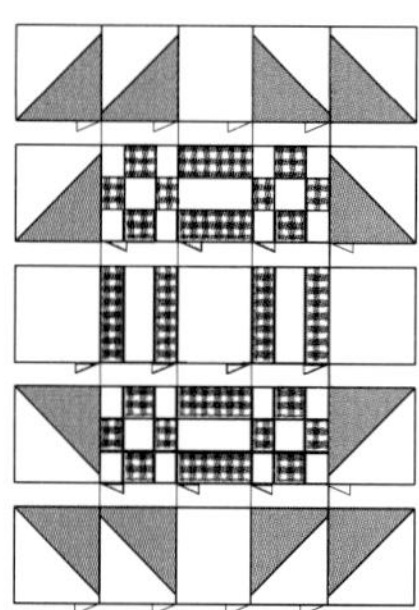

8. Sew rows together, locking seams on Nine-patches. Press seams in one direction.

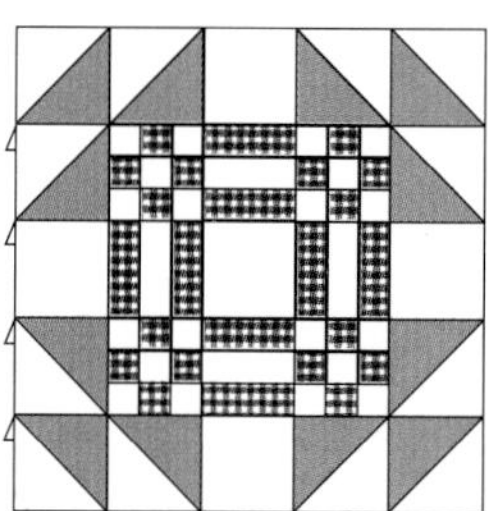

Classic Goose in the Pond Quilt *75" x 96"*
Pieced by Unknown Quilt Maker
Long Arm Quilted by Judy Jackson

This vintage Goose in the Pond quilt is circa 1950s. Though it is not known who pieced this charming quilt, it stands the test of time to be as pertinent today as it was the day it was made. In history, blue and white quilts are the second most popular color way. This classic Goose in the Pond Quilt has three sizes of Nine-Patches. Block Nine-Patches are 3" square, Lattice Nine-Patches are 6" square, and Corners are 9" square. It's an easy quilt to make, with simply strips and pieced squares.

Goose in the Pond Quilt

Fabric Selection

Select two contrasting fabrics like blue and white or red and white for a classic looking quilt.

Cutting Chart for Quilt

	Finished Size 75" x 96"
Background	**5½ yds**
Pieced Squares for Blocks	(4) 8" strips cut into (18) 8" squares
Stripes and Nine-Patch for Blocks	(18) 1½" strips
Lattice	(18) 2½" strips
Lattice Nine-Patch	(1) 2½" strip
Borders	(14) 3½" strips
Border Nine-Patch	(1) 3½" strip
Binding	(9) 3" strips
Dark	**4¼ yds**
Pieced Squares for Blocks	(4) 8" strips cut into (18) 8" squares
Squares for Blocks	(6) 3½" strips cut into (60) 3½" squares
Stripes and Nine-Patch for Blocks	(15) 1½" strips
Lattice	(9) 2½" strips
Lattice Nine-Patch	(2) 2½" strips
Borders	(7) 3½" strips
Border Nine-Patch	(2) 3½" strips
Backing	**5 yds**
Batting	84" x 104"

Making Pieced Squares for Twelve Blocks

1. Place 8" squares of light and dark right sides together.
2. Draw an X on top, and pin.
3. Sew ¼" seam from both sides of diagonal line.
4. Cut into fourths.
5. Cut on diagonal lines.

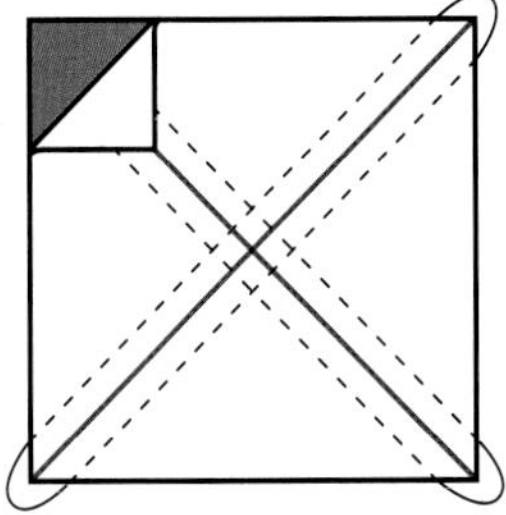

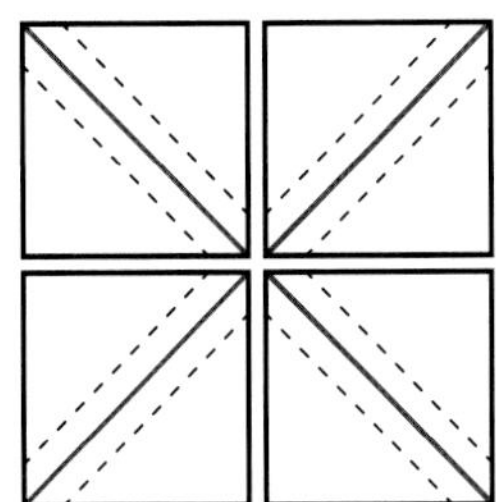

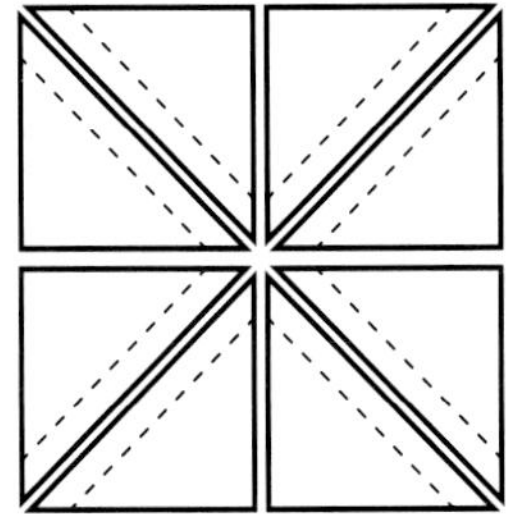

6. Square one hundred forty-four 3½" squares with 6½" Triangle Square Up Ruler.

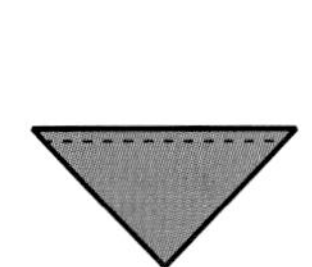

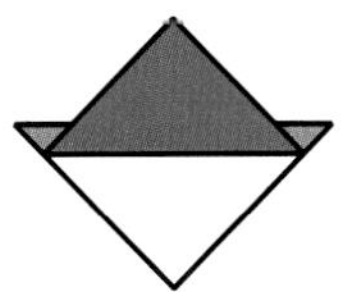

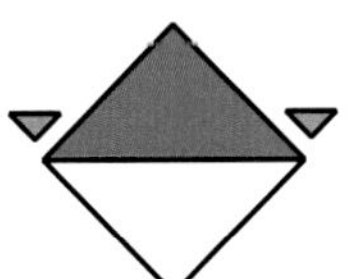

Make 144

7. Press seams toward dark side, and trim tips.

Making Stripes and Nine-Patch for Twelve Blocks

1. Sew seven sets of 1½" strips together.
2. Press seams toward dark.
3. Cut into forty-eight 3½" squares.
4. Cut remainder into forty-eight 1½" strips.

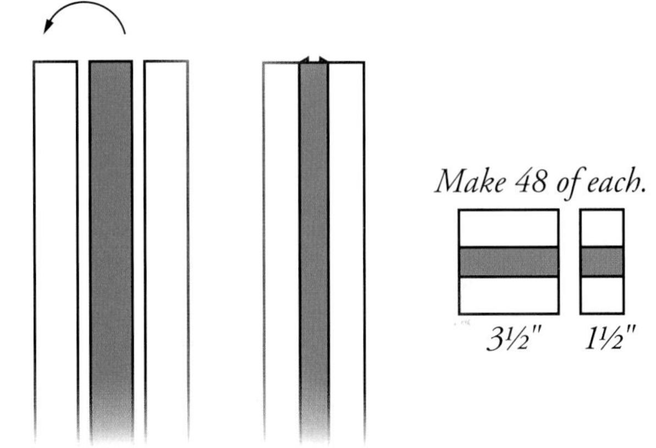

Bkgrnd/Dark/Bkgrnd

5. Sew four sets of 1½" strips together.
6. Press seams toward dark.
7. Cut into ninty-six 1½" strips.
8. Sew strips into forty-eight Nine-Patch.

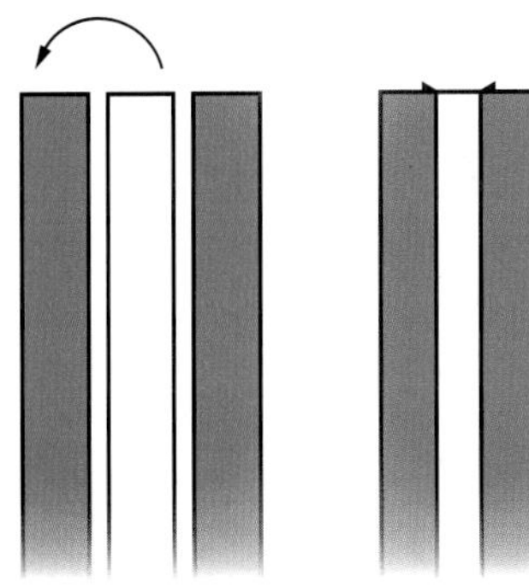

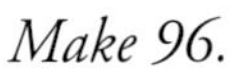

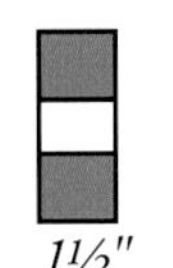

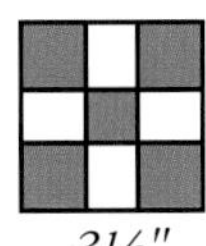

Making Twelve Blocks

1. Lay out blocks.
2. Assembly-line sew together.
3. Measure size of block and record.

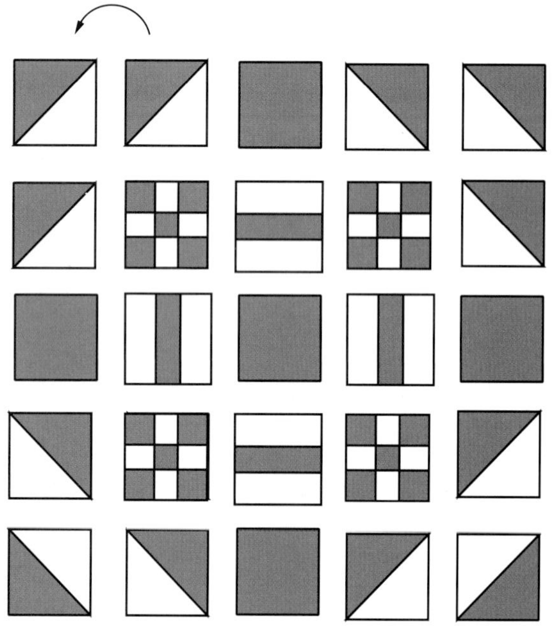

Making Seventeen Lattice and Six Nine-Patch

1. Sew nine sets of 2½" strips together.
2. Press seams toward dark.

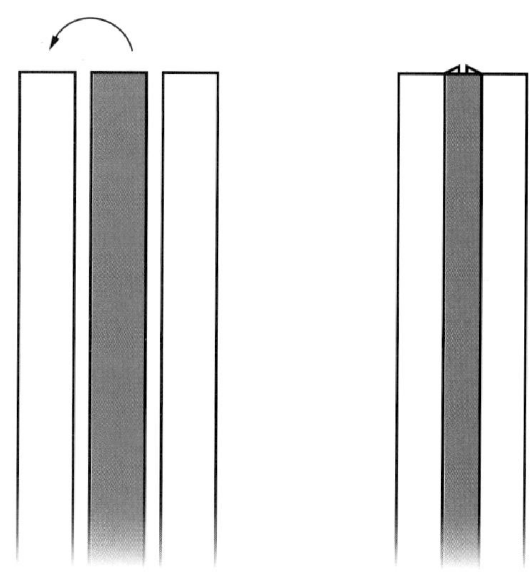

3. Cut seventeen Lattice same size as block.
4. Cut remainder into six 2½" pieces.

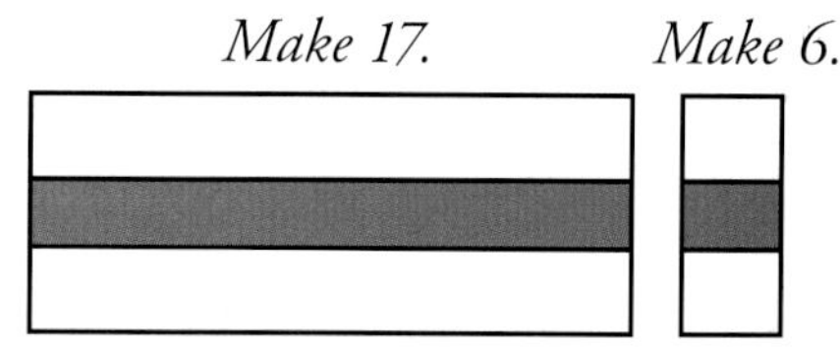

5. Sew one set of 2½" strips together.
6. Press seams toward dark.

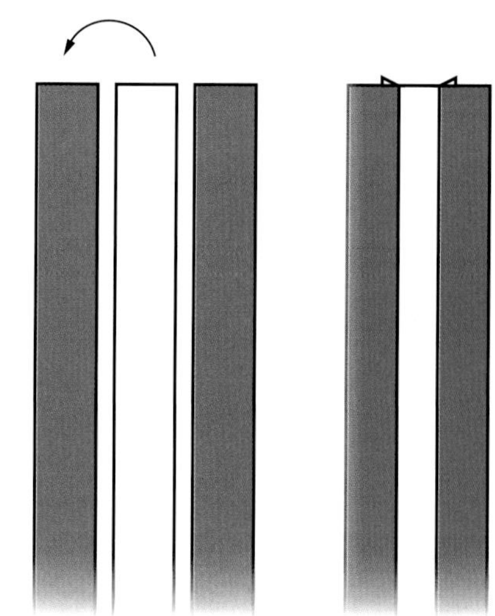

7. Cut into twelve 2½" strips.
8. Sew six Nine-Patch together.

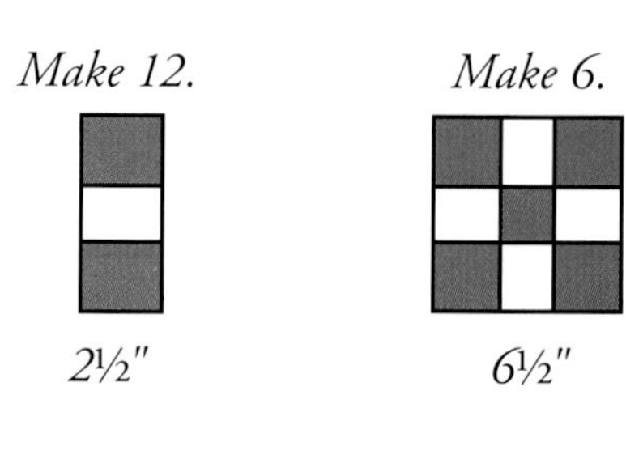

Making Four Borders and Four Nine-Patch

1. Sew seven sets of 3½" strips together end-to-end into long strips.
2. Sew long strips together. Press seams toward dark.

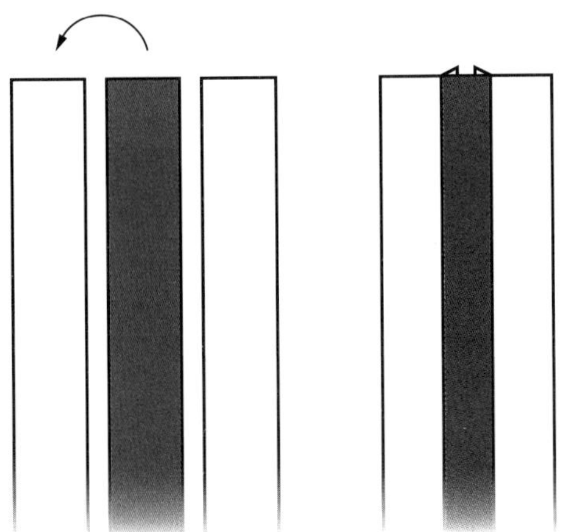

3. Measure Sides and Top and Bottom.
4. Cut two Borders for Sides.
   Cut remainder into four 3½" pieces.

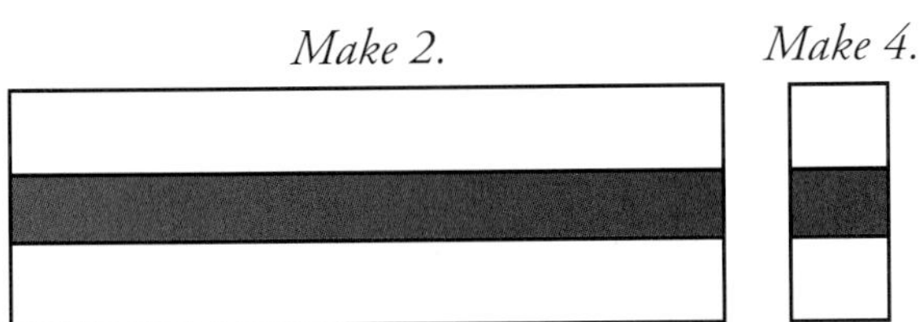

5. Sew one set of 3½" strips together.
6. Press seams toward dark.

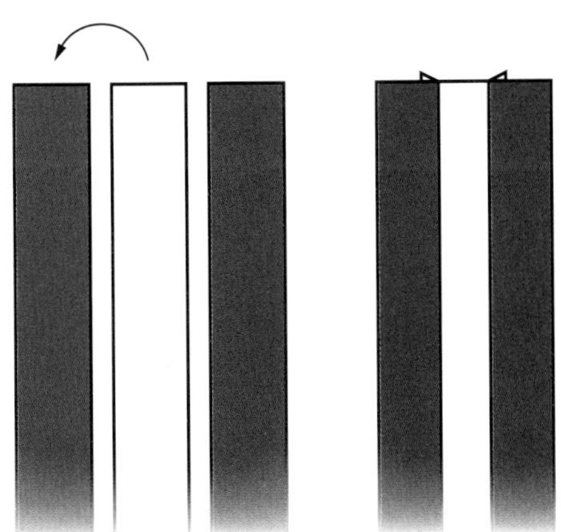

7. Cut into eight 3½" strips.
8. Sew four Nine-Patch together.

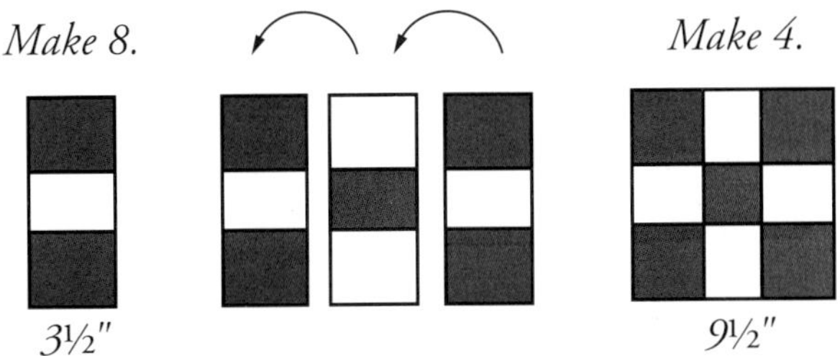

9. Sew Sides to quilt top. Press seams toward Border.
10. Cut two Borders for Top and Bottom.
11. Sew Nine-Patches to ends, locking seams. Press seams toward Borders.

12. Sew to quilt top. Press seams toward Border.
13. Layer, quilt, and bind.

Crow's Nest Quilt

Crow's Nest appeared in Nancy Page's column, a syndicated mail-order column written by Florence LaGanke Harris, which appeared in many periodicals in the late 1920's – 40's. She also called it Attic Window. Kansas City Star Newspaper named this block Friendship Quilt in 1938. Friends signed their name in the background fabric.

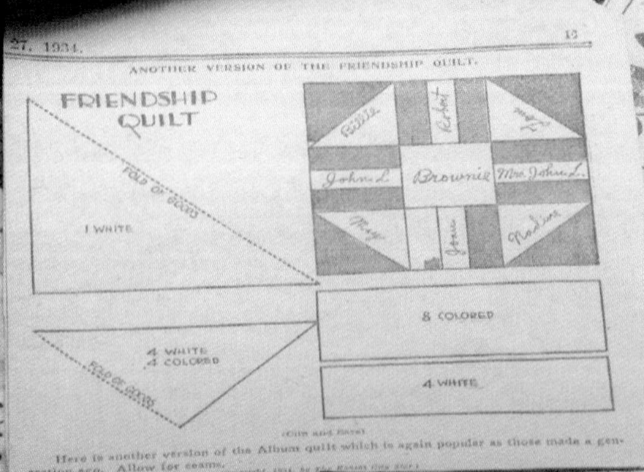

ANOTHER VERSION OF THE FRIENDSHIP QUILT.

FRIENDSHIP QUILT

FOLD OF GOODS

1 WHITE

Brownie

John L.

Mrs. John L.

8 COLORED

4 WHITE
4 COLORED

FOLD OF GOODS

4 WHITE

Here is another version of the Album quilt which is again popular as those made a generation ago. Allow for seams.

Antique Crow's Nest Quilt *65" x 76"*
Quiltmaker Unknown

This forty-two block Crow's Nest top was made around 1880 and finished some time later with polyester batting and bias tape on the wrong side. There is an interesting variety of scrap bag fabrics from paisley prints, homespun, black mourning prints and plain black, red polka dots, checks, stripes, and solid blue chambray. A striking print with black rosettes has beautiful federal blue dots in one, and stripes in another. Surprise blocks of beige and red are unevenly disbursed throughout the quilt. Eleanor Burns purchased the quilt in Julian, California.

Crow's Nest

A Crow's Nest is a small, partly enclosed lookout platform near the top of the ship's mast.

Fabric Selection

Select a light and one medium small scale print or plaid.

Cutting Chart for Three Blocks

	Finished Size 9" Square
Light	
Pieced Squares	(3) 4" x 8"
Stripes	(1) 1½" strip
Medium	
Center Squares	(3) 3½" squares
Pieced Squares	(3) 4" x 8"
Stripes	(2) 1½" strips

Supplies

6½" Triangle Square Up Ruler
6" x 12" Ruler
InvisiGRIP
Glow-Line™ Tape
Cutting Mat

Making Twelve Pieced Squares

1. Place three medium 4" x 8" pieces right side up.
2. Place light 4" x 8" right sides together.

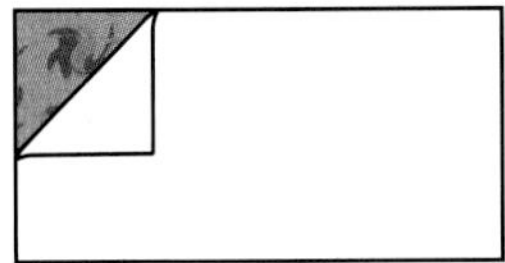

Make three sets.

3. On wrong side of light, draw a line at 4".

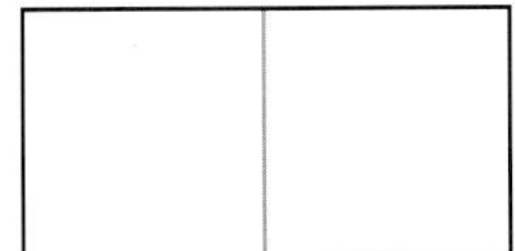

4. Draw diagonal lines with 6½" Triangle Square Up Ruler.

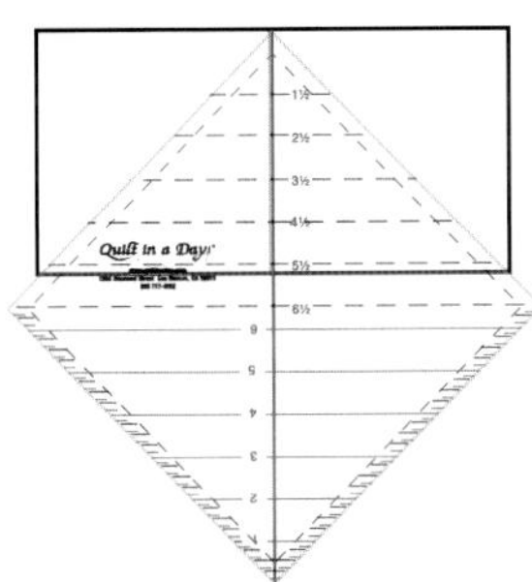

5. Assembly-line sew ¼" away from diagonal lines.

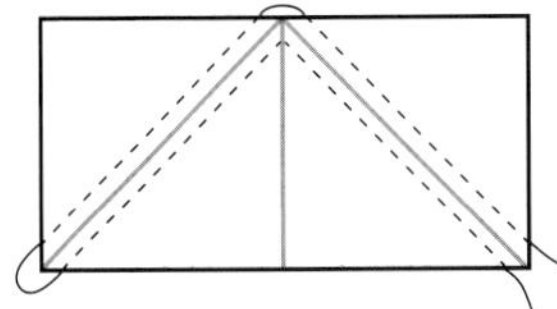

6. Cut on diagonal lines. Cut on straight line.

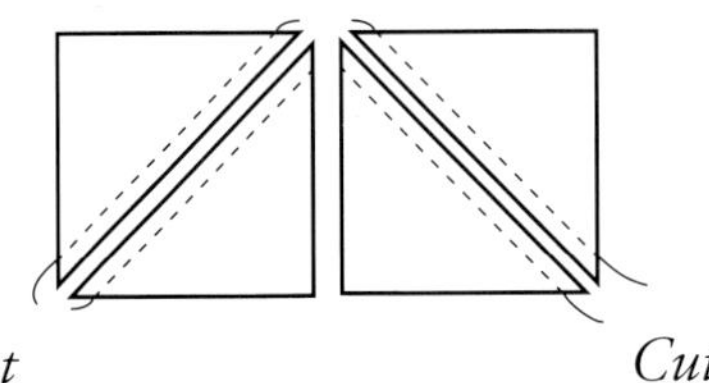

7. Select 4½" or 6½" Triangle Square Up Ruler. Put Glow Line tape under 3½" line.

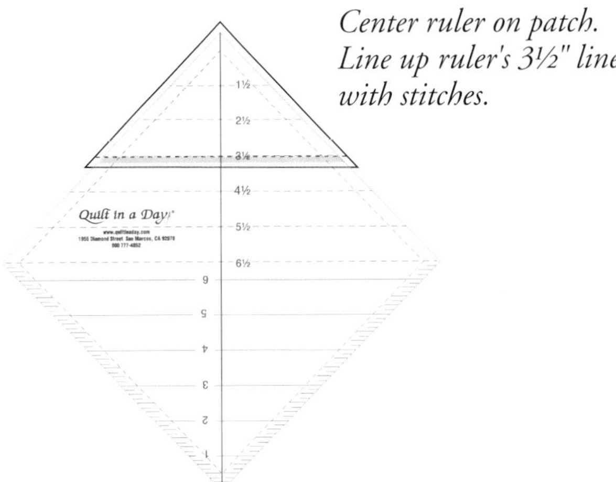

8. Trim patches to 3½" with Triangle Square Up Ruler.

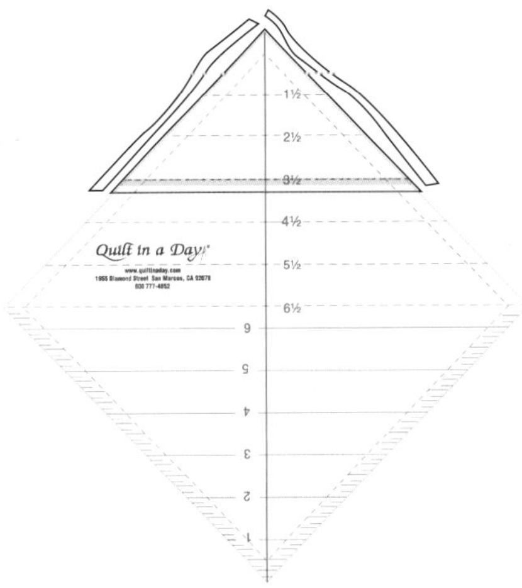

9. Set seams with medium on top. Open, and press toward medium. Trim tips.

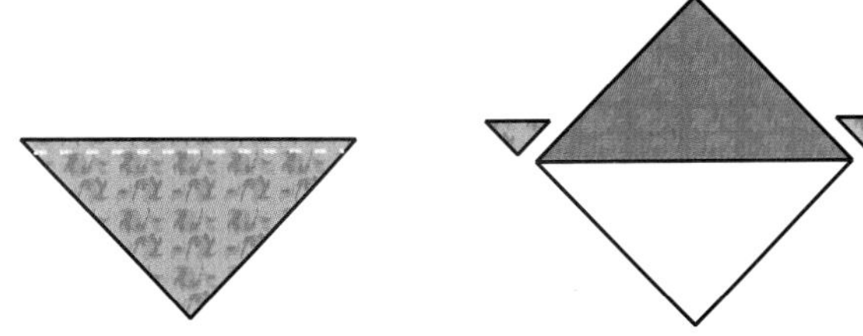

Sewing and Cutting Stripes

1. Lay out 1½" strips.
2. Sew with ¼" seam.

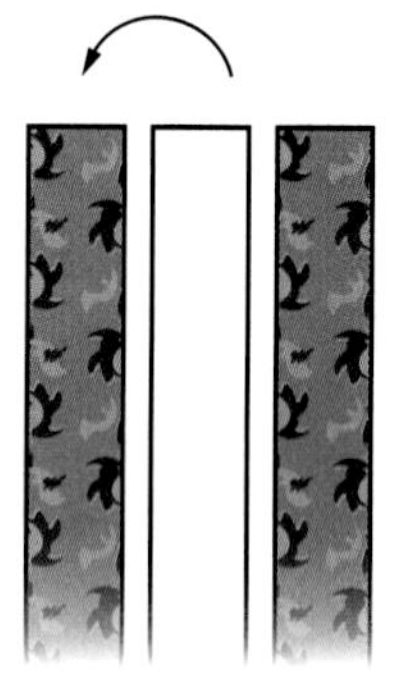

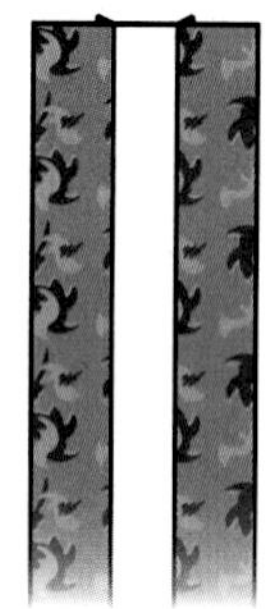

Medium Light Medium

3. Set seams with medium on top. Open, and press seams toward medium. Strips should be 3½" wide.
4. Straighten end. Cut twelve 3½" squares.

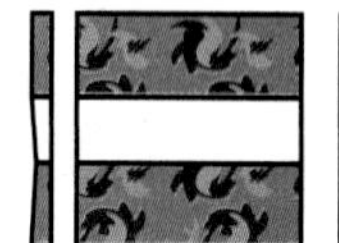

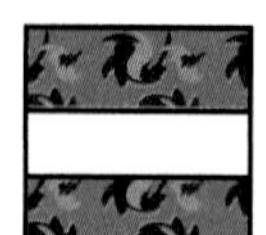

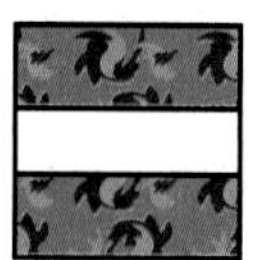

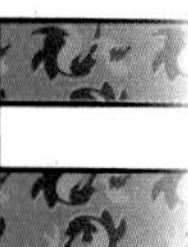

Sewing Blocks Together

1. Lay out pieces.
2. Flip middle vertical row to left vertical row, right sides together.

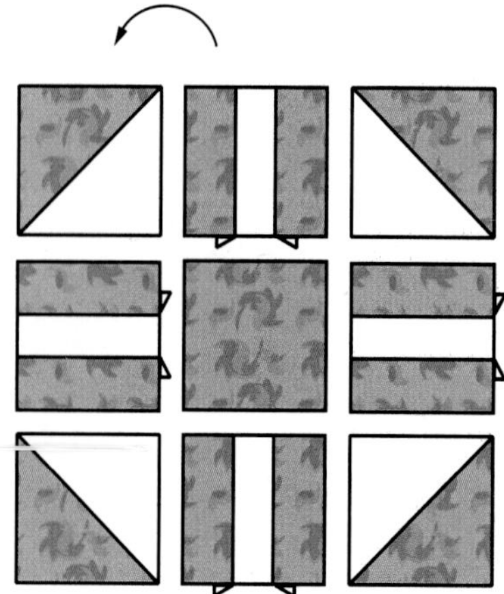

3. Assembly-line sew.

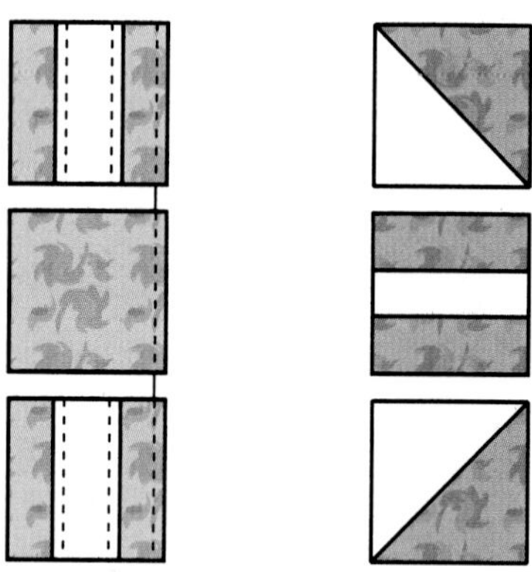

4. Open. Flip right vertical row to middle vertical row, right sides together.
5. Assembly-line sew.

6. Turn.
7. Sew remaining rows, pressing seams away from Stripe and toward Center Square.
8. Press last seams away from middle row.

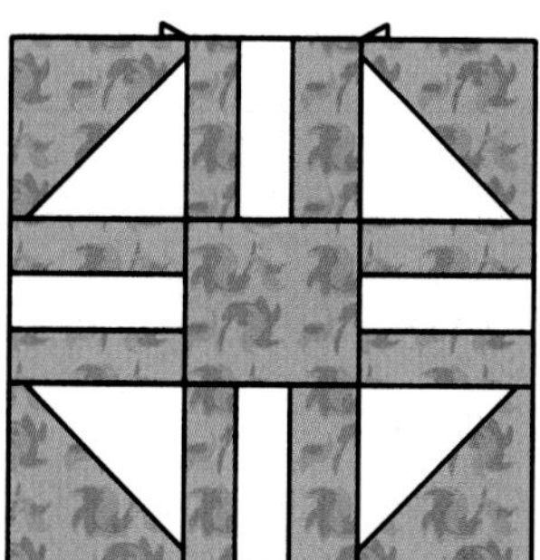

Fussy Cut Crow's Nest Quilt *38" x 38"*
Pieced by Patricia Knoechel
Quilted by Amie Potter

Using the Crow's Nest block in two contrasting colors adds interest to Patricia's wallhanging. She used narrow lattice and cornerstones on each block and repeated it for a framing border. Her choice of a large scale print for her outside border provides the perfect finish.

Reproduction Crow's Nest Quilt

Pieced by Eleanor Burns
Quilted by Judy Jackson

36" x 54"

Eleanor recreated the antique Crow's Nest Quilt to hang in her log home in Julian, California. She used a primitive line of fabric for most of her blocks, plus threw in a couple of scrappy blocks for a surprise element. Of course, some of the blocks had to be red!

Cutting Chart for Twenty Four Blocks Finished Size 36" x 54"

This yardage makes three identical blocks from each set of light and medium ¼ yd pieces.

	Cut from Each
Eight Lights ¼ yd of each	**Cut from Each**
Pieced Squares	(3) 4" x 8"
Stripes	(1) 1½" strip
Eight Mediums ¼ yd of each	**Cut from Each**
Center Squares	(3) 3½" squares
Pieced Squares	(3) 4" x 8"
Stripes	(2) 1½" strips
Binding	**½ yd**
	(5) 3" strips
Backing	**1¾ yds**
Batting	**42" x 60"**

Crow's Nest Quilt

On a block to block quilt, reverse pressing on half of the blocks so seams lock together.

1. Make Pieced Squares for twenty-four blocks following block directions.

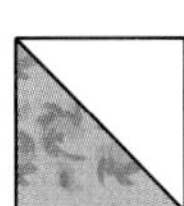

2. Sew and press **twelve blocks.**

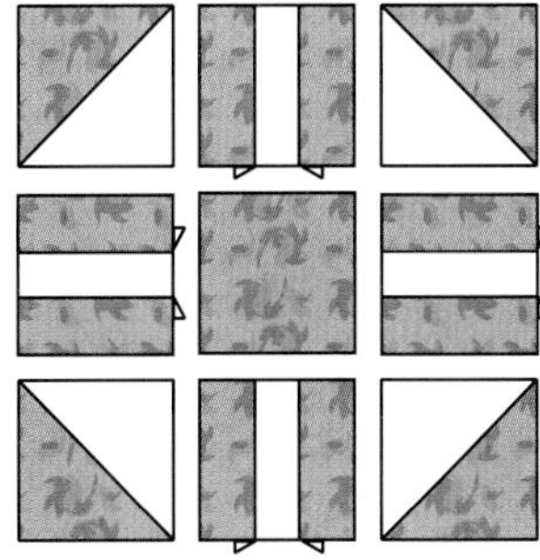

Reverse Pressing on Second Twelve

1. Press seams on Stripe toward light.

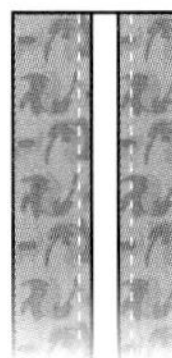

2. On vertical rows, press seams toward Stripe and away from Center.

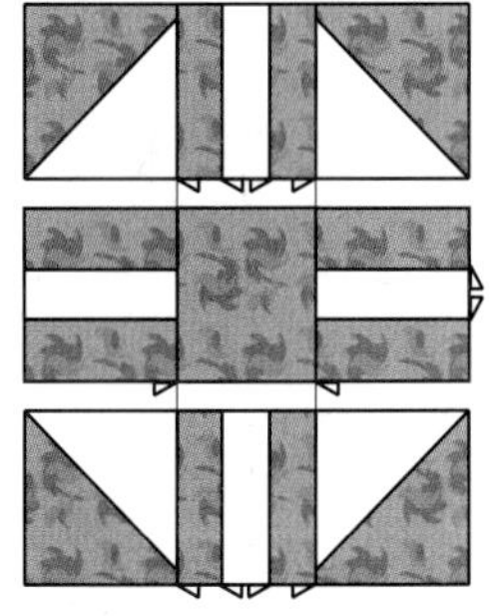

3. Press last seams toward middle row.

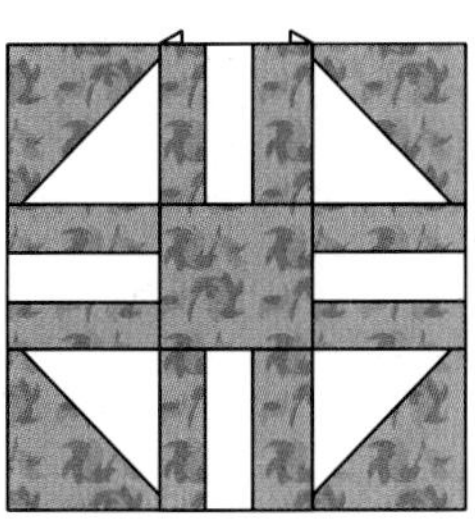

4. Alternate blocks when setting them together.
5. Layer, quilt, and bind.

Positive and Negative Crow's Nest Quilt

Pieced by Sue Bouchard
Quilted by Judy Jackson

45" x 63"

Sue made this quilt from Nine Fat Quarters. Each Fat Quarter makes two Positive Blocks and two Negative Blocks.

Cutting Chart for Thirty-five Blocks

Finished Size 45" x 63"

Background	**2¼ yds** (8) 4" strips cut into (36) 4" x 8" (27) 1½" strips cut in half (2) 3½" strips cut into (18) 3½" squares
Nine Fat Quarters	**From each Fat Quarter cut** (6) 1½" x 21½" strips (1) 8" strip cut into (4) 4" x 8" (2) 3½" squares
Binding	**⅝ yd** (6) 2¾" strips
Batting	**53" x 71"**
Backing	**3¼ yds**

Cutting Fat Quarters

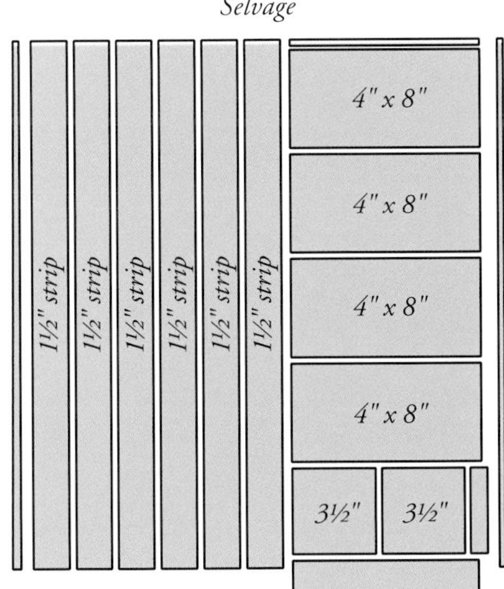

1. For Blocks, press your seams away from the Background. The blocks lock when you sew them together.
2. When arranging your blocks, place your positive blocks on the design wall. Then fill in with your negative blocks.

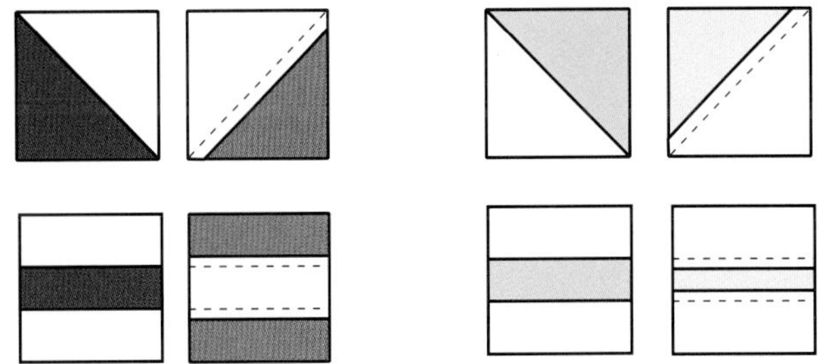

For patches, press seams toward the dark for both Positive and Negative.

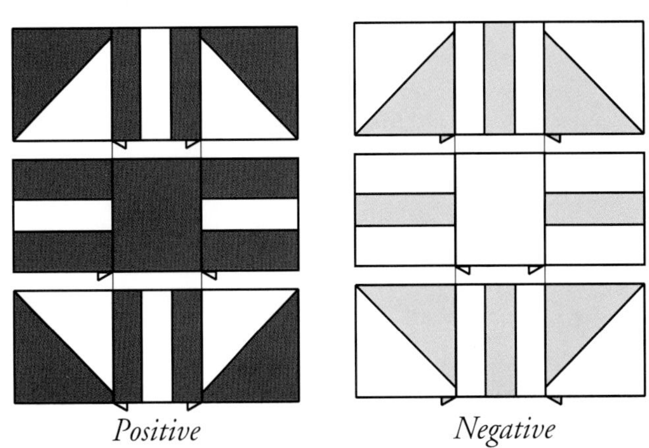

Arrow Quilt

The origin of this pattern has been attributed to Aunt Martha's Studio. Like Betty Crocker, Aunt Martha was not a real person. At the beginning of the Depression, Jack and Clara Tillotson of Kansas City, Missouri, started the company cutting quilt block kits. They discovered their customers preferred ten cent paper patterns over the costly kits. The Aunt Martha byline began in February 1931 with a first person, chatty narrative called *Easy Quilts.*

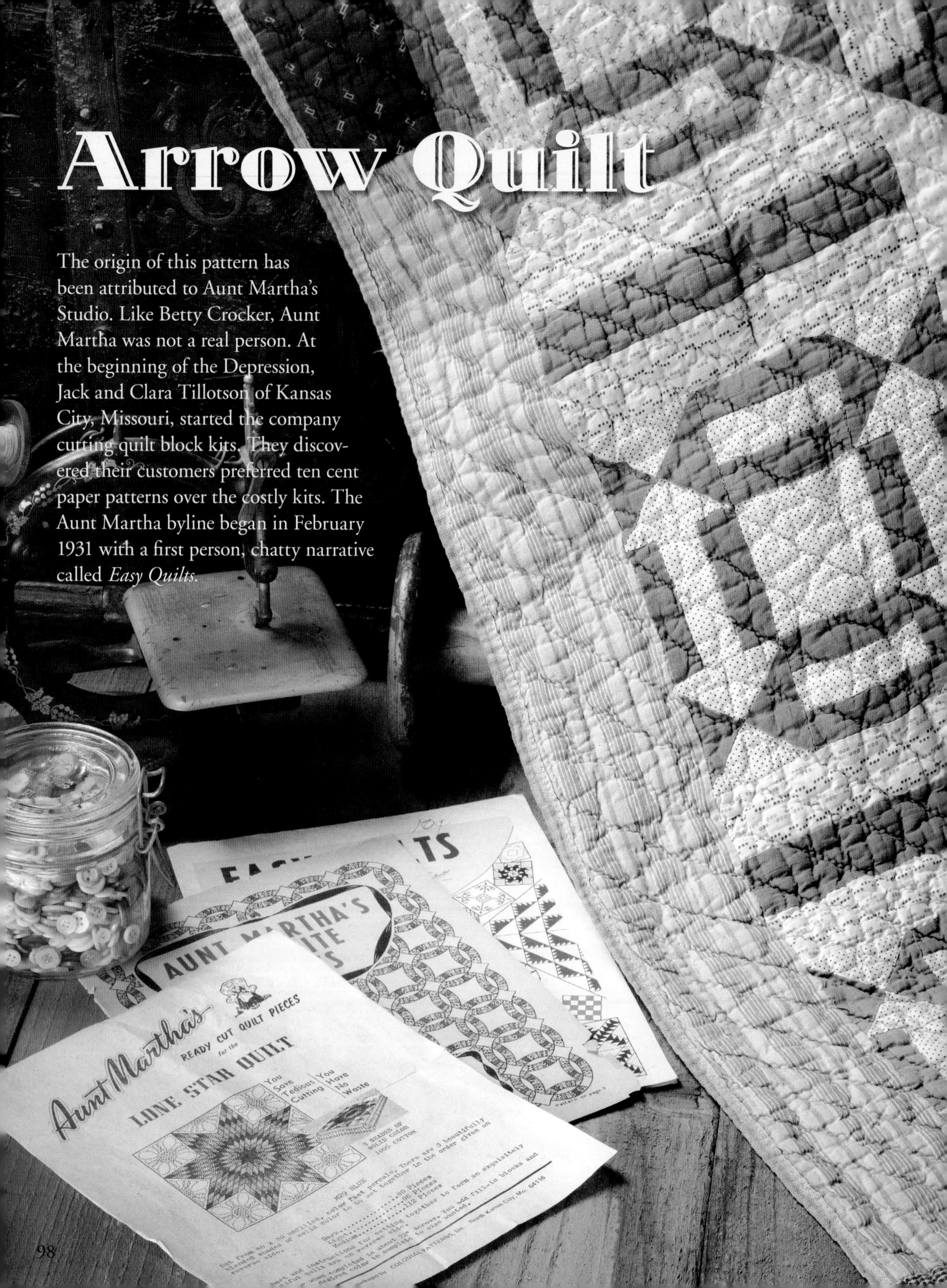

Antique Arrow Quilt

Quilt Maker Unknown *63" x 72"*

This thick Arrow Quilt was made in the late 1800's. Arrows in small prints of indigo blue and grey head in all directions across the quilt. There appears to be no rhyme or reason as to which direction they are headed. Arrows in the Lattice tend to pull the blocks together. A pieced border adds interest to the quilt, whether to be used as a "whisker cloth" or to just give a little extra width to the quilt.

Grey striped homespun backing was brought to the front, and finished with diagonal lines of quilting through a very thick batting.

Arrow

Fabric Selection

Select Background and one Medium small scale print or plaid.

Cutting Chart for One Block

	Finished Size 9" Square
Background	
Center Square	(1) 3½" square
Quarter Squares	(2) 4½"squares
Stripes	(1) 1½" x 21"
Medium	
Quarter Squares	(2) 4½"squares
Stripes	(1) 1½" strip Cut in half

Supplies

3½" Fussy Cut Ruler
6" x 12"Ruler
InvisiGRIP
Large Cutting Mat

Making Four Quarter Square Patches

1. Place two sets of 4½" squares right sides together. Draw diagonal lines.

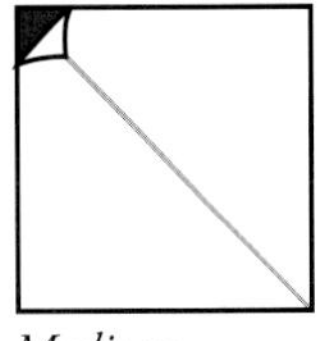

Medium and Background

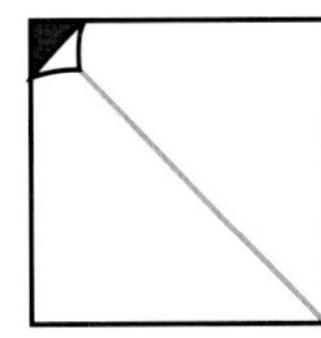

Medium and Background

2. Sew ¼" from both sides of diagonal line. Use 15 stitches per inch, or 2.0 on computerized machine.

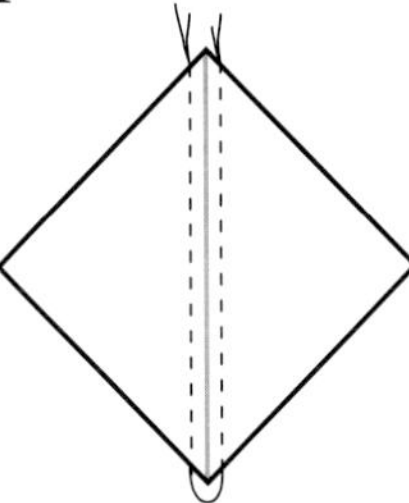

3. With rotary cutter and ruler, cut squares in half on diagonal line.

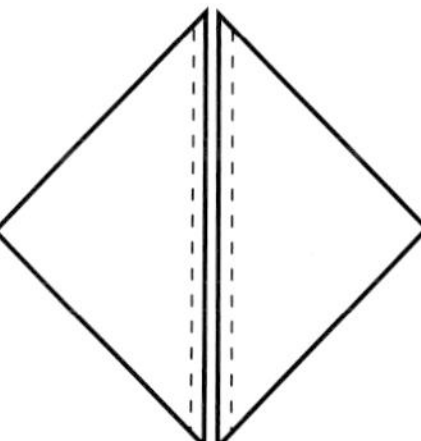

4. Set seams with medium on top.

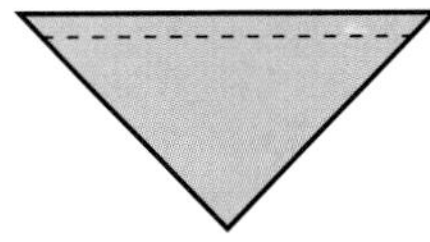

5. Open, and press seams toward medium.

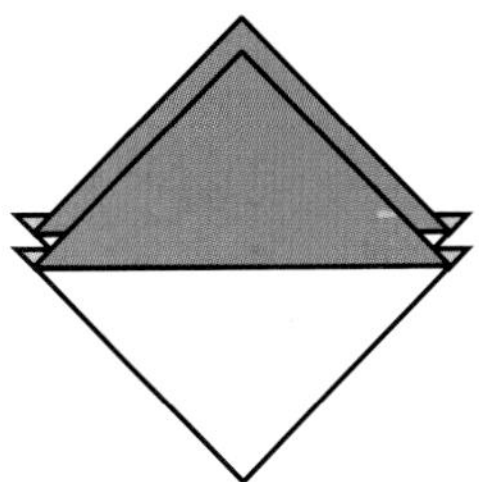

Make two sets of each.

6. Lay out sets. Flip patch on right to patch on left, right sides together.

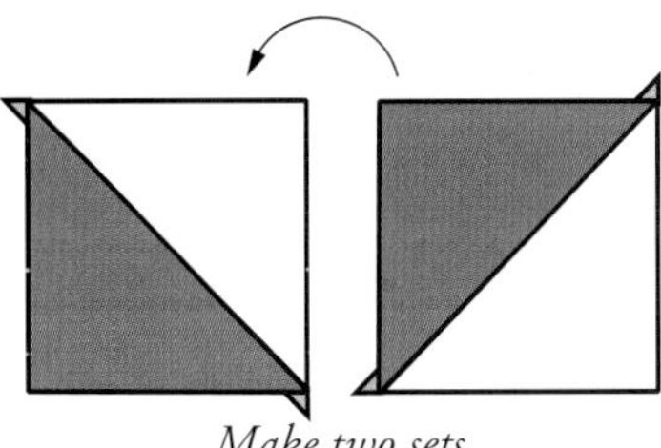

Make two sets.

7. Lock center seams. Draw diagonal line.

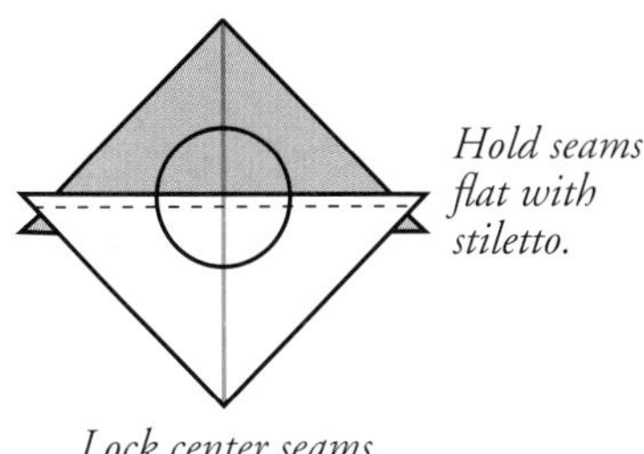

Lock center seams.

8. Assembly-line sew ¼" from line on both sides.
9. Cut on diagonal line.

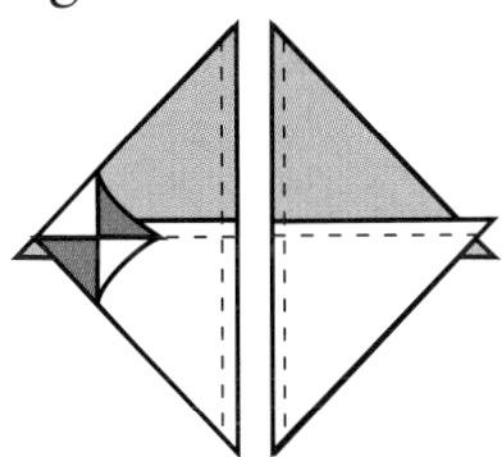

10. Place on flat surface wrong side up.
11. "Swirl" two patches clockwise, and two counter clockwise. Open center, and press Four-Patch flat. Swirl seams around center.

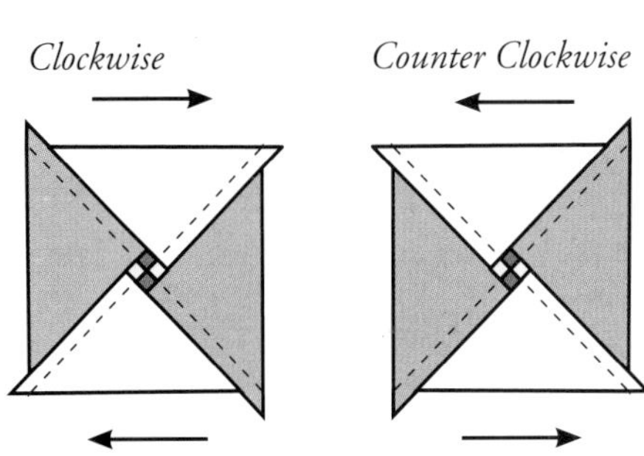

This technique creates a little Four-Patch in the center.

12. Place patch on a small cutting mat right side up.
13. Place 3½" Fussy Cut Ruler on top with lines on seams.

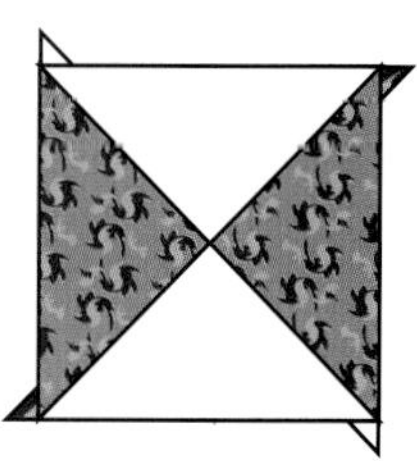

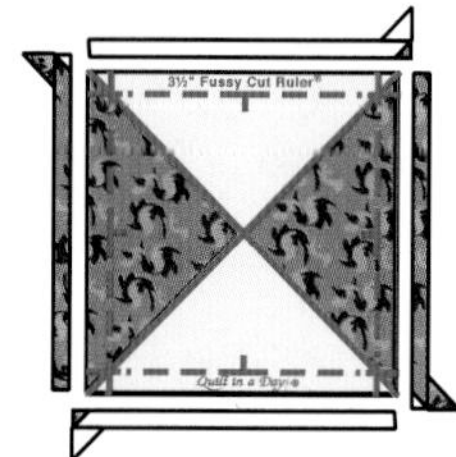

14. Trim on four sides.

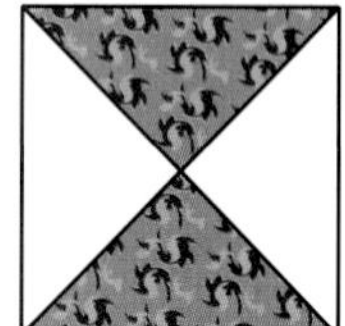

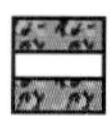 Sewing and Cutting Stripes

1. Place 1½" half strips.
2. Sew with ¼" seam.

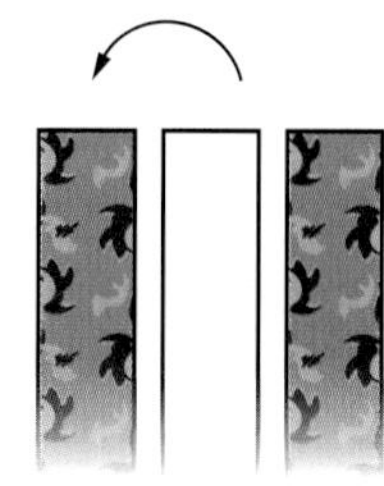

Medium Bkgrnd Medium

3. Set seams with medium on top. Open, and press seams toward medium.
4. Measure width of strips. Strips should be 3½" wide. Resew if necessary.

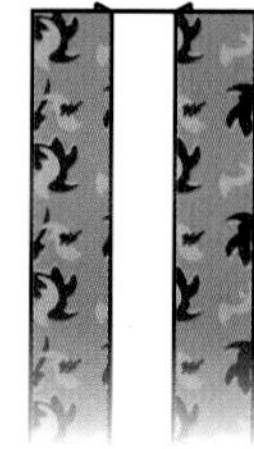

5. Straighten end. Cut four 3½" squares with 3½" Fussy Cut Ruler.

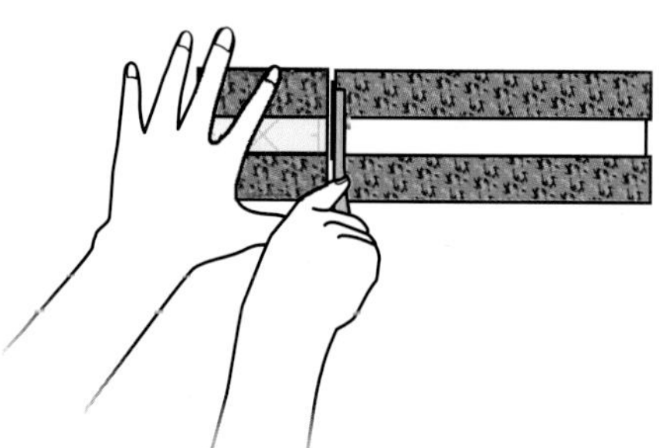

Sewing Block Together

1. Lay out pieces.
2. Flip middle vertical row to left vertical row, right sides together.

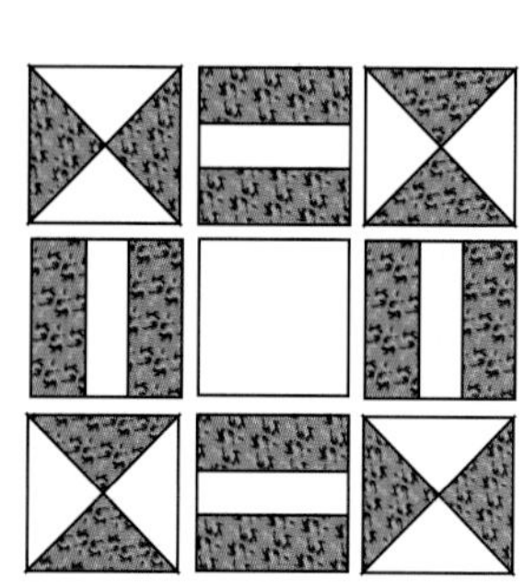

3. Assembly-line sew.

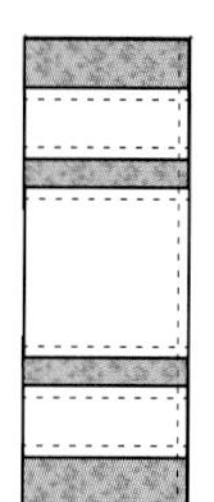

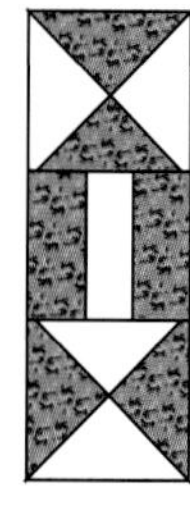

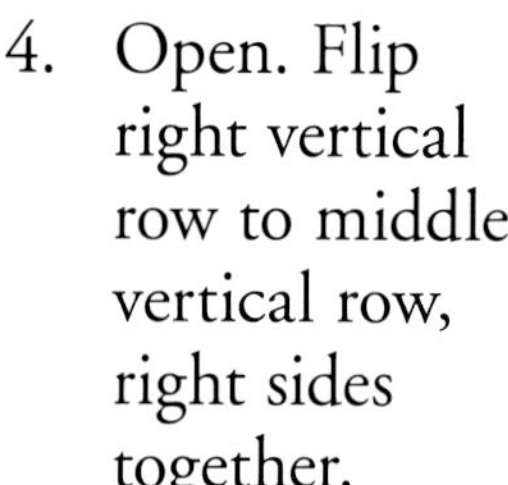

4. Open. Flip right vertical row to middle vertical row, right sides together.

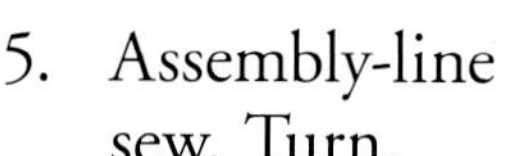

5. Assembly-line sew. Turn.

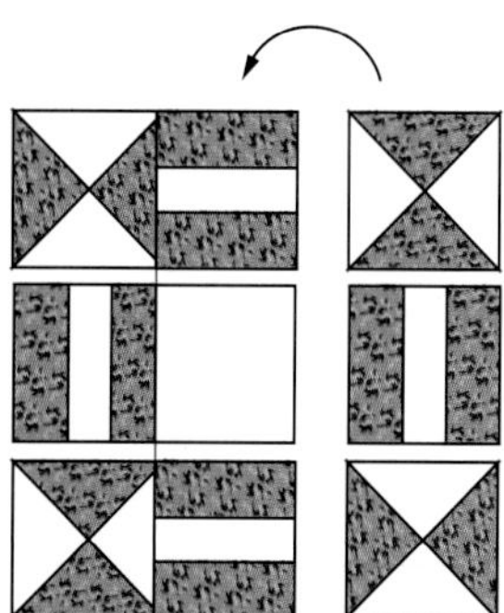

6. Sew remaining rows, pressing seams away from Pieced Squares and Center Square.
7. Press seams toward middle row.

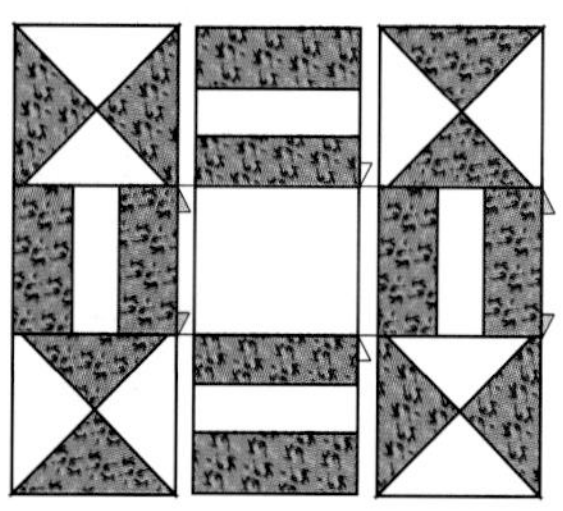

This Way, That Way Arrow Quilt *42" x 56"*
Pieced by Teresa Varnes
Quilted by Judy Jackson

Teresa Varnes pieced this beautiful two color Arrow quilt. After studying the antique quilt, she decided to simplify the quilt and make only two versions of blocks. You can have fun too, making your arrows go any which way. Just don't get lost!

Arrow Quilt

Yardage and Cutting Chart for Twelve Blocks

Background	**2 yds**
Center Squares	(1) 3½" strip cut into (12) 3½" squares
Quarter Squares	(3) 4½" strips cut into (24) 4½" squares
Stripes	(5) 1½" strips
Lattice	(16) 2" strips
Cornerstones	(2) 6" strips cut into (10) 6" squares
Medium	**2¼ yds**
Quarter Squares	(3) 4½" strips cut into (24) 4½" squares
Stripes	(10) 1½" strips
Lattice	(8) 2" strips
Cornerstones	(2) 6" strips cut into (10) 6" squares
Binding	(6) 3" strips
Batting	**53" x 65"**
Backing	**3 yds**

Supplies

3½" Fussy Cut Ruler
6" Square Up Ruler
6" x 12" Ruler
InvisiGRIP *Place on under side of rulers.*
Cutting Mat

Making Twelve Blocks

Four blocks are turned one way and eight are turned the opposite way.

1. Make forty-eight 3½" Quarter Square Patches and forty-eight 3½" Stripe Patches.
2. Sew four together as first Arrow.

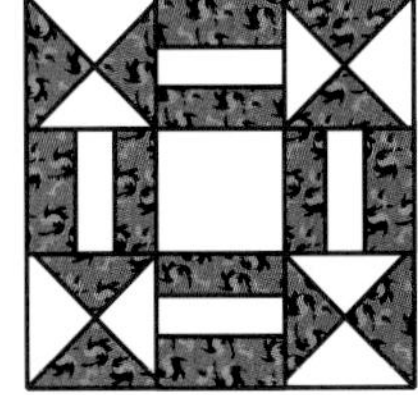

Make 4

Sewing Eight Blocks Together

Sew eight as second Arrow, or any direction Arrow you choose.

1. Lay out pieces.
2. Flip middle vertical row to left vertical row, right sides together.

3. Assembly-line sew.

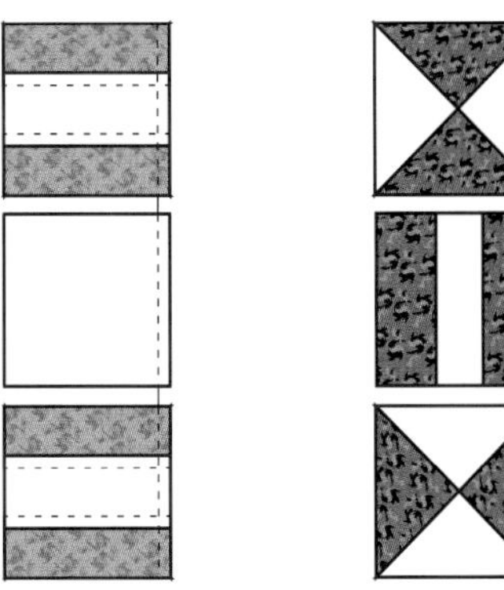

4. Open. Flip right vertical row to middle vertical row, right sides together.

5. Assembly-line sew. Turn.
6. Sew remaining rows, pressing seams away from Pieced Squares and Center Square.

7. Press seams toward middle row.

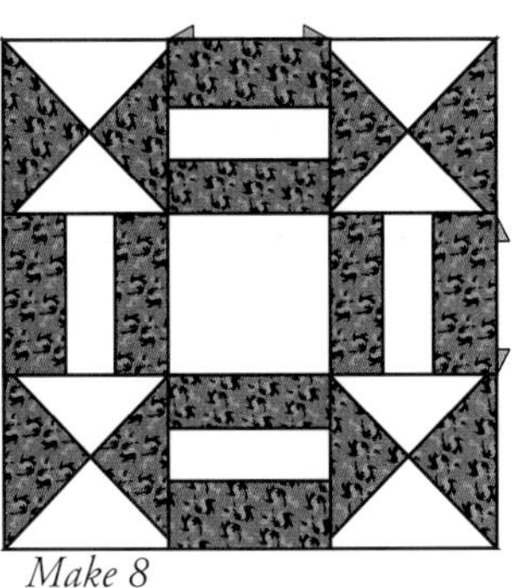

Make 8

Making Twenty Quarter Square Patches for Cornersones

1. Place ten sets of 6" squares right sides together. Draw diagonal lines.
2. Sew following directions on page 101.
3. Place patch on a small cutting mat right side up.
4. Square with a 6" Square Up Ruler to 5".

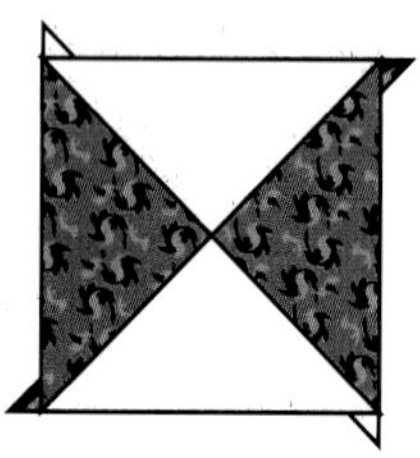
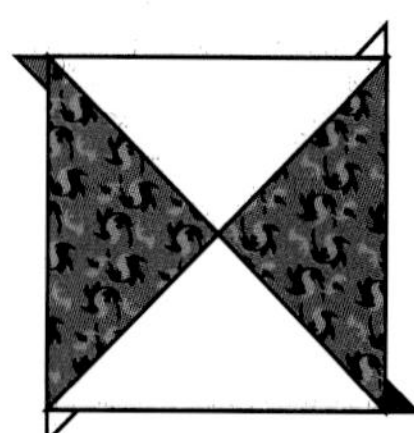

5. Trim on four sides.

Sewing and Cutting Lattice

1. Place 2" strips.
2. Sew with ¼" seam.

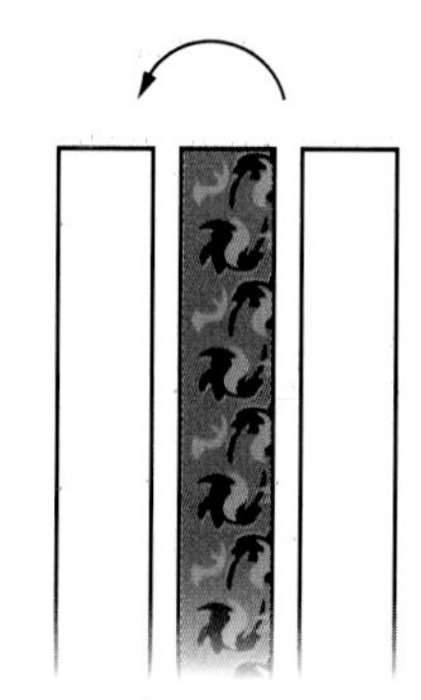

Light Medium Light

3. Set seams with medium on top. Open, and press seams toward medium.
4. Measure width of strips. Strips should be 5" wide. Resew if necessary.

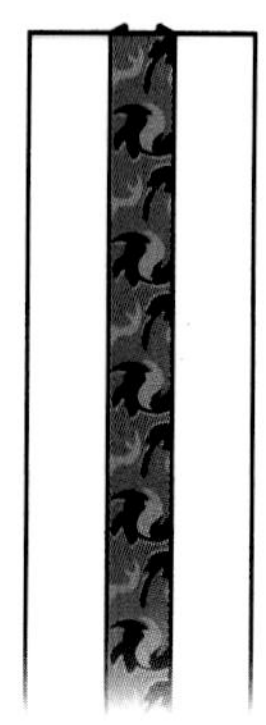

5. Straighten end. Cut thirty-one 5" x 9½" strips with 6" x 12" Ruler.

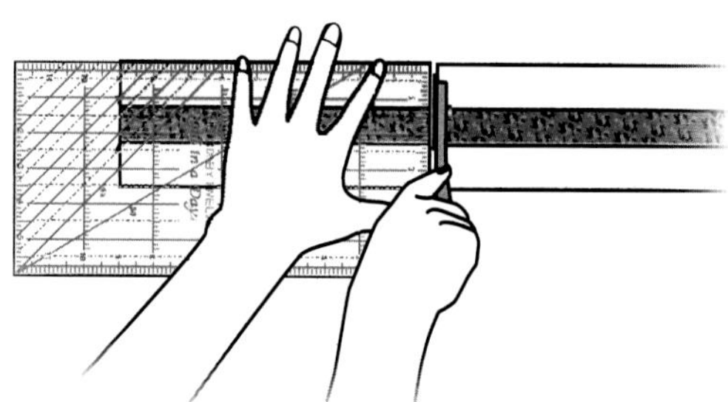

Sewing Top Together

1. Lay out Blocks with Lattice and Cornerstones following photograph.
2. Sew vertical rows.
3. Press all seams toward Lattice.
4. Sew remaining rows. Press seams towards Lattice.
5. Layer, quilt, and bind.

Arrows Chasing Crows Around the Pond *46" x 46"*
Pieced and Quilted by Jo Ann Bender

Jo Ann combined three quilt block patterns to make her impressive quilt. She used the Arrow Block for her corners and alternated them with Crow's Nest blocks. For her centerpiece, she stitched a large Goose in the Pond block and framed the quilt using fabric scraps from all of her blocks.

English Flower Garden Quilt

In 1928, Ruby McKim began writing for the Kansas City Star, which launched 1,000 full size patterns printed over three decades. This pattern is #81.

Ruby McKim was a trend setter in the industry with her book, *"101 Patchwork Patterns"* published in 1931.

Antique English Flower Garden Quilt designed by Ruby McKim *72" x 84"*
Unknown Quilt Maker

In the early 1920's, Ruby McKim and her husband Arthur, founded McKim Studios, a home based business with syndicated quilt patterns and kits. It was quite successful at a time when women had little money to spend on their hobby.

English Flower Garden

Fabric Selection

Select one green for Stem and Leaves, one check for Flower Pot and three small prints for Flowers.

Cutting Chart for One Block

Finished Size 16" Square

Background	(1) 17" square
Green	
Stem	(1) 9" square
Leaves	(1) 4½" x 7½"
Prints	
Flowers	(3) 4½" squares
Flower Pot	(1) 4½" x 6½"
Yo yos (Optional)	(3) 4½" squares
Light Weight Non-Woven Fusible Interfacing	**⅓ yd**
Leaves	(1) 4½" x 7½"
Flower Pot	(1) 4½" x 6½"
100% Cotton Batting	
Flower Pot	(1) 4½" x 7½"
Freezer Paper	
Flowers	(3) 4½" squares

Supplies

½" wide Bias Tape Maker
6" x 12" Ruler
Hemostat
Wooden Iron
Frixion Pen
8½" x 11" Freezer Paper
Sewline Fabric Glue Pen (Optional)
Template Plastic

Making Flower Pot and Leaves

1. Trace patterns on template plastic with template marking pen. Cut out shapes.

2. Turn 4½" x 6½" pieces non-woven fusible interfacing **smooth side up.** With permanent marking pen, trace four Leaves on smooth side of interfacing with ½" space between each, and one Flower Pot on second piece.

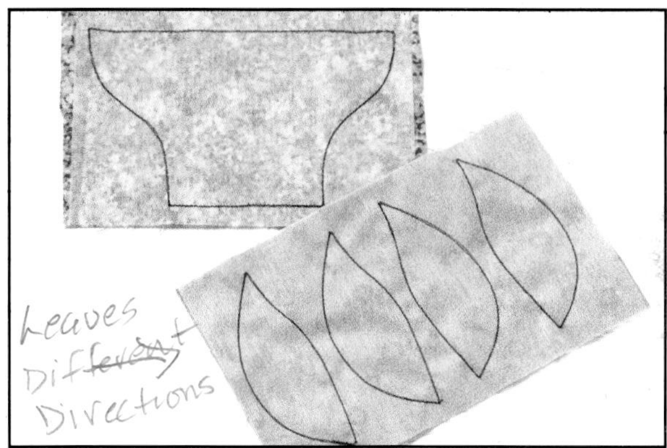

Trace two leaves in one direction, and two leaves in the other direction.

3. Place **rough, fusible side** of interfacing against right side of 4½" x 6½" fabrics for Flower Pot and green Leaf fabric. Pin.
4. With 20 stitches per inch or 1.8 on computerized machines, sew on drawn lines with metal open toe foot.
5. Trim seams to ⅛".

6. Cut small opening in center of interfacing. Insert straw into hole. Push straw against fabric.

7. Place ball of ball point bodkin on fabric stretched over straw. Gently push fabric into straw with bodkin to start turning piece.

Use straw to turn out correct way

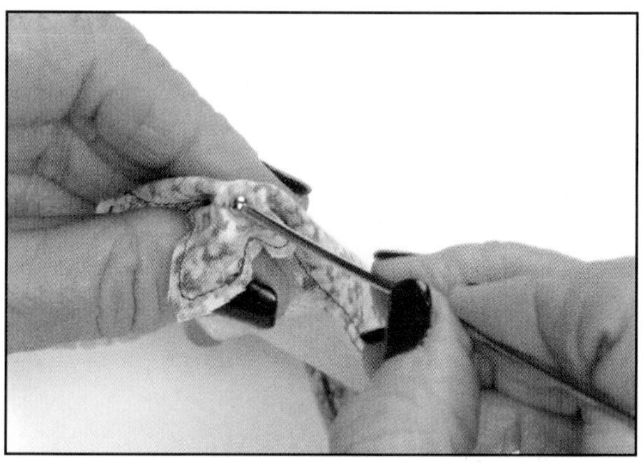

8. Remove straw and bodkin. Insert straw in second half, and turn right side out with bodkin. Run bodkin around inside edge, pushing out seams.
9. Pick out points on Leaves with stiletto.

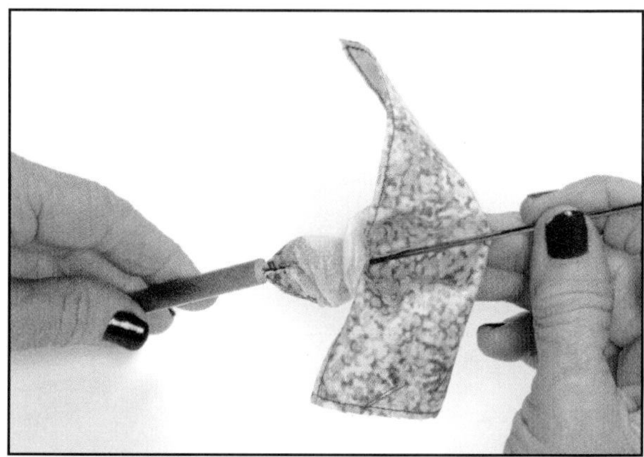

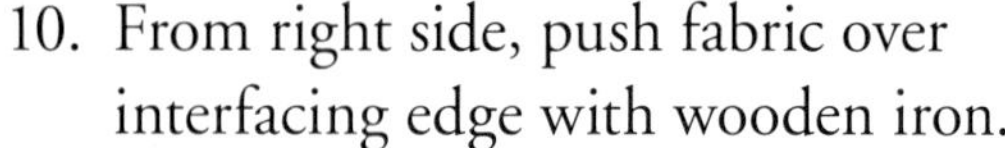

10. From right side, push fabric over interfacing edge with wooden iron.

Push from inside out.

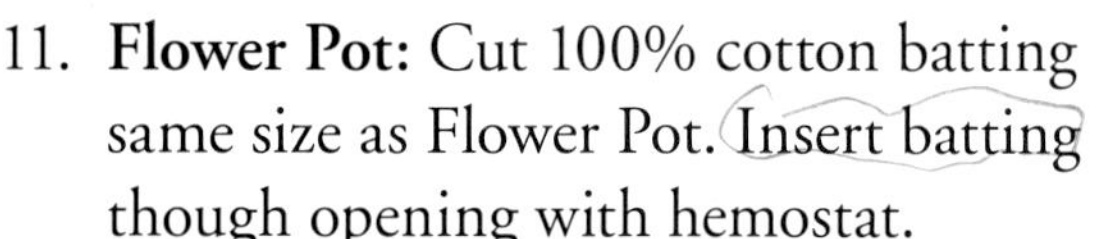

11. **Flower Pot:** Cut 100% cotton batting same size as Flower Pot. Insert batting though opening with hemostat.

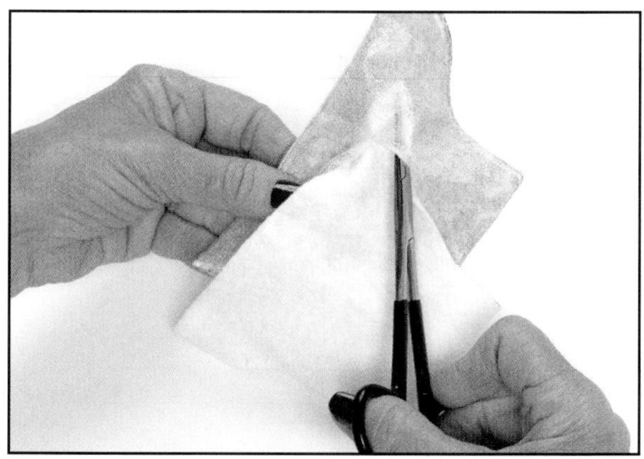

Making Bias Stem

1. Cut 9" square on diagonal.

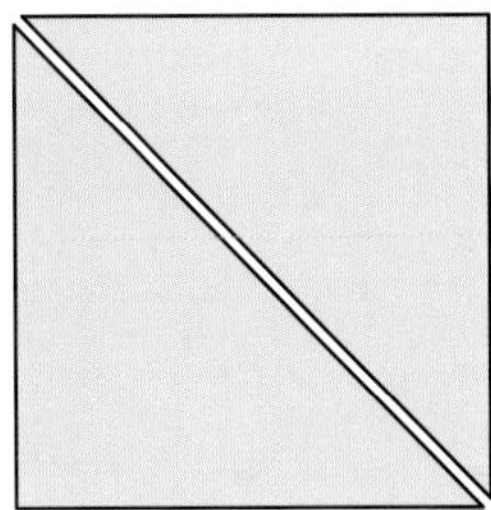

2. Cut 1" strips from both sides of center.

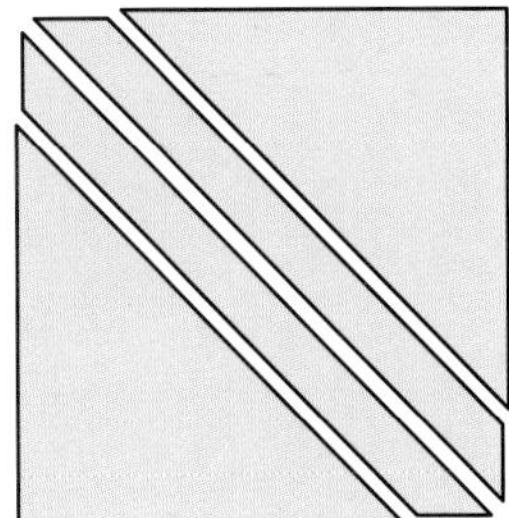

3. Feed bias strip into ½" or 12mm Bias tape maker. Use a stiletto to help start fabric if necessary.

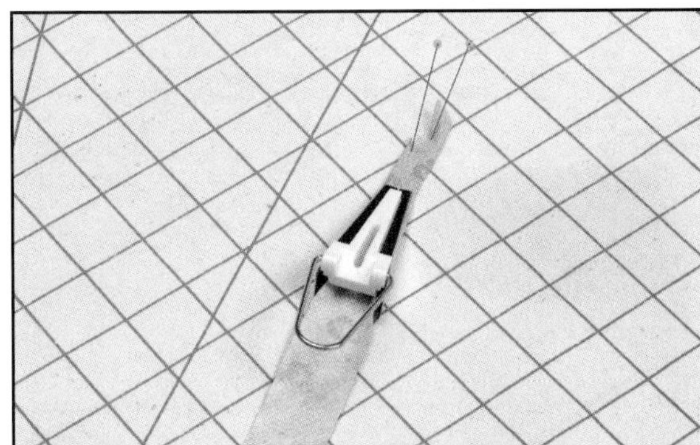

4. Press Bias strip with raw edges centered.

Making Durable Templates

1. Cut freezer paper in half.
2. Trace three hexagons on dull side of freezer paper.

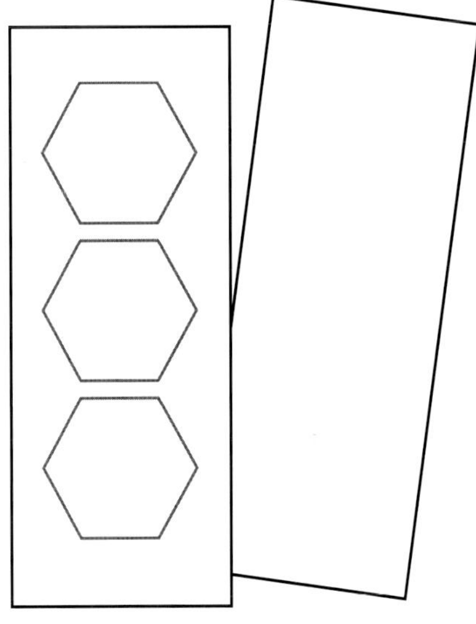

3. Place two sheets together, shiny side of marked paper to dull side.
4. Press on applique pressing sheet **shiny side down. Do not use steam.**

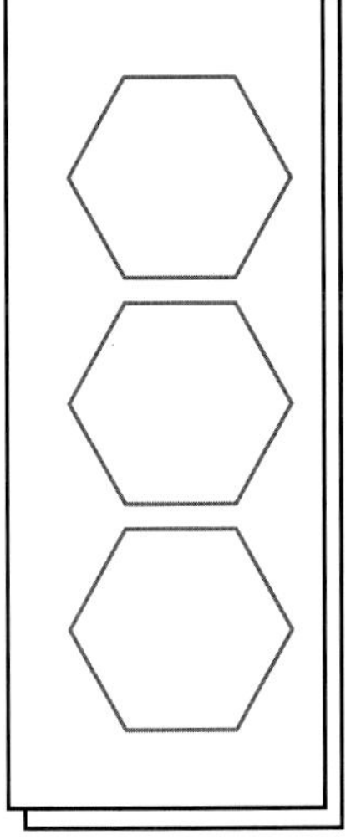

5. Let template cool. Cut three hexagon templates out of freezer paper.

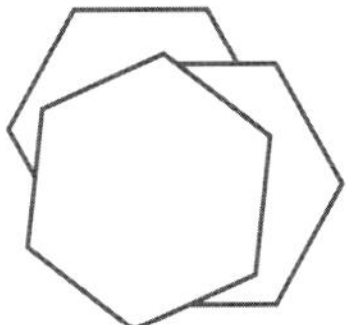

Making Hexagon Flowers

1. Center hexagon on wrong side of fabric square, shiny side against wrong side of fabric. Press.

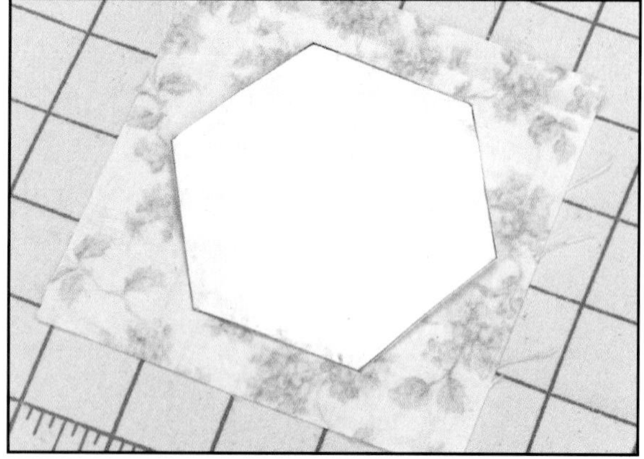

2. Trim excess fabric from each corner, leaving ⅜" seam allowance.

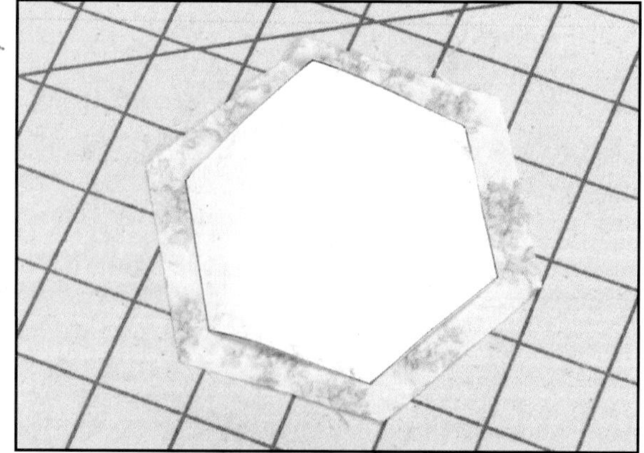

3. Using fingers and thumb, fold fabric over first edge.
4. Miter and fold fabric over corner. Press in place with hot iron. (Optional: Glue in place with Sewline Fabric Glue Pen.)

5. Circle around hexagon, folding and pressing each miter in place.

6. Press from right side of fabric. Let cool.

7. Remove freezer paper.

Sewing Bias Stem to Background

1. Fold 17" Background in half and crease.
2. Draw placement lines 1½" in on Background square with **disappearing marker as Frixion pen.** It disappears when pressed with steam.
3. Fold one bias strip in half. Pin center on center line 7" up from bottom edge. Curve slightly. Pin ends.
4. Edge stitch with matching thread.

5. Place 9" bias strip on center line 3½" from bottom edge. Pin top and bottom.
6. Edgestitch.

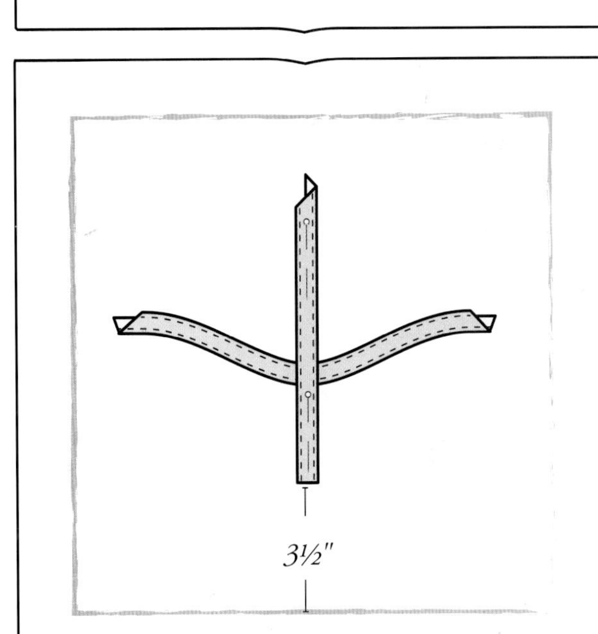

Placing Flower Pot, Flowers and Leaves

1. Crease Flower Pot in half. Place on center line 1½" up from bottom.
2. Line Flower's straight edges on 1½" lines.
3. Place Leaves. Tuck Leaves under Basket and Stem.
4. Fuse Leaves and Flower Pot in place.
5. Pin Flowers in place.

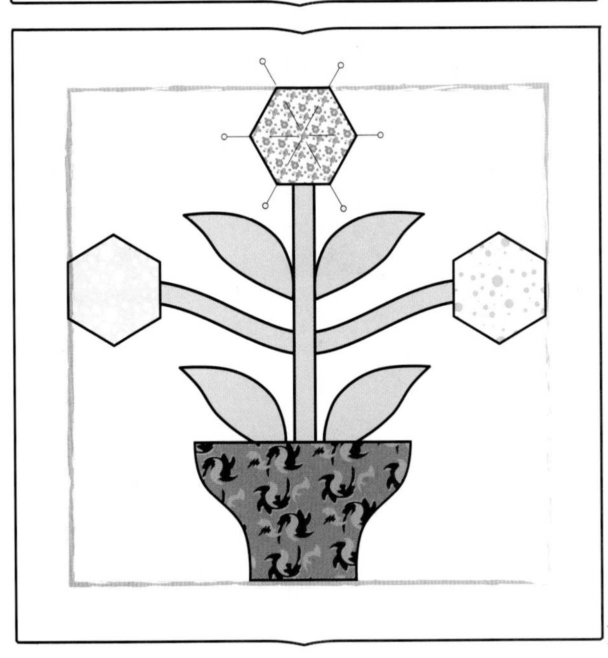

Sewing Outside Edges

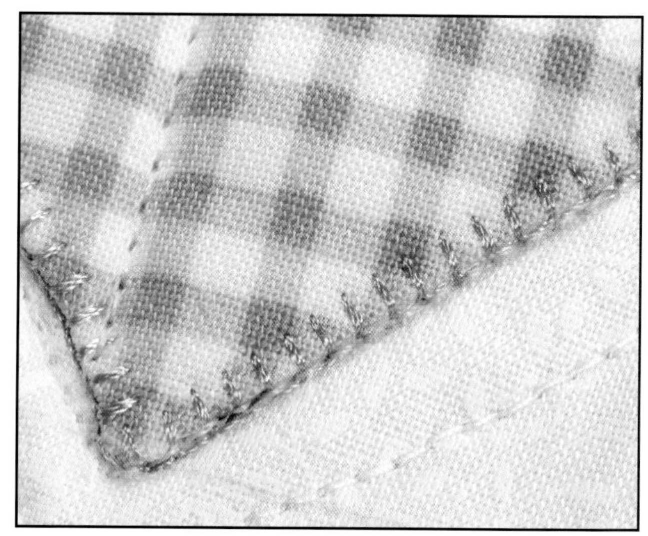

1. Sew outside edges of Leaves, Flower Pot, and Flowers with straight stitch or blanket stitch.
2. Remove outside line.
3. Sew buttons or Yo Yos to center of Flowers. To make sure block fits in layout.
4. Square block to match size of adjoining blocks.

Making Yo Yo Centers

1. Cut circles with a 3½" diameter from fabric. A circle template is handy for drawing circles with diameters 1¼" to 3½".

2. **Double thread a hand sewing needle** with quilting thread or regular matching thread. Knot the end.
3. Sew circle into a Yo Yo by turning under the edge ¼" to the wrong side, and basting. Pull tight, push the needle to the back, and knot.
4. Attach to center of Flower with thread and bar tack stitch.

Spring Garden
Pieced by Teresa Varnes
Quilted by Amie Potter

44" x 44"

Using fresh green to set off her blocks against her snowy white background, Teresa chose pink, blue and yellow for her flowers and added yo yo centers for dimension. By adding quarter square patches in green and white, she created a large 8-point star.

For the four Quarter Squares, cut two 14" squares of green and Background. Sew the quarter squares together following directions in the Arrow blocks on page 101. Square the four on point English Flower Garden blocks and quarter squares to the same size, approximately 13" to 12½".

Posey Quilt

This block pattern was originally designed by Eveline Foland for the Kansas City Star on June 8, 1929. When the block is repeated in a quilt it is most popularly known as Posies Round the Square. Other names given to the quilt are Sweetheart's Garden and Spiced Pinks.

Eveline Foland created 130 modern designs which were printed in the Kansas City Star from 1929 through 1932. Her bold signature set her designs apart.

Antique Posey Quilt designed by Eveline Foland *72" x 84"*
Unknown Quilt Maker

This lovely vintage quilt looks as fresh and cheerful as the day it was made. The quilter chose a shade of lavender for her squares and border on a fresh clean white background. Her pretty pink posies with bright yellow centers gives her quilt a spring time garden appearance.

Posey

Fabric Selection

Select one Background, a print for Quarter Circles, two fabrics for Flower and one for Leaves. *Decide how many Posey blocks you need for your quilt layout. This chart is for only one block, and you may want more blocks.*

Cutting Chart for One Block

	Finished Size 12" Square
Background	
Square	(1) 9" square
Triangles	(2) 7½" squares
Framing Border (optional)	(2) 3" strips
Print	
Circle	(1) 8½" square
Four Flowers	(1) 3" x 10"
Leaves	(1) 3" x 12"
Bias Stem	(1) 9½" square
Fusible Interfacing	
Circle	(1) 8½" square
Flowers	(1) 3" x 10"
Leaves	(1) 3" x 12"
Template Plastic	(1) 10" x 12"

Supplies

½" wide Bias Tape Maker
Four Buttons for Flower Center
Point Turner
Frixion Pen
Applique Pressing Sheet
9½" Square Up Ruler

Making Circle

1. Trace 8" Circle on smooth side of non-woven fusible interfacing.
2. Place bumpy side of fusible interfacing against right side of Circle fabric. Pin in place.
3. Put metal open toe foot on machine. Adjust settings to 1.8 stitch length and lighten pressure on foot. Use needle down feature if available to pivot as you turn.
4. Sew on drawn line. Overlap stitches ½".
5. Trim outside Circle ⅛" away from stitches.

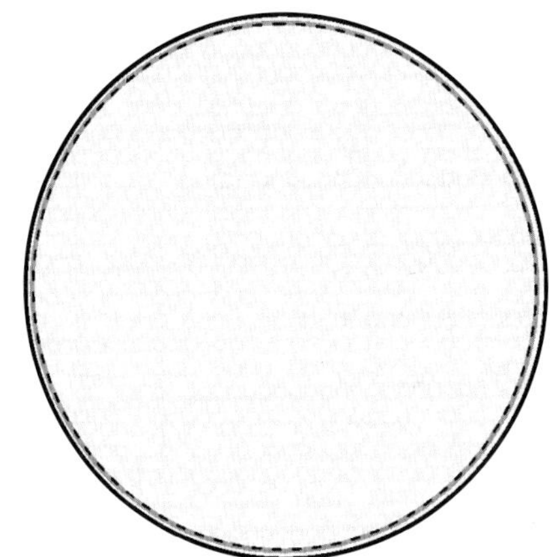

6. Pull fusible away from Circle fabric. Snip a small slit in center of fusible.
7. Carefully turn Circle right side out through slit. Use point turner to smooth out edges. Push fabric over edge from center out with wooden iron.

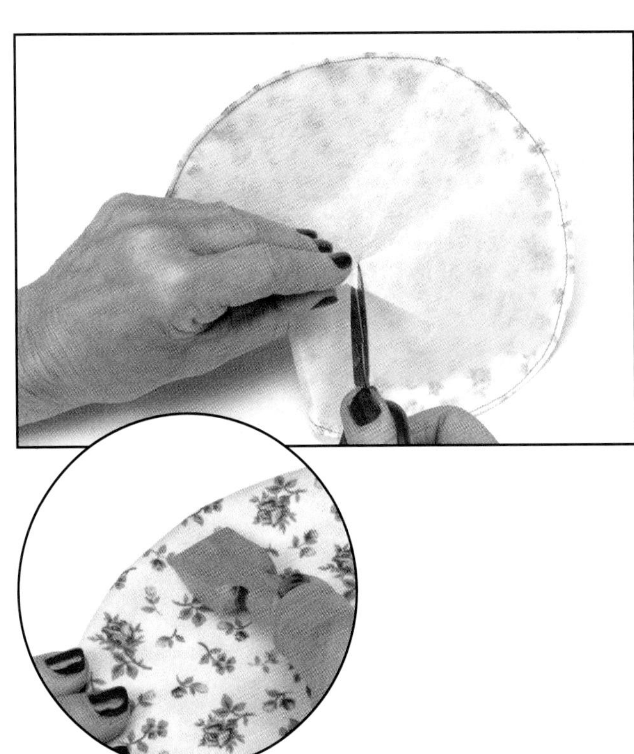

8. Place Circle on applique pressing sheet. Gently press Circle from center out.

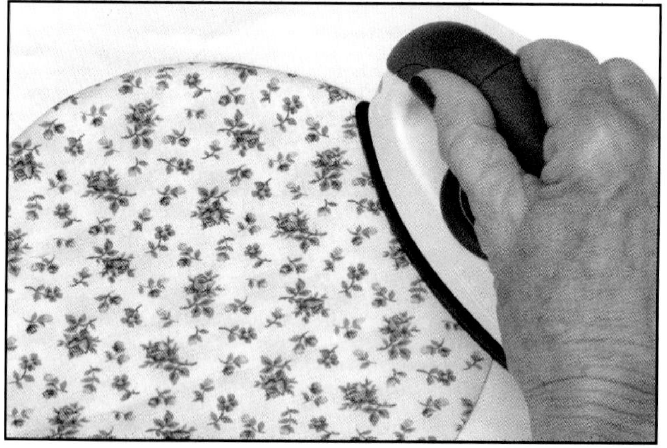

9. Finger press Circle in fourths. Take a little snip at quarter marks.

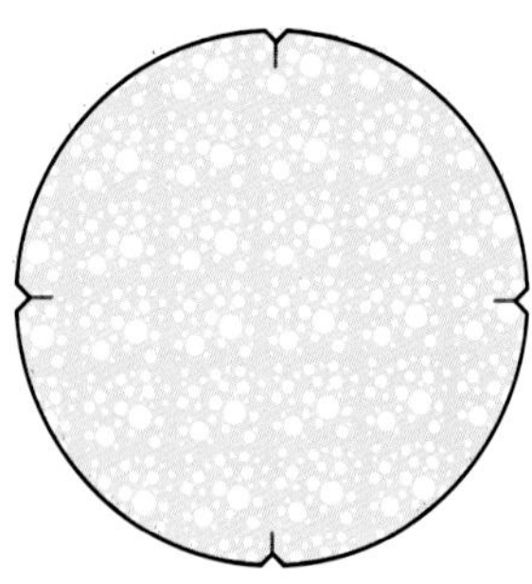

10. Cut Circle into fourths with ruler and cutter.

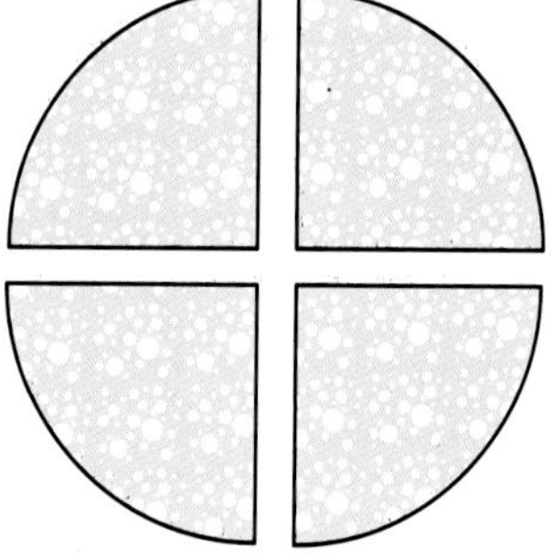

11. Place Quarter Circles on Background and press.

12. Turn patch over with Quarter Circles on bottom, and press.

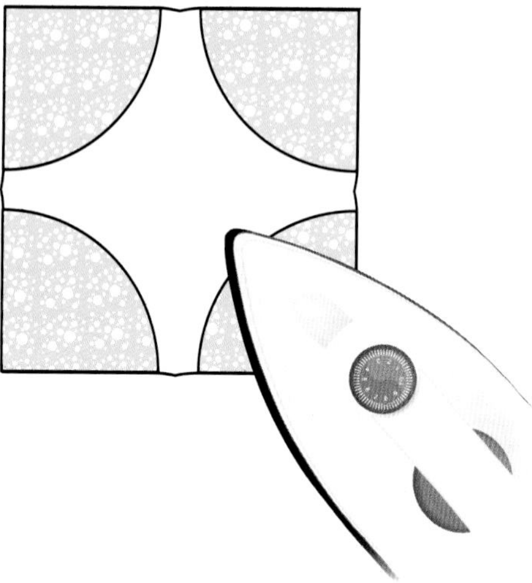

13. Place matching or contrasting thread in machine. Select a straight, blanket or blind hem stitch on machine. Stitch around appliqué.

Making Bias Stem

1. Feed 1" x 12" bias strip into ½" or 12mm Bias tape maker. Use a stiletto to help start fabric if necessary.

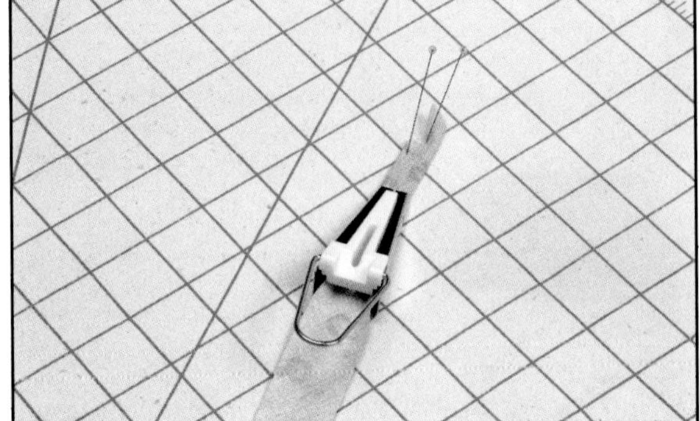

2. Press Bias strip with raw edges centered.

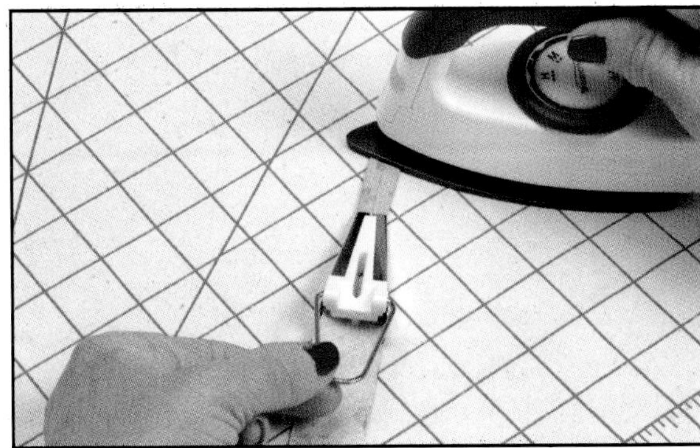

3. Straighten left end. Cut strip into four 2½" strips.

4. Center Stems on patch with open side up. Pin. Baste Stems in place ⅛" away from edge. Remove pins.

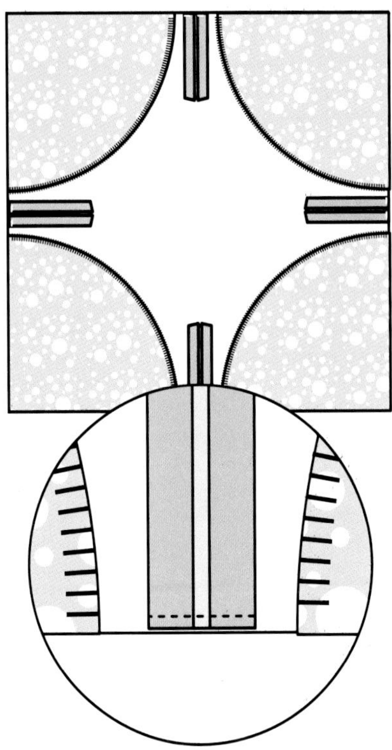

Adding Triangles

1. Layer cut 7½" Background squares in half on one diagonal.

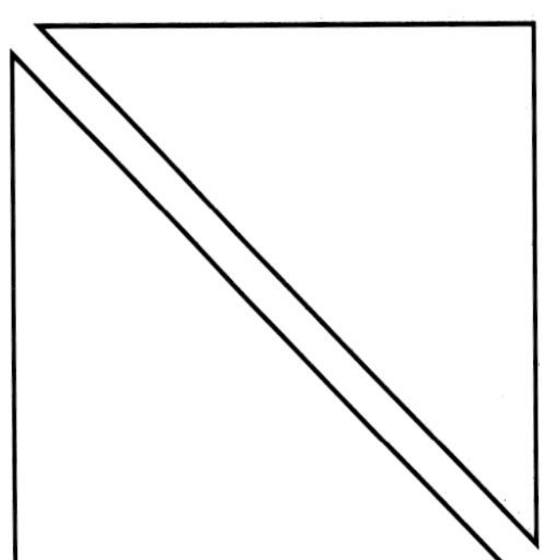

2. Fold Triangles in half. Crease centers.
3. Center Triangles on opposite sides of square.

4. Flip Triangles right side together with equal tips on both sides. Pin in place.

5. Sew Triangles with a ¼" seam and 15 stitches per inch.
6. Press seams toward Triangle. Trim off tips.
7. Add remaining Triangles with equal tips hanging out. Press toward Triangles.

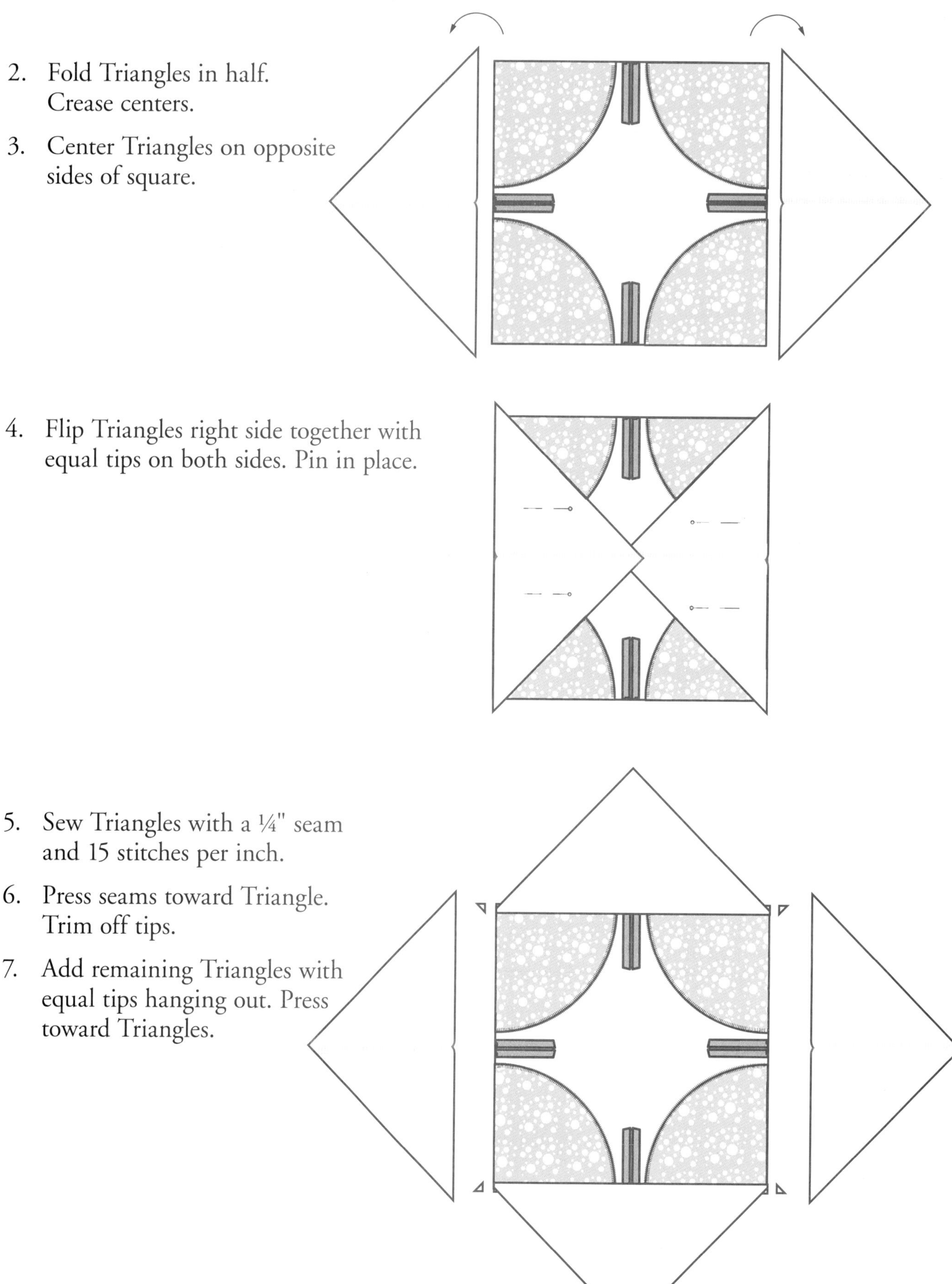

Adding Applique

1. Make Templates of Flowers and Leaves.
2. Trace Flowers and Leaves on smooth side of fusible interfacing.
3. Place bumpy side of fusible right side together to fabric.

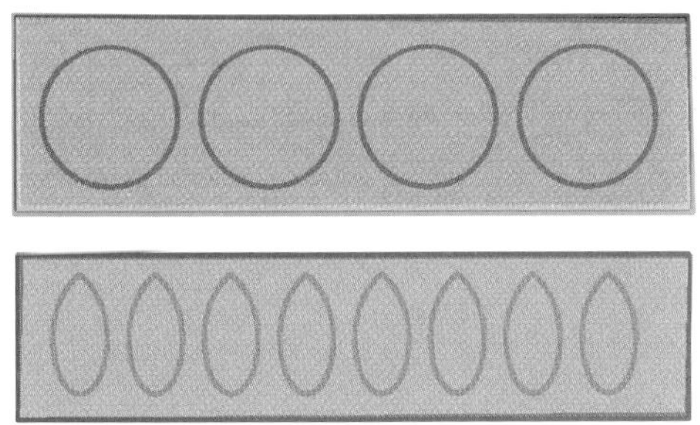

4. Sew on lines using 20 stitches per inch.

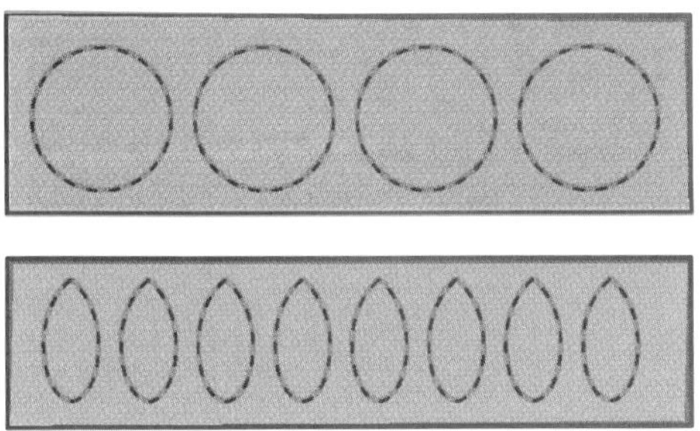

5. Trim ⅛" inch away from stitches. Clip excess at Leaf tips.
6. Turn Leaves and Flowers following directions on *English Flower Garden Block*.

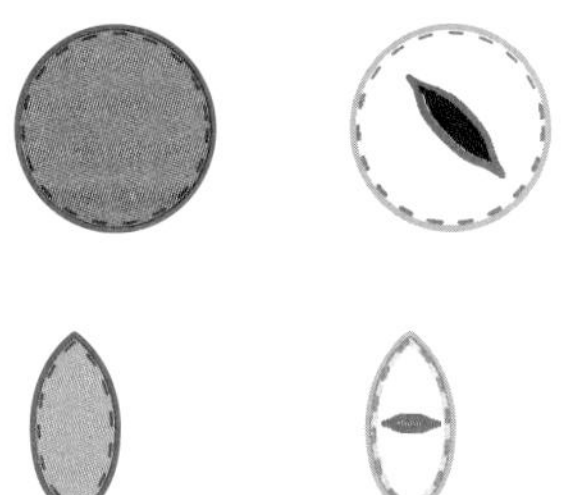

Finishing Block

1. Tuck Stem behind Flower. Arrange Leaves.
2. Steam press in place.
3. Place matching or contrasting thread in machine. Use a straight, blanket or blind hem stitch on block. Stitch around applique.
4. Square block to 12½".
5. Finish with button or embellishment of choice.

Optional: Adding Framing Border

Add a 3" strip to Posey if you choose to place the Posey block next to the Dresden Plate block in your layout.

1. Sew 3" strips around block.
2. Press toward Framing Border.
3. Square block to 16½".

Teresa's Cheery Posey Quilt

Pieced by Teresa Varnes
Quilted by Amie Potter

60" x 60"

Spring is definetly in the air with Teresa's pretty Posey Quilt. She used crisp white background for her blocks, lattice and borders. Cheerful bright pink poseys with coordinating quarter circles pop! Her selection of small print fabric for her corner and side triangles highlighted her center arrangment perfectly. Her addition of a scalloped border offers the perfect finishing touch.

Cheery Posey Wallhanging

Fabric Selection

Select one Background, a small print for Triangles, plus fabric for Cornerstone, Framing Border and Folded Border.

Cutting Chart for Quilt Setting

	Finished Size 60" x 60"
Background	**1¾ yds**
Lattice	(6) 3" strips cut into (16) 3" x 14"
Outside Border	(6) 6" strips
Cornerstones	**⅛ yd**
	(1) 3" strip cut into (12) 3" squares
Triangles	**1¼ yds**
Sides	(1) 25" square
Corners	(2) 15½" squares
Framing Borders for Blocks	**⅓ yd**
	(7) 1¼" strips
Folded Border	**⅓ yd**
	(7) 1¼" strips
Bias Binding	**½ yd**
	(1) 16" strip cut into 2¼" bias strips
Backing	**4 yds**
Batting	**68" x 68"**

Supplies

½" wide Bias Tape Maker
Scallop Ruler (Optional)

Making Blocks

1. Make five blocks.
2. Square blocks to 12½".
3. Sew 1¼" Framing Border to four sides of block.

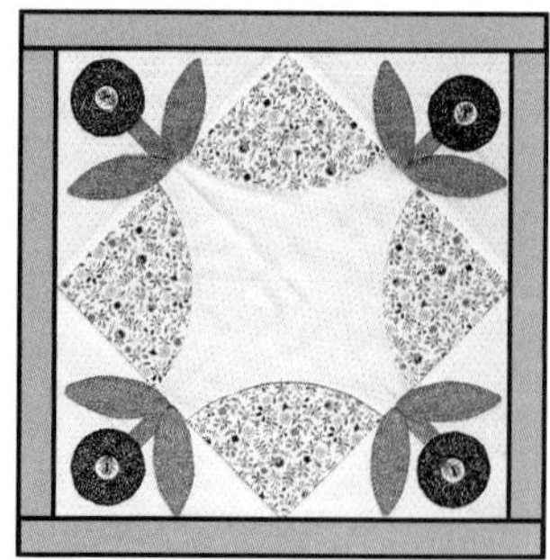

Finishing Wallhanging

1. Lay out five blocks on point with Lattice and Cornerstones.
2. Cut one 25" square on both diagonals into four Side Triangles. Place on sides.
3. Cut two 15½" squares on one diagonal into four Corner Triangles. Place at Corners.
4. Sew blocks together, and press toward Lattice.
5. Sew rows together, and press toward Triangles.
6. Square outside edge, leaving ½" away from points.
7. Piece 1¼" Framing Border strips together. Press in half, wrong sides together to form Folded Border.
8. Line up raw edge of Framing Border and sew corners. Press. Do not open.
9. Sew remaining two sides, overlapping Framing Border in corners. Press. **Do not open.**
10. Sew outside Border.
11. Mark for Scallop following directions in Quilt in a Day's Scallop Ruler package, item 2019.
12. Layer, quilt and bind.

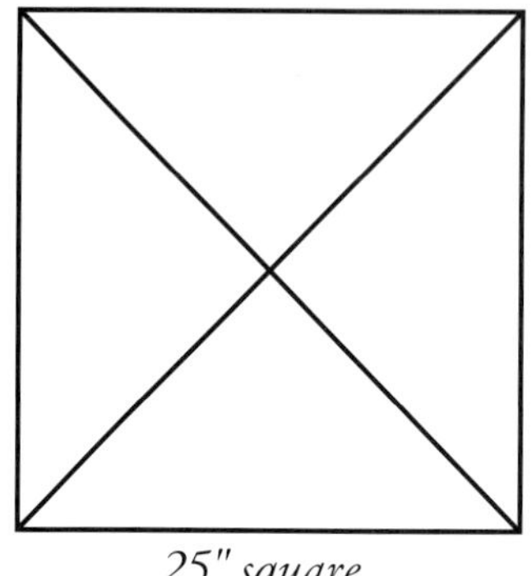

25" square

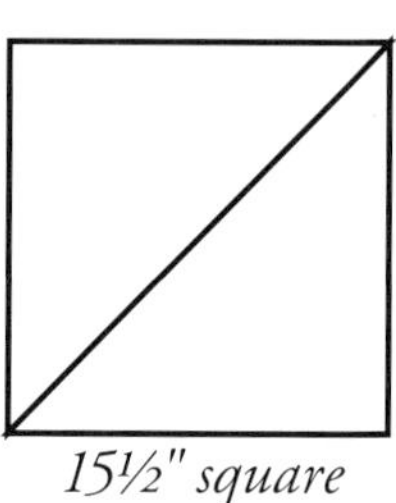

15½" square

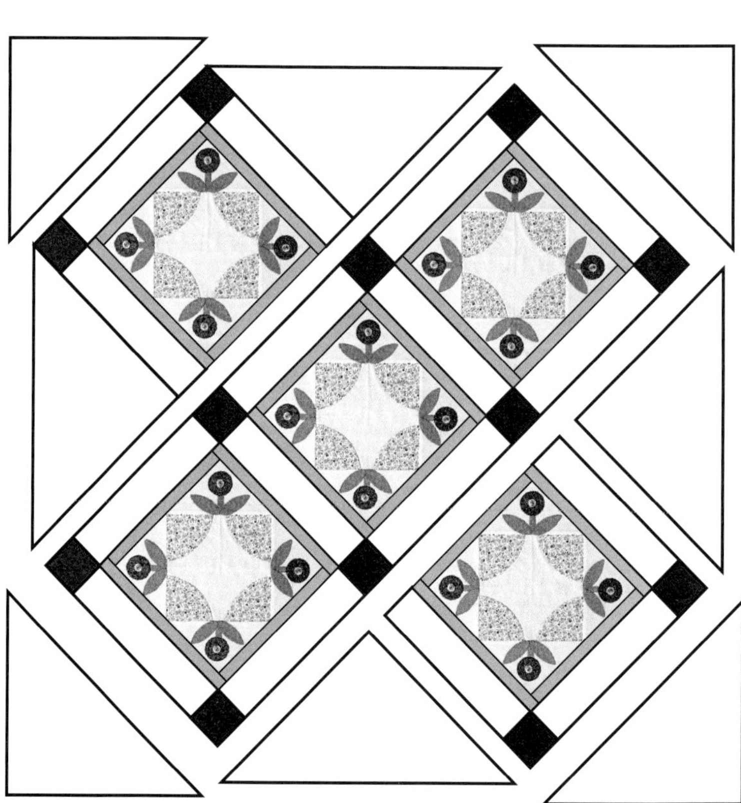

Unknown Quilter 70" x 82"

A creative quilter designed her own English Flower Garden quilt from Ruby McKim's pattern.

Spider Web Quilt

The *Orange Judd Farmer*, a periodical which originated in 1870, referred to this pattern as a Cobweb Quilt. In 1930, the Kansas City Star called it Spider Web with just two fabrics.

In Ruby McKim's book, *One Hundred and One Patchwork Patterns*, she described the Spider Web with rather particular piecing to make them lie perfectly flat when done.

Amish Spider Web Quilt with Floral Border *47" x 47"*
Unknown quilt maker

Ruth Finley, author of America's second quilting book *Old Patchwork Quilts and the Women Who Made Them*, was published in 1929. She named this four color quilt Spider Web, proclaiming influence from the great outdoors. She said this pattern would hardly have originated with an indoor person. The comfy quilt was found in a thrift store and sold for $5.00. Eleanor Burns was gifted this charming country quilt by Mary Ann Byerly.

Spider Web

Fabric Selection

Select two fabrics in light and dark that contrast with each other. For interest, select two prints in different scales.

Two Blocks

The first block is the one described in Ruby McKim's book, and is the most traditional Spider Web block. It's easily made with just two strips sewn together and finished with an easy technique known as "swirling", for a flat finish. The second block is a "no waste" block made from triangles left over from the first block.

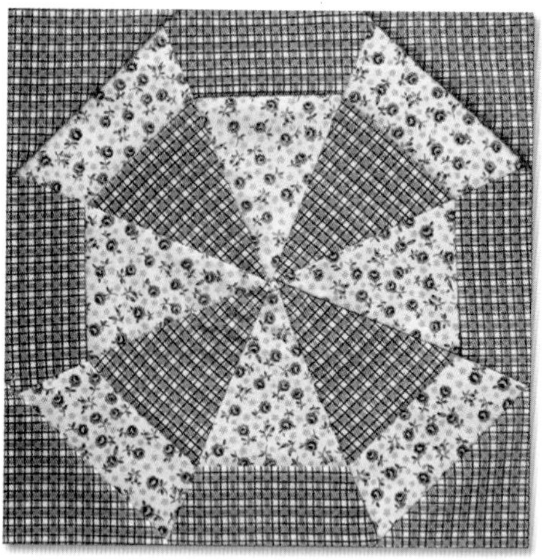

First Block

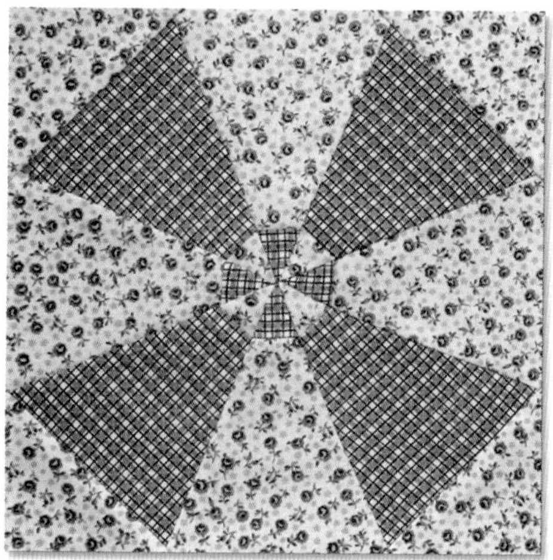

Second Block

Cutting Chart for Two Blocks

Finished Size 8" Square

Light	
Triangles	(1) 3¾" x 21" strip
Base of Triangles	(1) 1¾" x 21" strip
Corners	(2) 3½" squares
Dark	
Triangles	(1) 3¾" x 21" strip
Base of Triangles	(1) 1¾" x 21" strip
Corners	(2) 3½" squares

Supplies

Kaleidoscope Ruler
Invisigrip
Glow-Line Tape™
Seam Ripper
Stiletto

Sewing Strips Together

1. Use a ¼" seam. **Do not use a scant ¼" seam.**
2. Arrange two sets of strips.
3. Flip and sew right sides together with dark on top.

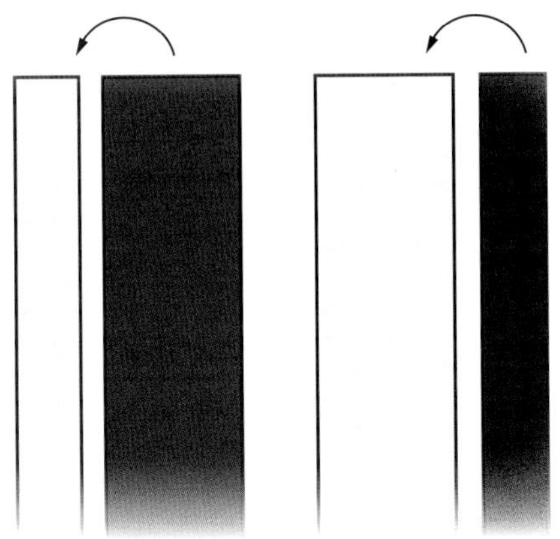

4. Set seams with dark on top.

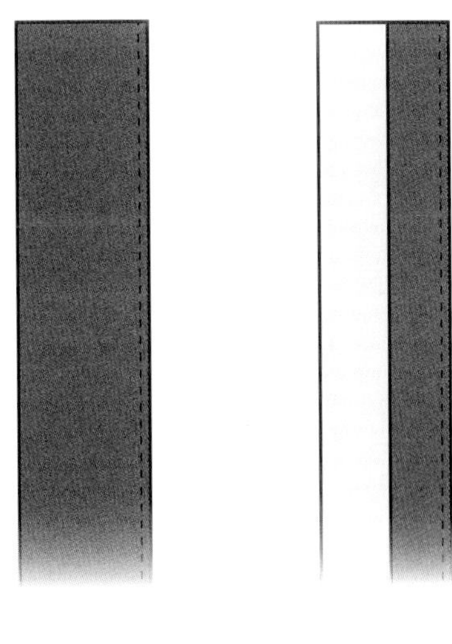

5. Open, and press toward dark.
6. Strip width should be 5".

Little Miss Seamstress is one of Eleanor's treasured gifts from daughter in law, Teresa Bones Burns.

Preparing Kaleidoscope Ruler

1. Place Glow-Line tape under 5" line.
2. Cut piece of Invisigrip ½" smaller than ruler, and apply to wrong side.

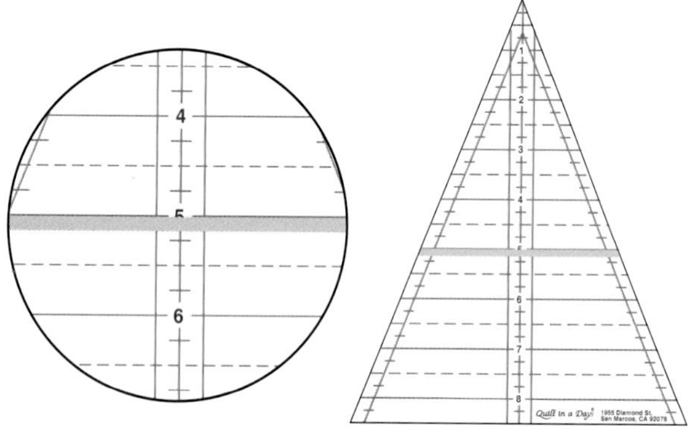

Cutting Triangles

1. Place strips with wide light on top, right side up.

2. Place strip with wide dark on top, right sides together.

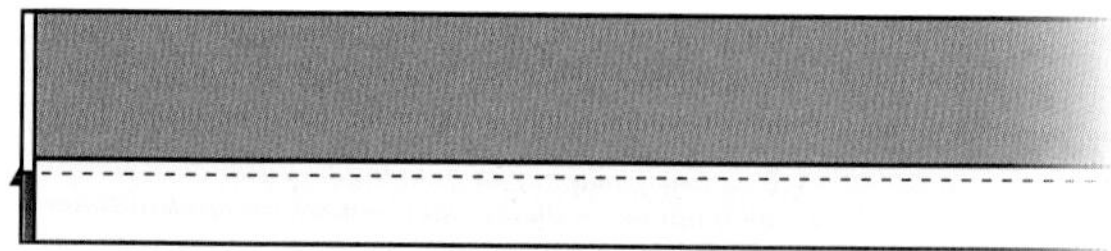

3. Place Kaleidoscope Ruler on strips, with 5" line across bottom.
4. Cut Triangle.

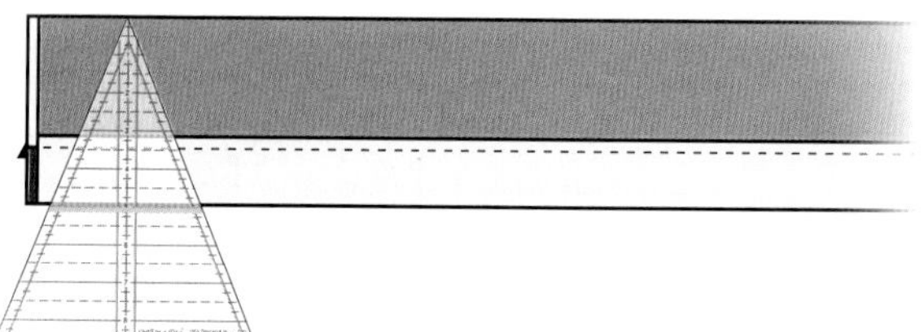

5. Turn ruler and line up ruler with cut edge.
6. Cut again. If necessary, sliver trim to correct the cut.
7. Continue to cut eight pairs.
Do not open.

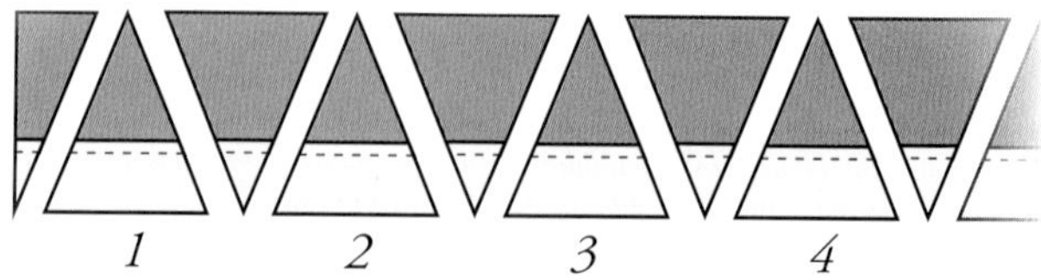

8. Pick up four pairs, every other one, and stack for first block.

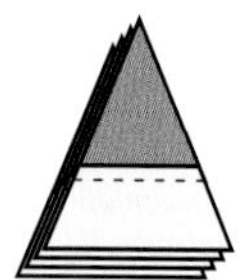

9. Stack remaining four pairs for second block.

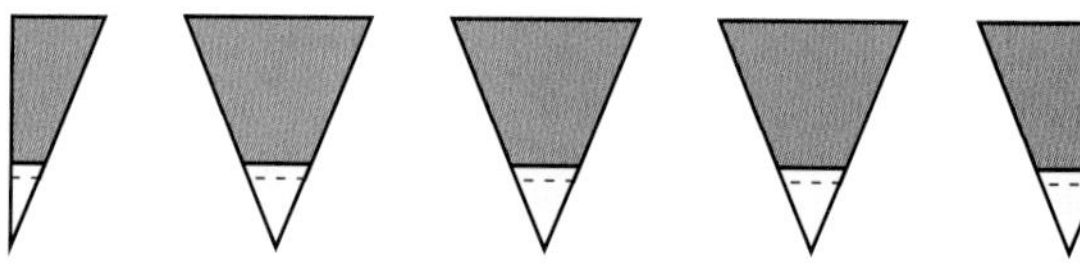

10. Flip stack of second blocks over to sew with locking seams. Set aside.

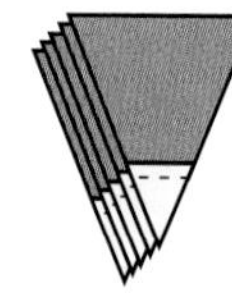

Erwin Knoechel made this intricate sewing box for his second daughter Eleanor.

Sewing Triangles into Circles

1. Begin sewing with first stack.
2. Assembly-line sew. Use a jumper scrap to get started.

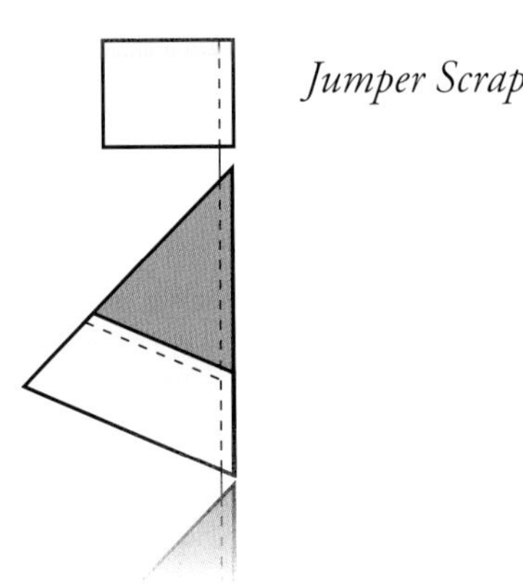

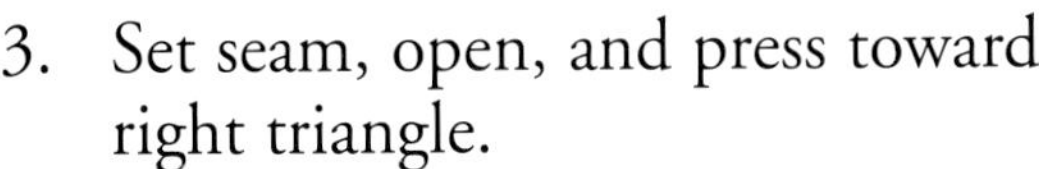

3. Set seam, open, and press toward right triangle.
4. Trim tips even with triangles.

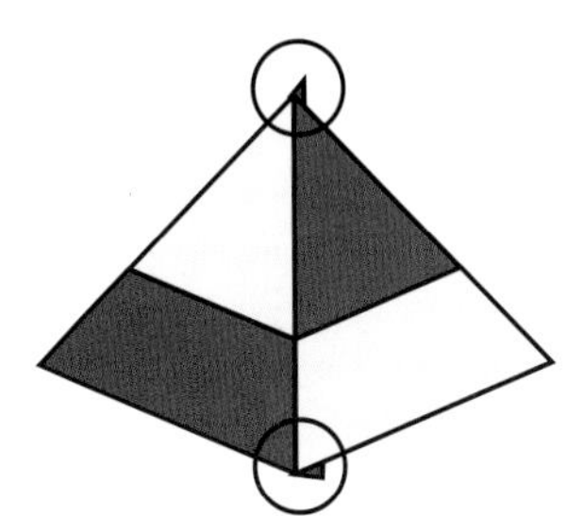

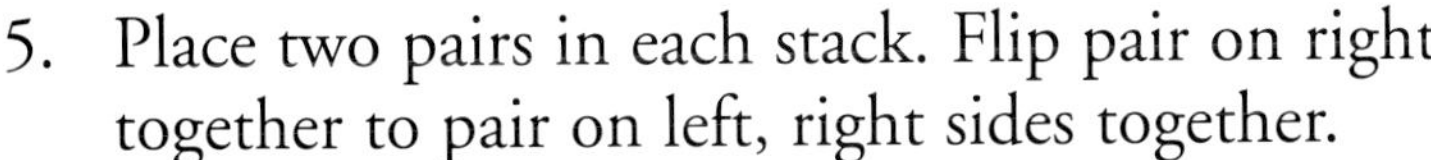

5. Place two pairs in each stack. Flip pair on right together to pair on left, right sides together.

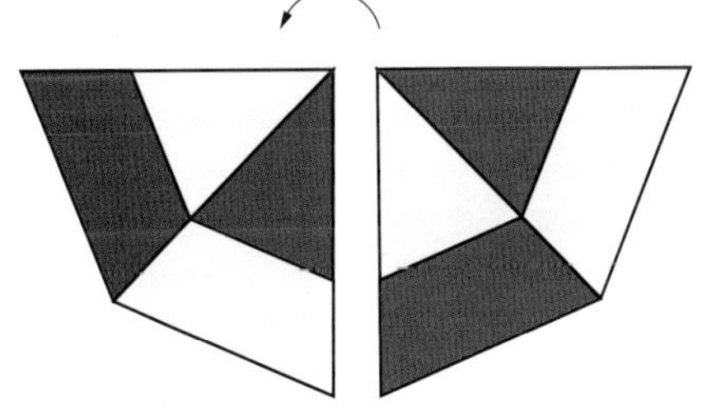

6. **Lock seams**, and assembly-line sew.

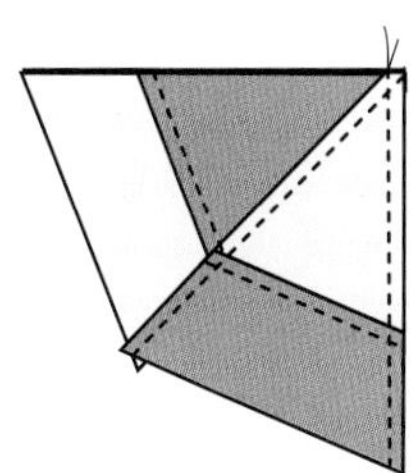

7. Set seam, and press to right.
8. Trim tips.

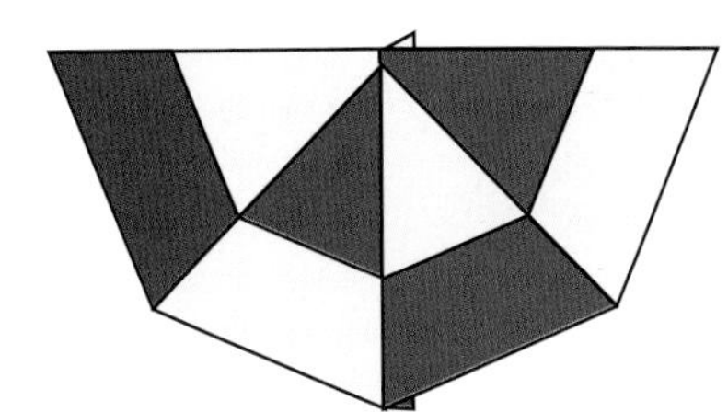

Swirling Center

1. Flip pairs right sides together.

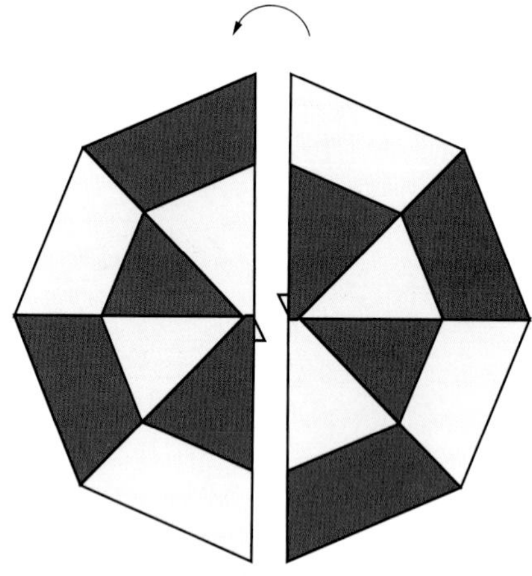

2. Lock center seam, pushing top seam up, and underneath seam down.

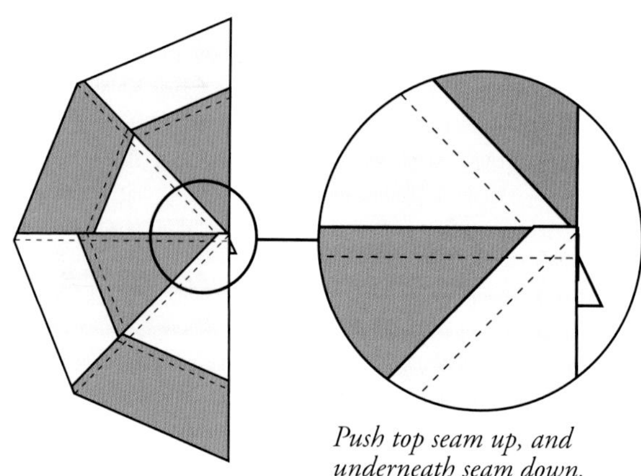

Push top seam up, and underneath seam down.

3. Remove three straight stitches in seam allowance on both sides of vertical seam. See thread to remove in red.

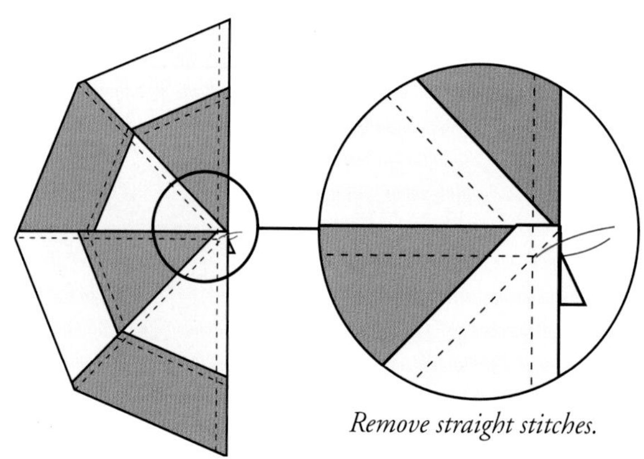

Remove straight stitches.

4. Lay block flat wrong side up.

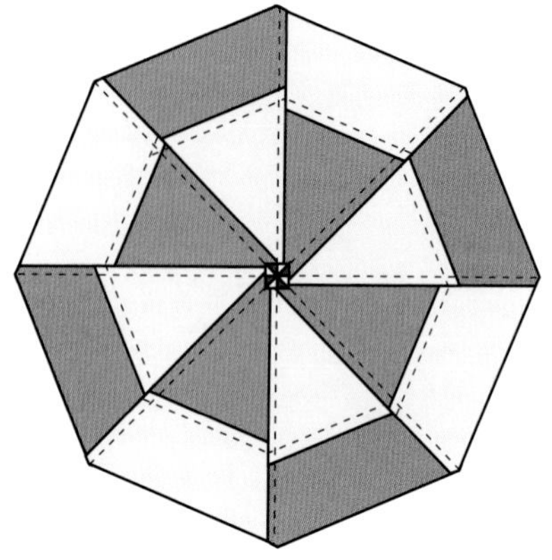

5. Open center and press flat, swirling seams around center.

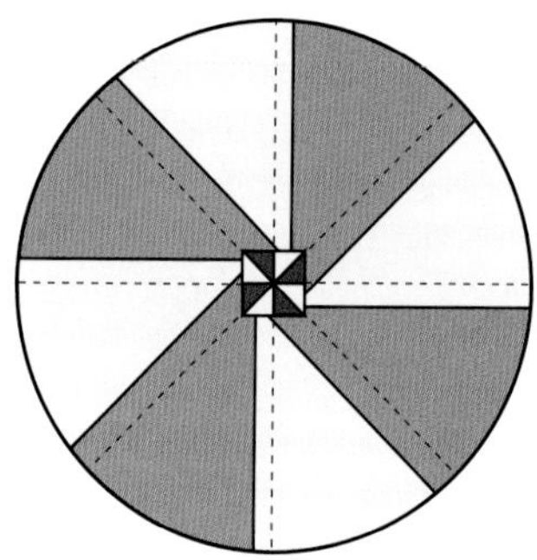

6. Sew Second Block like Block One.

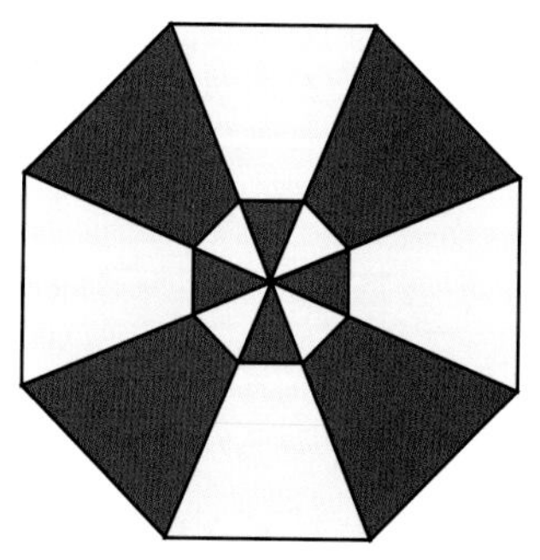

Adding Corners

1. **Change seam allowance to a generous seam allowance. On most machines a perfect ¼" setting is 3.5. Move needle to 3.0 for a generous ¼".**
2. Make two separate stacks of Block One and Block Two.
3. Cut 3½" squares for Corners in half on one diagonal. Place four triangles against opposite color fabric around outside edge of blocks.
4. Turn blocks and corners wrong side up. *It's easier to center triangles.*
5. Center triangles on block corners and sew.
6. From right side, set seams, open, and press toward Corners.

Block One
Sew dark corners on light strips.

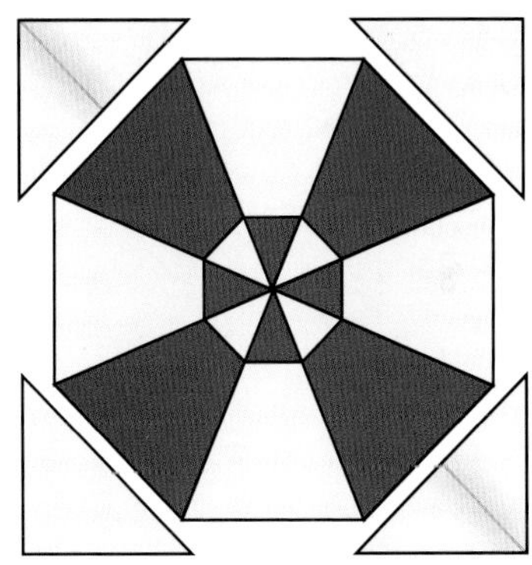

Block Two
Sew light corners on dark triangles.

Squaring Up Block to 8½"

1. Place 9½" Square Up Ruler on block with diagonal line and 4¼" line on center.
2. **Line up ruler's ¼" lines on points from seams.** Trim two sides.

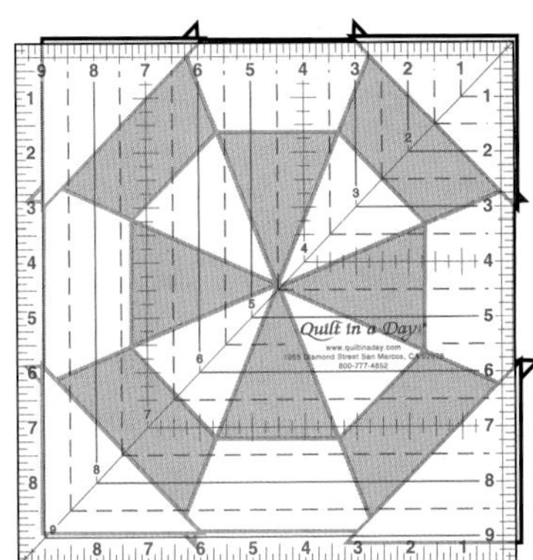

Allow a ¼" seam from points.

3. Turn block. Do not turn ruler. Repeat trimming two sides, allowing a ¼" seam from points. The approximate size is 8½" square. **It is more important to keep ¼" seams than have a perfect 8½" square.**

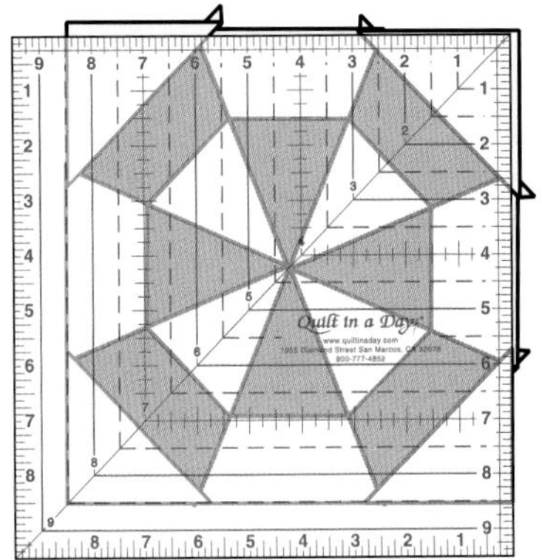

The approximate size is 8½" square.

"Use It Up" Quilt

Pieced by Teresa Varnes
Quilted by Judy Jackson

48" x 48"

Housewives have forever chanted "Use it up, wear it out, make it do, or do without." In this day and age, it's still admirable to "Use it up!" The Spider Web block combined with the No Waste block makes a charming presentation.

Sewing Blocks

1. Make three sets of blocks from each fabric. You will have eighteen blocks: sixteen are for the quilt. Lay out blocks 4 x 4, alternating between Block One and Two.

3. Place twenty 1½" x 8½" Short Lattice between blocks, and beginning and end of each row.

4. Assembly-line sew blocks into four horizontal rows, pressing seams toward Lattice.

5. Sew five Long Lattice between rows, top, and bottom. Press seams toward Lattice.

6. Add Borders. Layer, quilt, and bind.

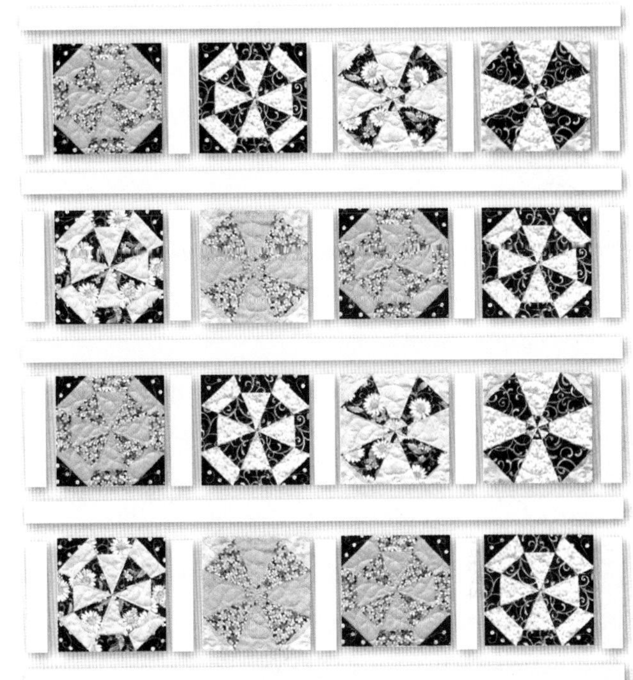

Six Fat Quarters in values from light to dark	**Layer Cut from Each** (3) 3¾" x 20" (3) 1¾" x 20"
Light	**½ yd**
Corners	(2) 3½" strips cut into (18) 3½" squares
First Border	(4) 2¼" strips
Dark	**1½ yds**
Corners	(2) 3½" strips cut into (18) 3½" squares
Second Border	(5) 4½" strips
Binding	(5) 3" strips
Lattice	**½ yd** (10) 1½" strips
Short Lattice	(5) 1½" strips cut into (20) 1½" x 8½"
Long Lattice	(5) 1½" x 42"
Backing	**3 yds**
Batting	56" x 56"

Ocean Waves Quilt

Ocean Waves is a very old pattern. The earliest example of an Ocean Waves Quilt goes back to 1850 – 60, according to *New Discoveries in American Quilts* by Bishop and Patricia Coblentz. Ruby McKim referred to the pattern as Ocean Waves in the Kansas City Star. *Hearth and Home* periodical, published from 1865 to 1930's, called the quilt Waves of the Ocean.

Antique Ocean Waves Quilt *56" x 70"*
Unknown Quilt Maker

This charming Ocean Waves Quilt has two dates: Sept. 24, 1947 and Dec 27, 1947 embroidered in two corners. Could those dates indicate the beginning and completion? The scrap bag quilt has feed sack patches with stripes, checks, and solids. Outside corners are cut off. The backing is loosely woven muslin brought around to the front. The batting is very thick, permitting the quilter to make only ½" stitches, definitely "toenail catchers".

Ocean Waves

Fabric Selection

For Background, select a solid fabric, small dot, or print that reads solid from a distance. Select ten different light to medium prints or checks, and ten different dark prints. Mix values and scales of prints.

Cutting Chart for One Block

Finished Size 16" Square

Background	
Large Triangles	(4) 5" squares
Ten Light Prints	
Pieced Squares	(1) 3" x 6" from each
Triangles	(1) 3" square from four
Ten Dark Prints	
Pieced Squares	(1) 3" x 6" from each
Triangles	(1) 3" square from four

Supplies

4½" or 6½" Triangle Square Up Ruler

Making Forty Pieced Squares

1. Place ten light 3" x 6" rectangles right side up.
2. Place ten dark 3" x 6" rectangles right sides together. Mix colors and prints.

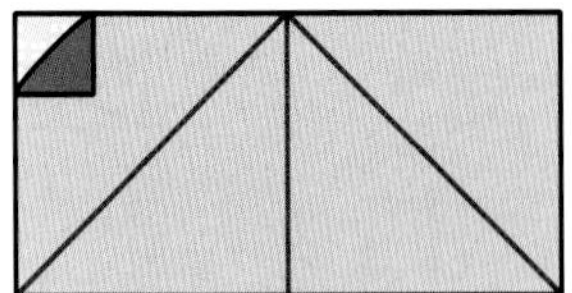

3. On wrong side of dark, draw a line at 3". Draw diagonal lines. Repeat on all pairs.
4. Assembly-line sew ¼" from both sides of diagonal lines.

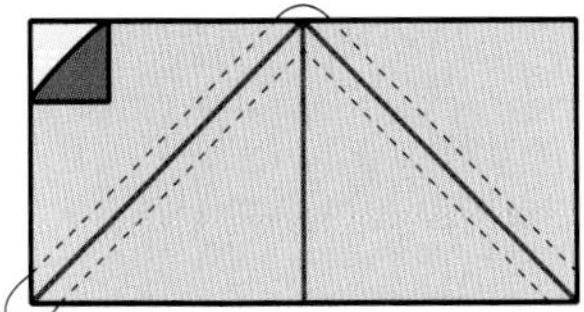

5. Cut on diagonal lines. Cut on straight line.

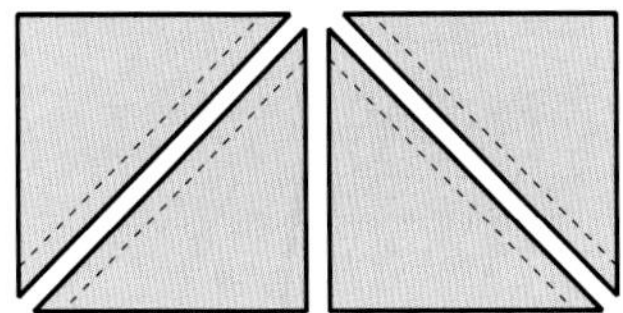

6. Select 4½" or 6½" Triangle Square Up Ruler. **Place 2½" line on stitches.** Trim.

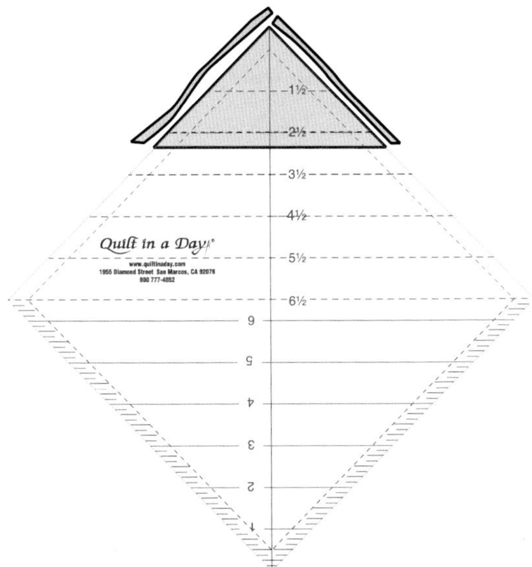

7. Square patches to 2½" with Triangle Square Up Ruler.
8. Set seams with dark on top. Open, and press toward dark. Trim tips.

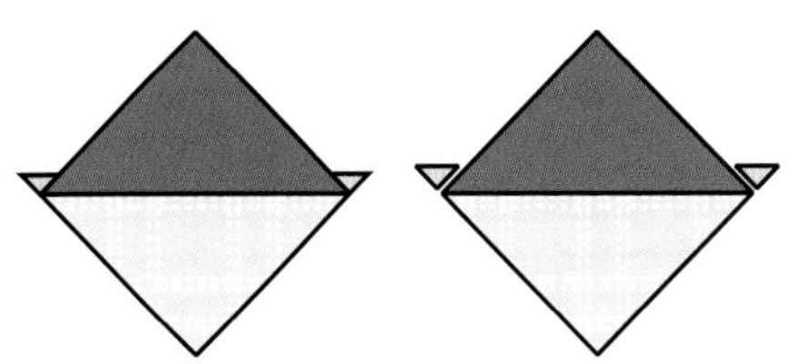

9. Stack four pieces alike and keep separated.

Cutting Triangles

1. Stack four 3" light squares. Stack four 3" dark squares.

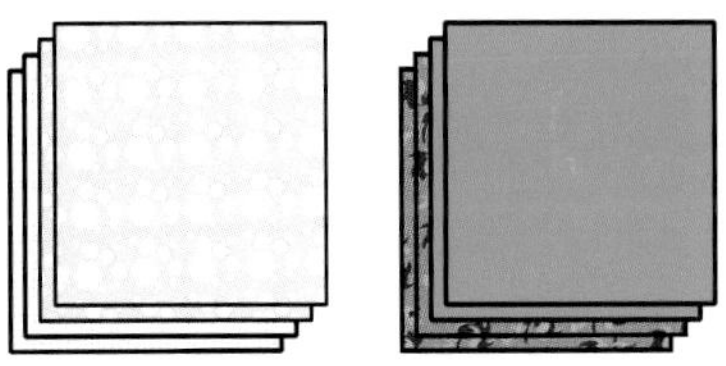

2. Cut squares on one diagonal.

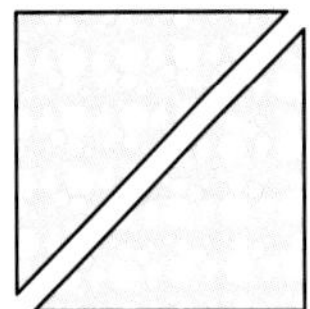
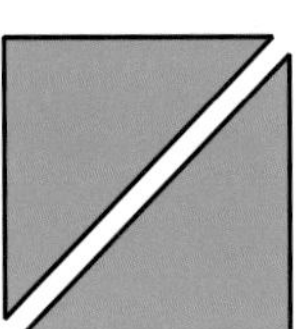

Stacking Quarters

One 16" block is made of four identical quarters. Each quarter is made of ten 2½" pieced squares, two light triangles, and two dark triangles.

1. Lay out one quarter of block.
2. Place the same four pieced squares in each stack. Triangles are different.
3. Divide into rows.

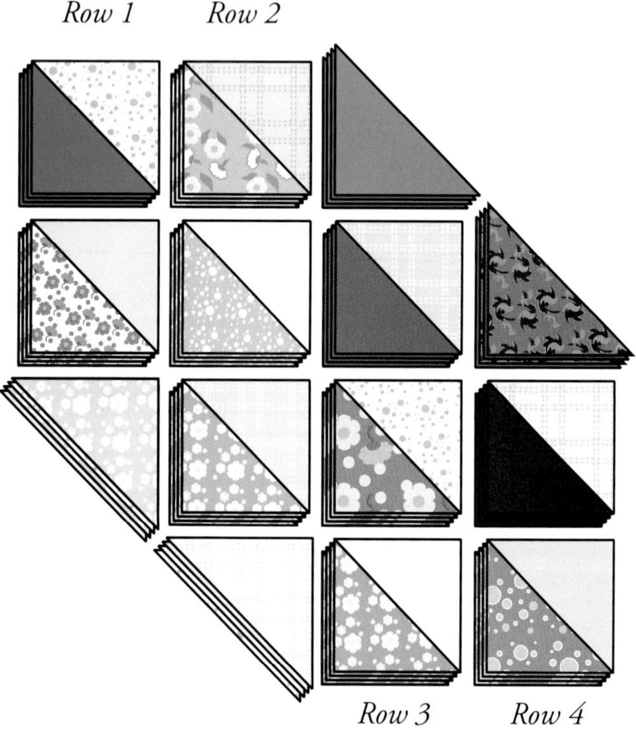

All four quarters can be made alike because they are turned before sewing them together.

Sewing Row One

1. Separate out Row One and turn for easy assembly-line sewing without fighting seams.
2. Flip middle row to left row.

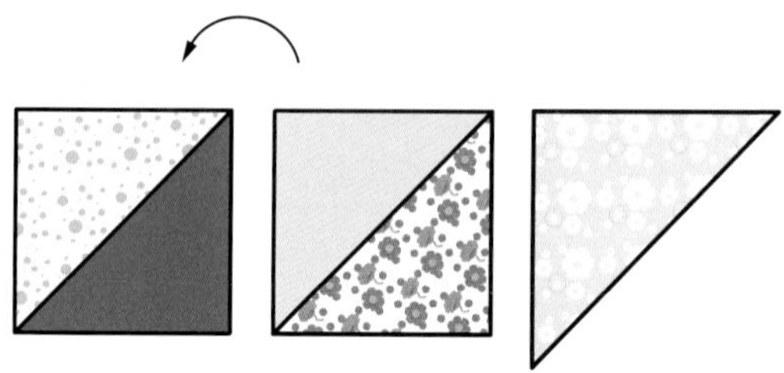

3. Assembly-line sew four sets.

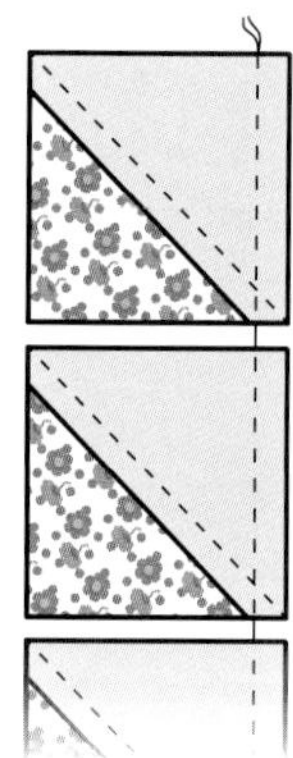

4. Open. Do not clip apart.
5. Add **Light** Triangle.

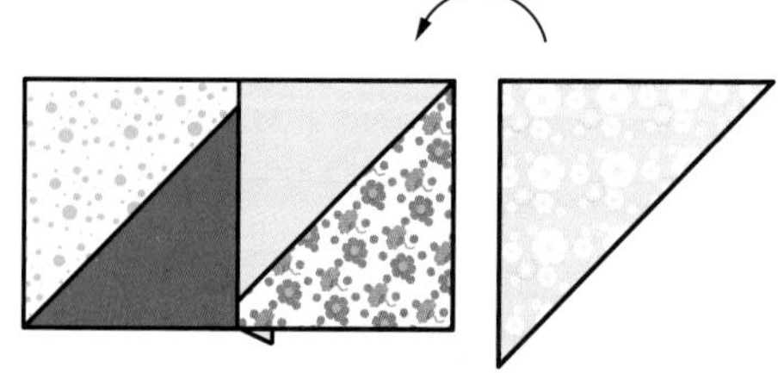

6. Press seams **toward Light Triangle**.

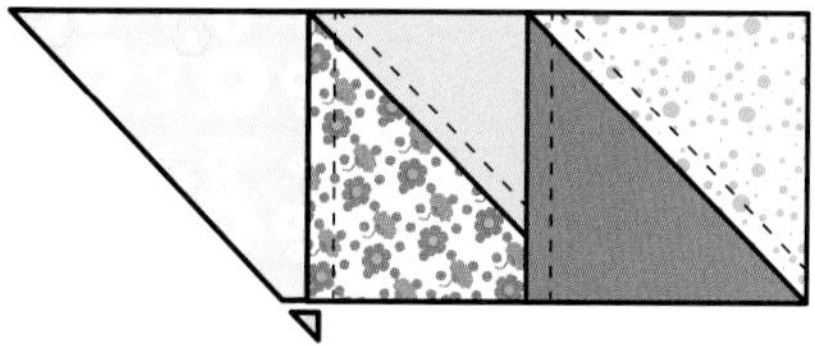

7. Cut off tips.

Sewing Row Two Together

1. Separate out Row Two and turn.
2. Assembly-line sew four sets.

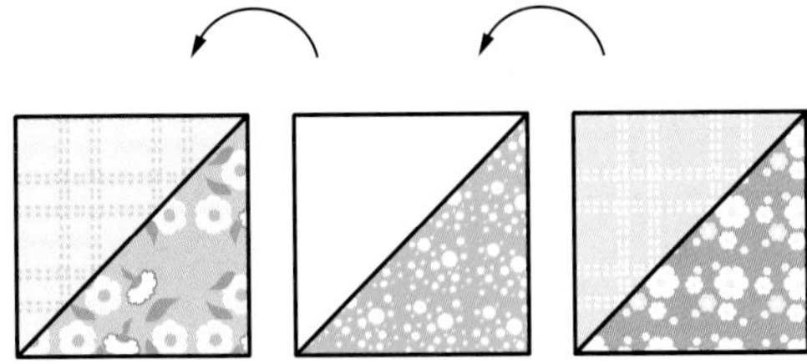

3. Add **Light** Triangles.

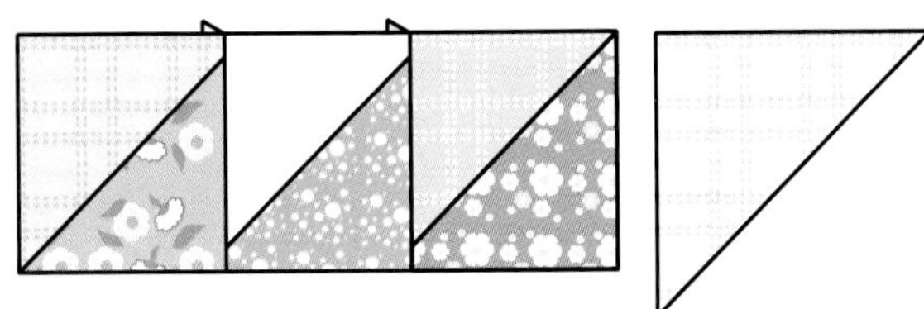

4. Press seams **away from Light Triangle.**

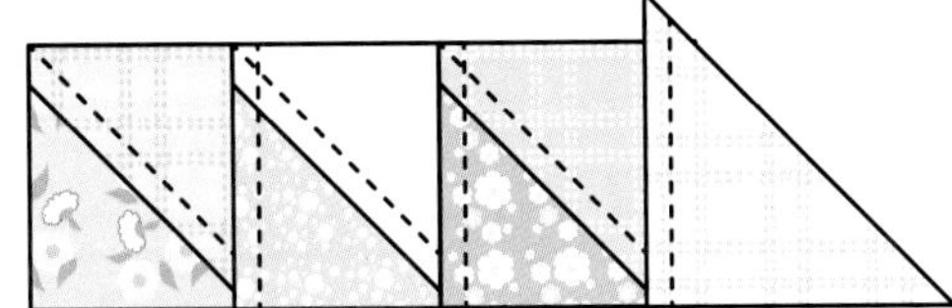

5. Cut off tips.

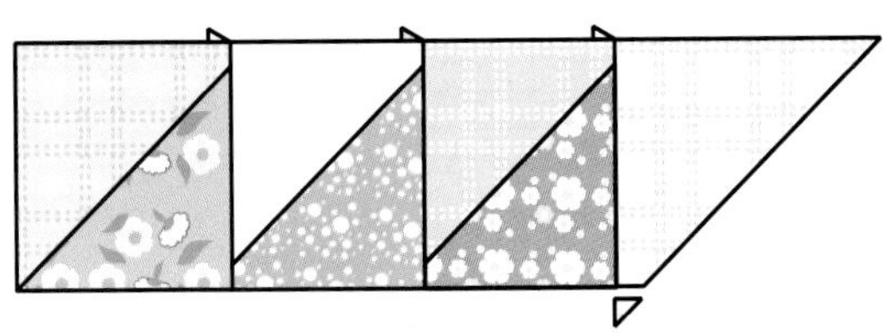

Sewing Row Three Together

1. Separate out Row Three.
2. Assembly-line sew four sets.

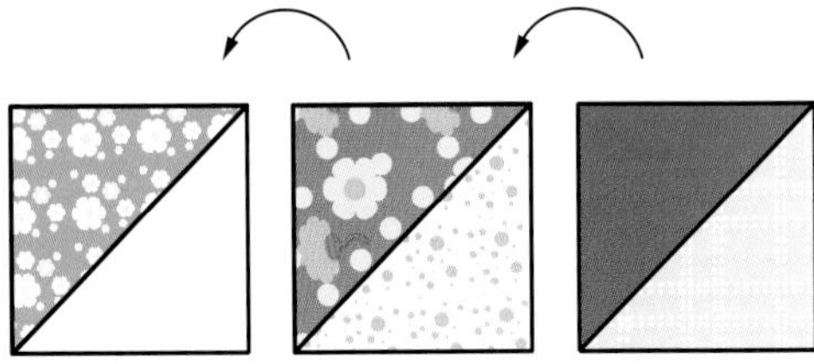

3. Add **Dark** Triangles.

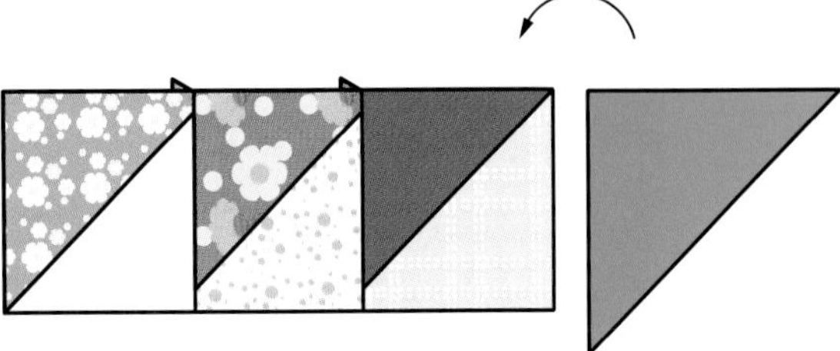

4. Press seams **away from Dark Triangle.**

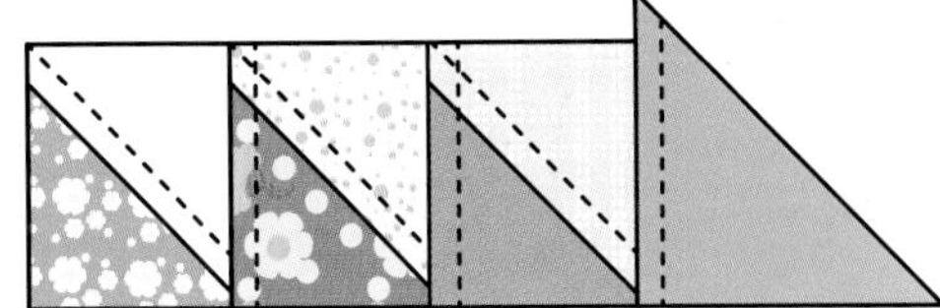

5. Cut off tips.

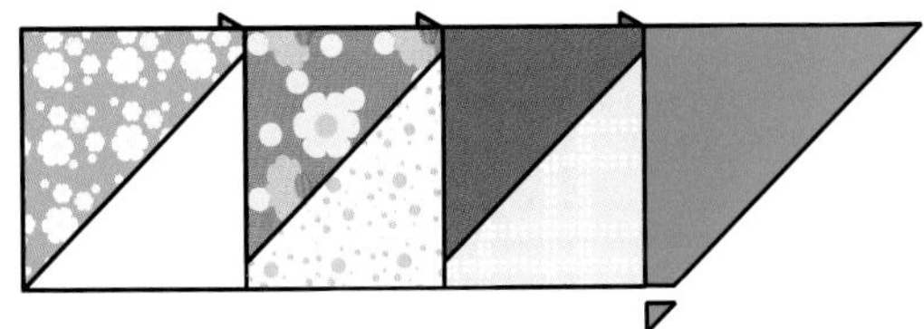

Sewing Row Four Together

1. Separate out Row Four.
2. Assembly-line sew four sets.

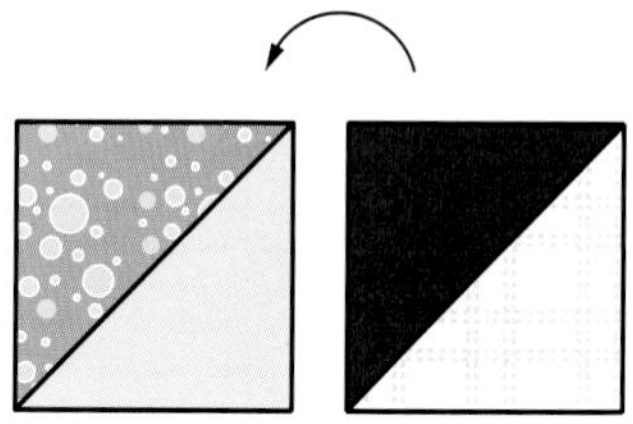

3. Add **Dark** Triangles.

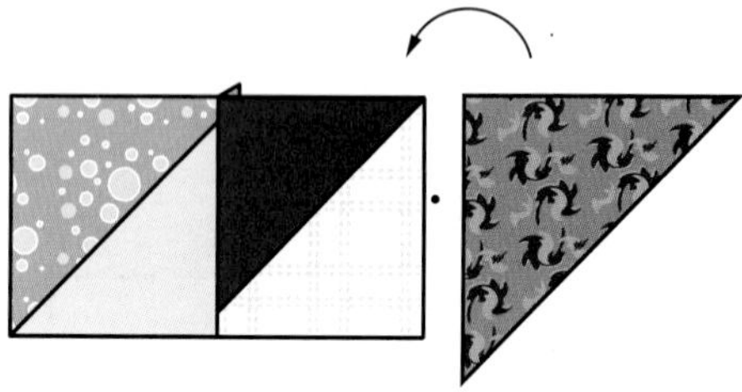

4. Press seams **toward Dark Triangle.**

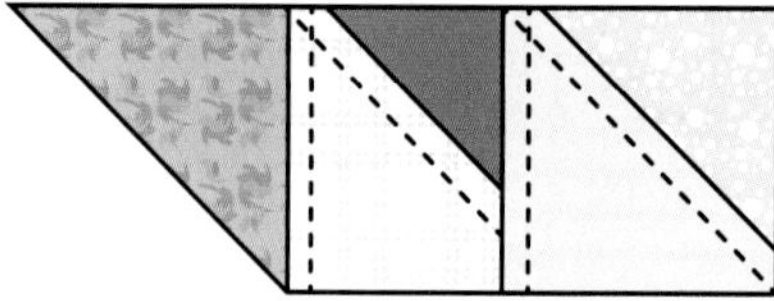

5. Cut off tips.

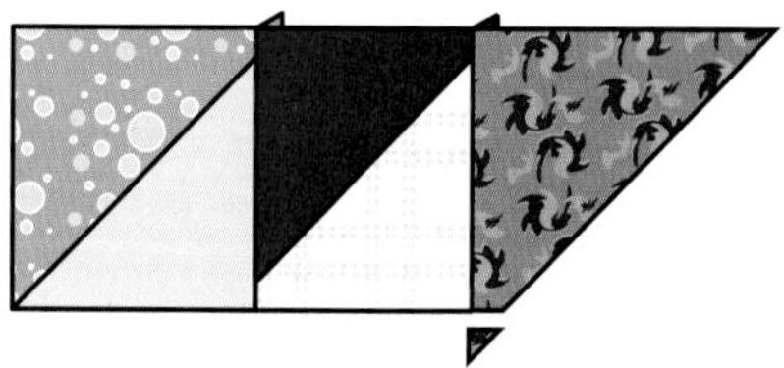

Sewing First Pairs Together

1. Place pressed stacks of Row One and Two.
2. Flip Row Two right sides together to Row One.
3. Lock seams. Assembly-line sew four sets.

First Pair

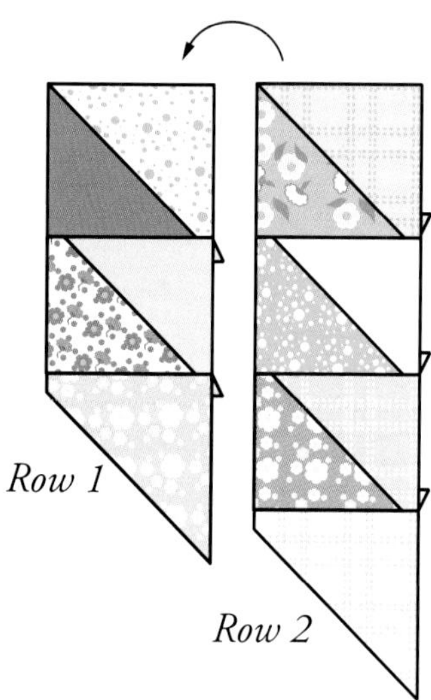

4. Press seams **toward Row One.**

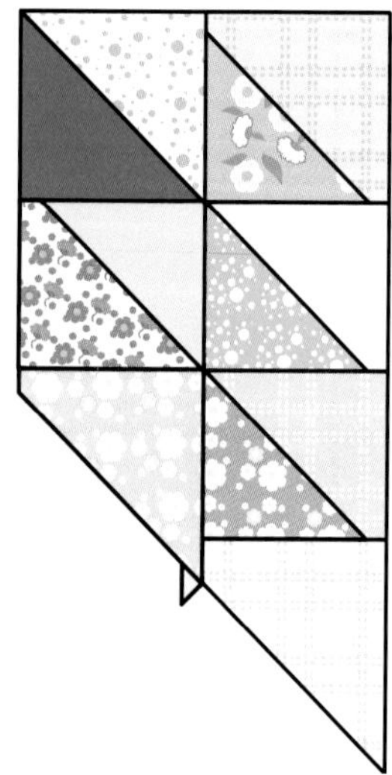

Sewing Second Pairs Together

1. Place pressed stacks of Row Three and Four.
2. Flip Row Three right sides together to Row Four.
3. Lock seams. Assembly-line sew four sets.

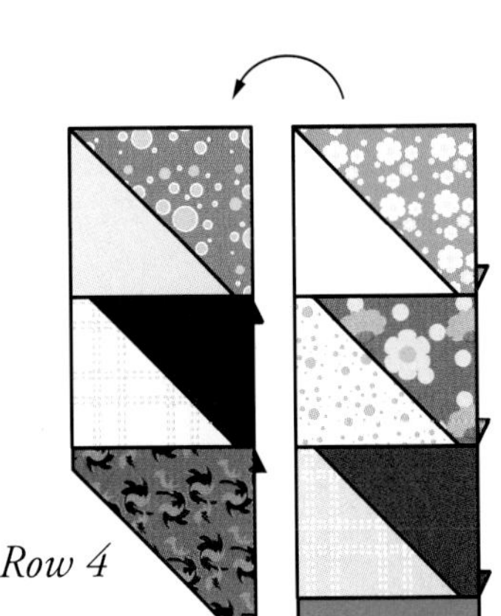

4. Press seams **toward Row Four.**

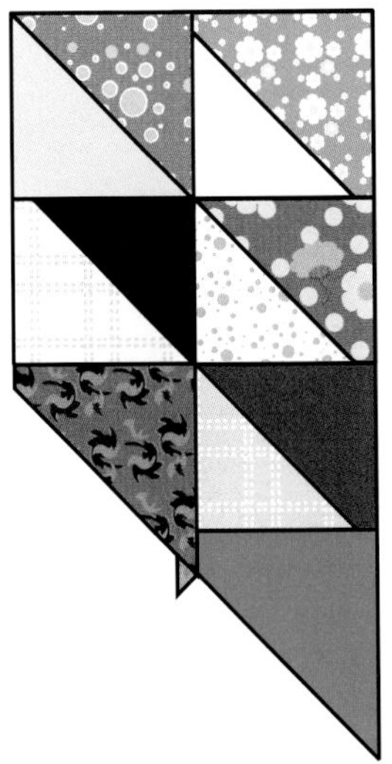

Sewing Two Pairs Together

1. Lay out two sets.
2. Flip Second Pair right sides together to First Pair.
3. Lock seams and assembly-line sew four sets.

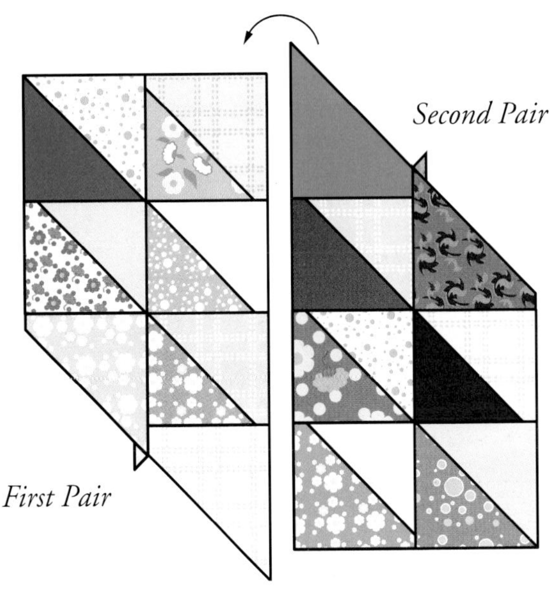

4. Press new seams toward First Pair.

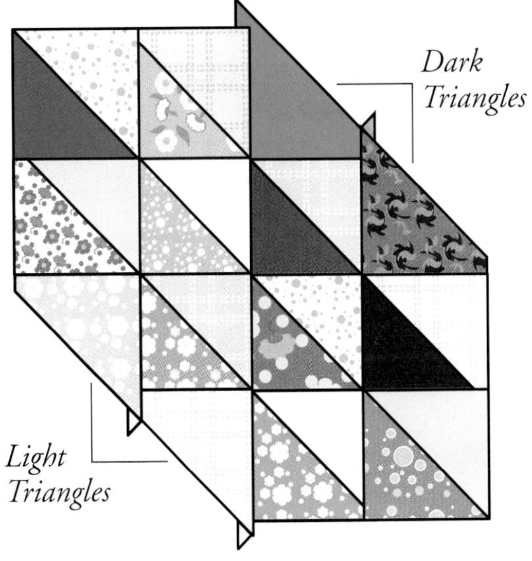

Squaring Up Quarters

1. Use a 6" x 12" Ruler.
2. Place ruler's 45° line on quarter seam.
3. Line up ruler's ¼" line on center seam and ⅛" lines positioned ⅛" out from corners.

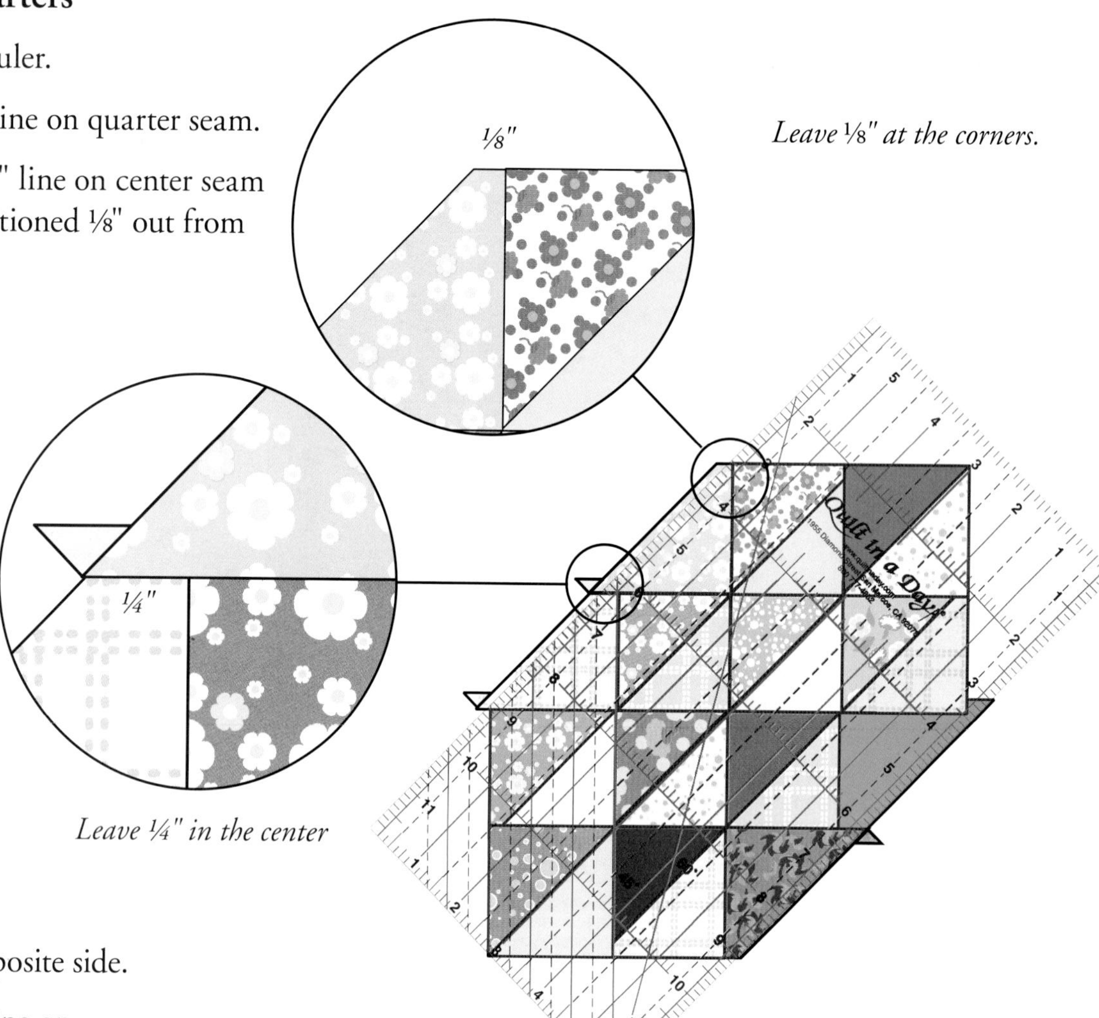

4. Move ruler to opposite side.
5. Place ruler's 45° line on quarter seam.
6. Line up ruler's ¼" line on center seam and ⅛" lines positioned ⅛" out from corners.
7. Check ¼" lines and ⅛" lines.
8. Trim tips.

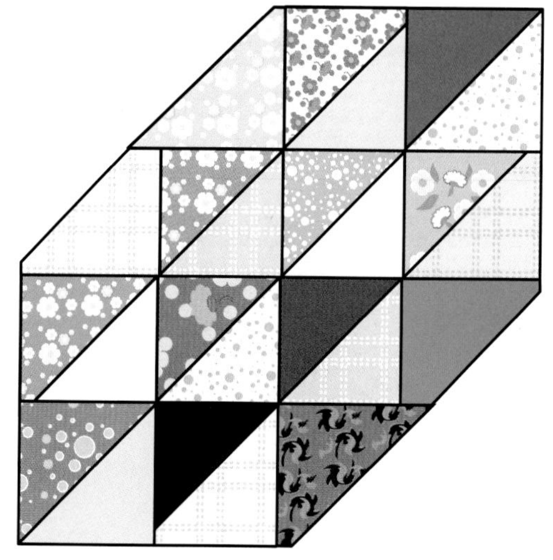

Sewing Background Triangles

1. Lay out four 5" Background squares.
2. Cut in half on one diagonal.
3. Make two stacks.

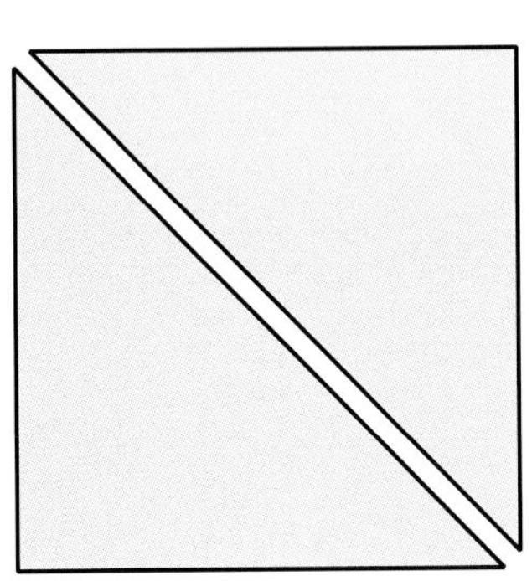

4. Center Triangles on four sides.
5. Turn Quarters wrong side up and sew with Triangles on bottom.

Add Triangles.

Pressing Large Triangles

Seams lock together by pressing two Triangles in one direction, and remaining two Triangles pressed in opposite direction.

1. Make two quarters with Triangle **seams pressed in.**

Make two with seams pressed in.

2. Make two quarters with Triangle seams **pressed out.** Place pins to mark two blocks with seams pressed out.
3. Square blocks to approximately 8½" square.

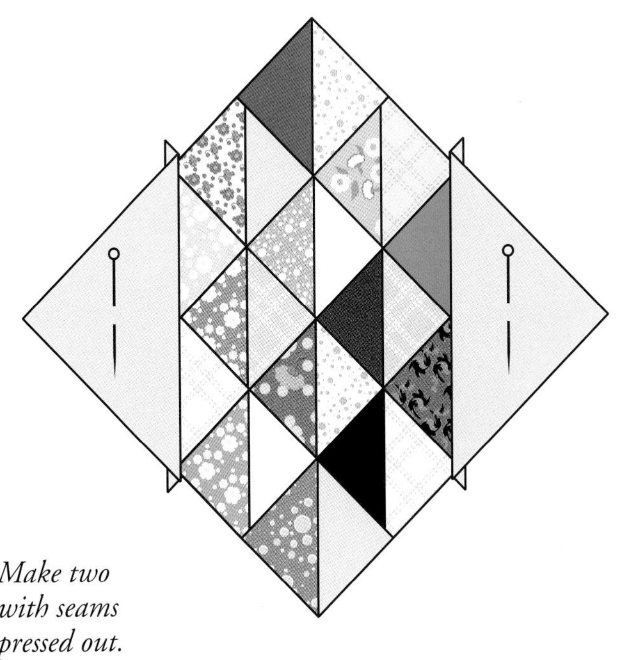

Make two with seams pressed out.

Sewing Block Together

1. Lay out one block with light and dark Triangles opposite each other.
2. Make sure seams are also pressed in opposite directions.

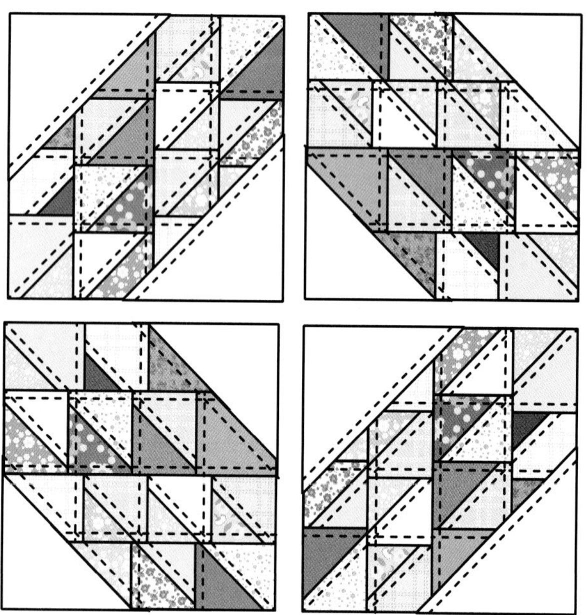

3. Turn right side up. Flip right sides together, locking seams. Assembly-line sew.

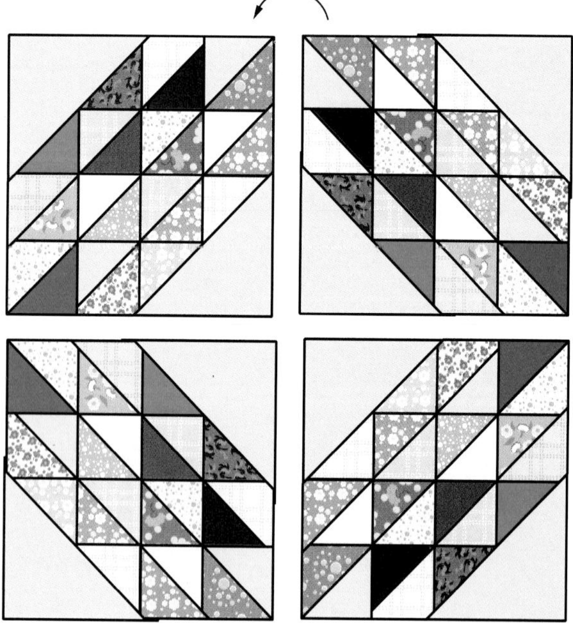

4. Turn. Sew remaining row, pressing top seam up, and underneath seam down.

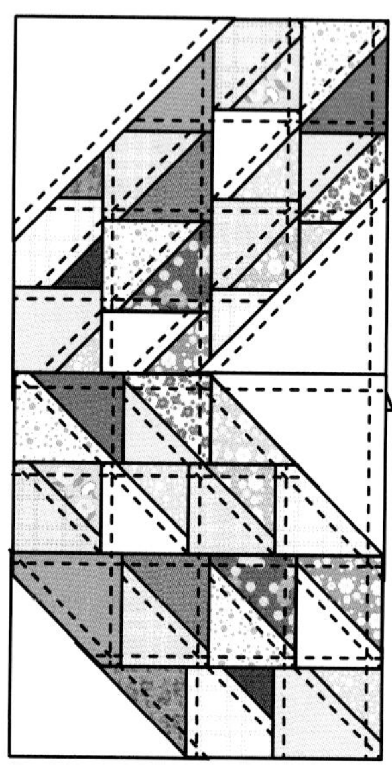

5. "Swirl" center seam into little Four-Patch.

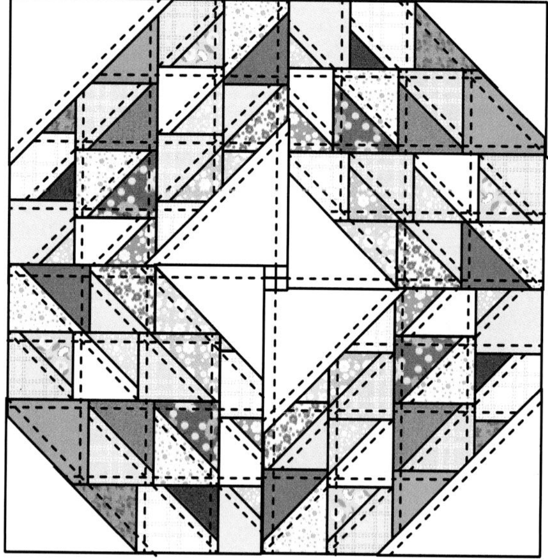

Tribal *68" x 68*
Pieced by Linda Carlson
Quilted by Judy Jackson

Linda chose brown, black and white for her blocks to achieve a tribal ambience. She arranged them perfectly to carry out an indigenous flavor for her quilt. Linda's clever use of color and layout make her quilt a work of art.

Three Color Ocean Waves

Fabric Selection

Select one Backround for Large Triangles, and one light print and one dark print for Pieced Squares and Triangles.

Pieced by Teresa Varnes
Quilted by Amie Potter
43" x 43"

Yardage Chart for Four Blocks

	43" x 43"
Background	**½ yd**
Large Triangles	(2) 5" strips cut into (16) 5" squares
First Border	(4) 1½" strips
Light Print	**¾ yds** (4) 6" strips cut into
Pieced Squares	(20) 6" squares
Triangles	(16) 3" squares
Dark Print	**1¾ yds** (4) 6" strips cut into
Pieced Squares	(20) 6" squares
Triangles	(16) 3" squares
Border	(4) 5" strips
Binding	(5) 3" strips
Backing	**1½ yds**
Batting	**50" x 50"**

Supplies

6½" or 4½" Triangle Square Up Ruler
9½" Square Up Ruler
Glow-Line Tape™
InvisiGRIP

Making 160 Pieced Squares for Four Blocks

1. Place 6" squares of light and dark right sides together.
2. Draw an X on top, and pin.
3. Sew ¼" seam from both sides of diagonal line.

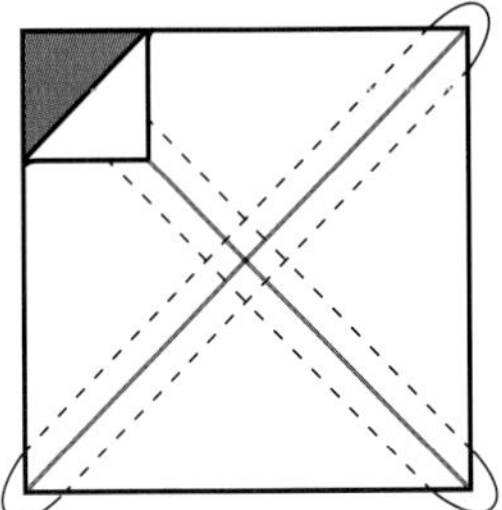

4. Cut into fourths.

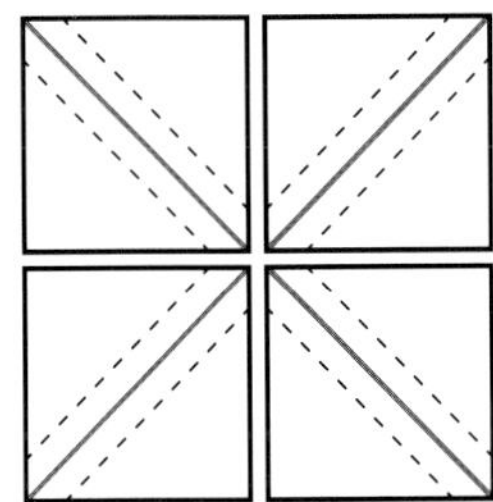

5. Cut on diagonal lines.

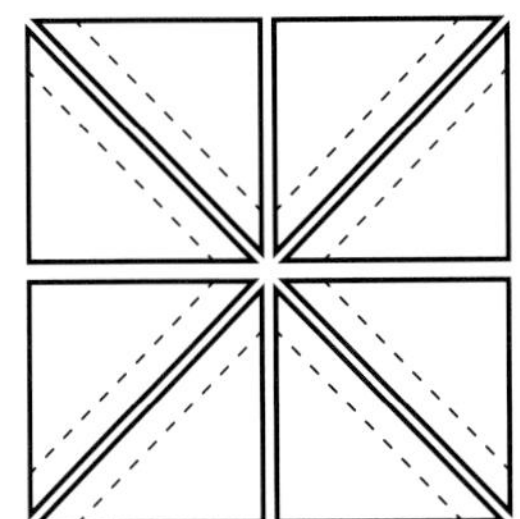

6. Square one hundred sixty 2½" squares with 6½" Triangle Square Up Ruler.

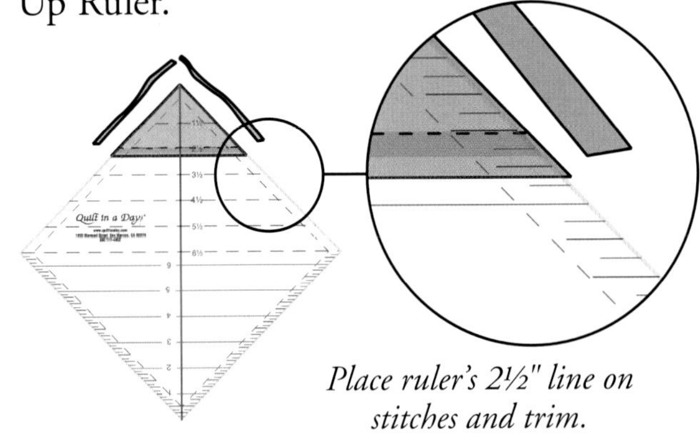

Place ruler's 2½" line on stitches and trim.

7. Press seams toward dark side, and trim tips.

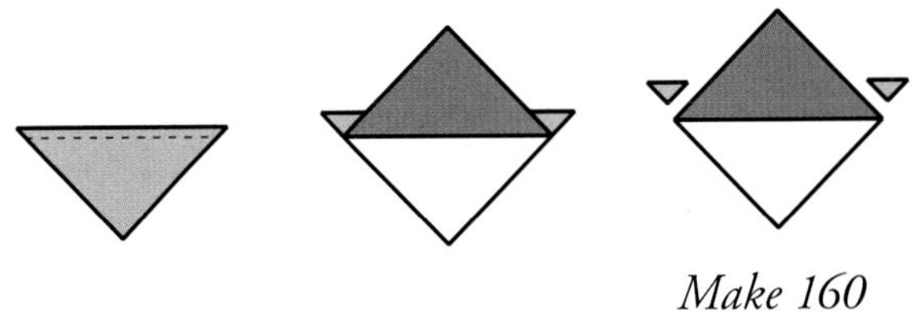

Make 160

Finishing Quilt

1. Sew four blocks together into top.
2. Add 1½" First Border.
3. Add 5" Second Border.
4. Layer, quilt, and bind.

Scrappy Ocean Waves Quilt

Yardage Chart

	Makes Four Blocks
Background	**2 yds for all**
Large Triangles	(2) 5" stripes cut into (16) 5" squares
Light Prints	**Coordinated Scraps**
Pieced Squares	(20) 6" squares
Triangles	(16) 3" squares
Dark Prints	**Coordinated Scraps**
Pieced Squares	(20) 6" squares
Triangles	(16) 3" squares
	Border Blocks (Refer to Arrow and Goose in the Pond for Instructions)
Background	
Arrow	(2) 4½" strips cut into (10) 4½" squares
	(2) 1½" strips
Goose in the Pond	(4) 1½" x 14"
	(1) 1½" x 7"
	(3) 4" x 8"
Dark	**Scrappy ⅔ yd**
Arrow	(2) 4½" strips cut into (10) 4½" squares
	(4) 1½" strips
Goose in the Pond	(2) 1½" x 14"
	(2) 1½" x 7"
	(3) 4" x 8"
Background for Setting	
Inside Border	(4) 3½" strips
Outside Border	(5) 2½" strips
Binding	(5) 3"strips
Backing	**3 yds**
Batting	**60" x 60"**

Pieced by Teresa Varnes
Quilted by Amie Potter

48" x 48"

The seas are churning with life in this beautiful Ocean Waves quilt. Using aquatic toned batiks to set the mood, Teresa selected various shades of blue, purple, and green on a pale green background to make her design burst forth. Notice the clever use of color to highlight pinwheels and stars in prominent areas. Her framing border is formed from Arrow patches and Goose in the Pond patches for a stunning finish.

Making Quilt

1. Make one hundred sixty pieced squares following piecing on page 153.
2. Sew four blocks together into top.

Make Border Blocks

1. **Arrow:** Make twenty 3½" quarter squares. Sew three strips together. Press and cut twenty at 4" long instead of 3½".
2. Sew four Borders with five quarter squares and five 4" long strips. Press.
3. Sew together to 3½" Border and press.
4. **Four Goose in the Pond Corners:** Follow piecing on page 76.
   Sew Borders to quilt.
5. Layer, quilt and bind.

Settings for Blocks from El's Attic

Individual blocks in El's Attic are modular and can be set together in many ways. There are four layouts included in this chapter, plus more for inspiration. You can use the information to adapt to your own layout. The fabric line in this quilt is called *Sunny Days* by Benatex.

Pieced by Teresa Varnes
Quilted by Judy Jackson

59" x 73"

Finished Block Sizes

There are three different block sizes to set together, including 16", 8", and 9" finished sizes. Three blocks require additional Framing Borders or Spacers to bring them up to designated sizes.

16" Finished Size Blocks

Ocean Waves
English Flower Garden
Dresden Plate
Goose in the Pond with Framing Border
Posey with Framing Border

9" Finished Size Blocks

Crow's Nest
Arrow

8" Finished Size Blocks

Traditional Fan
Scalloped Fan
Spider Webs
Fan Basket plus 5½" x 8½" Spacers

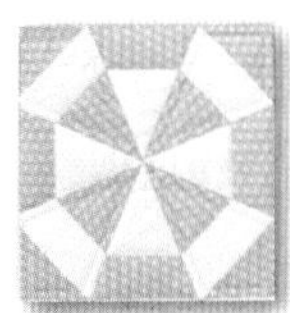
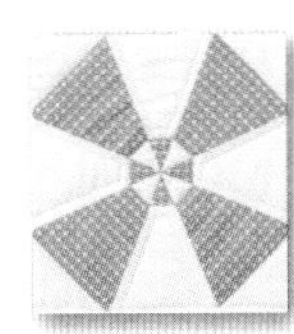

Setting One Blocks

Make blocks following instructions in book.

You need this many blocks:

- Seven Traditional Fans
- Two Fan Baskets
- Three Sets of Spider Webs
- One English Flower Garden
- One Ocean Wave
- One Goose in the Pond with 1¼" Framing Border
- Two Posey Blocks with 3" Framing Border
- One Dresden Plate
- Two Arrow Blocks
- One Crow's Nest Block

Pieced by Teresa Varnes
Quilted by Judy Jackson *59" x 73"*

Additional Yardage Chart for Setting One

Background	**2⅓ yds**
Framing Borders	(4) 1¼" strips
	(4) 3" strips
Spacers	(2) 5½" x 8½"
	(2) 7½" x 9½"
Dividers	(2) 3" x 16½"
Border	(7) 7½" strips
Backing	**5 yds**
Straight Binding	**¾ yd** Cut into (8) 3" strips
or Bias Binding	**1 yd** (2) 16" strips cut into 2¼" strips cut on bias
Batting	**70" x 86"**

Row One

Measurements are for unfinished sizes.

1. Sew three Traditional Fans and one Spider Web together. Swirl center.
2. Sew two 5½" x 8½" Spacers to **Fan Baskets**. Trim Spacers so block measures 16½". Sew two Fan Baskets together and press seam to one side.
3. Sew blocks together with English Flower Garden block. Press seams to left.
4. Measure. Height should be approximately 16½" and Width approximately 48½".

Row Two

1. Sew three Traditional Fans together with one Spider Web. Swirl center.
2. Sew 1¼" Framing Border to Goose in the Pond and square to 16½".
3. Sew blocks together with Ocean Waves. Press seams to right.

Row Three

1. Sew one Traditional Fan together with three Spider Webs. Swirl center.
2. Sew 3" Framing Borders to two Posey blocks for 16½" squares. One is for Row Three and the other is for Row Four.
3. Square Dresden Plate block to 16½".
4. Sew three 16½" blocks together. Press seams to left.

Row Four

1. Sew 7½" x 9½" Spacers to Arrow and Crow's Nest. Press seams toward Background.
2. Sew two 3" x 16½" Dividers between Arrow and Crow's Nest. Press seams toward Background.
3. Sew blocks with Spacers and Dividers with one 16½" Posey block.
4. Press seams to right.

Sewing Rows Together

1. Sew rows together.
2. Press seams toward bottom.

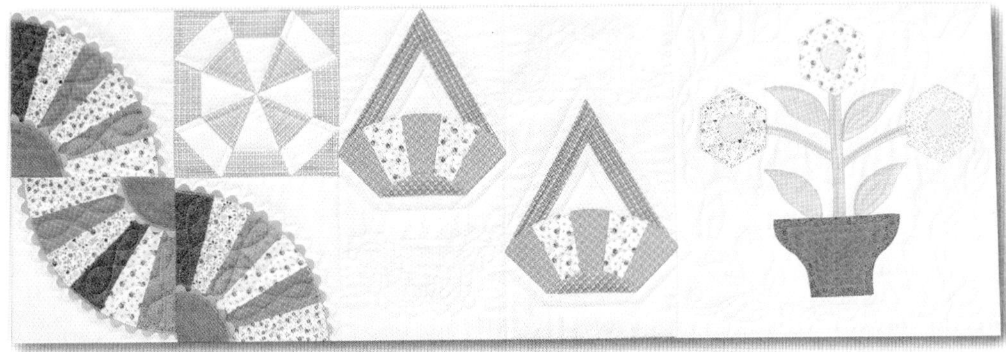

Row 1

Row 2

Row 3

Row 4

Adding Borders

1. Sew 7½" Borders to four sides.
2. **Optional:** Follow directions on Quilt in a Day's Scallop Ruler. Mark off nine 8¼" Scallops on sides, and seven 8¼" Scallops on top and bottom.
3. Layer and quilt.
4. Cut and sew Bias Binding for Scallops or Straight Binding.

Neutral and Dark *60" x 68"*
Pieced and Quilted by Diana Edgemon

Diana created a stunning, original setting for her twenty-nine blocks. Half of the blocks are stunning in just two fabrics, and others are brighten with accent fabrics in soft blue and brown. Blocks are nicely balanced in opposite corners while open blocks fill the center space. Visually pleasant to look at, the quilt is spectacular.

Setting Two

Pieced by Teresa Varnes and Eleanor Burns
Quilted by Merry Jo Rembold

59" x 73"

Setting Two Blocks

Make blocks following instructions in book.

You need this many blocks:

Two Fan Baskets
Three Sets of Spider Webs
One English Flower Garden
One Ocean Wave
One Goose in the Pond with 1¼" Framing Border
Two Posey Blocks with 3" Framing Border
One Dresden Plate
Two Arrow Blocks
One Crow's Nest Block

Additional Yardage Chart for Setting Two

Background	**2⅓ yds**
Solid Squares	(2) 8½" squares
Framing Borders	(2) 1¼" strips
	(4) 3" strips
Spacers	(2) 5½" x 8½"
	(2) 7½" x 9½"
Dividers	(2) 3" x 16½"
Border	(7) 7½" strips
Backing	**5 yds**
Straight Binding	**¾ yd** Cut into (8) 3" strips
Or Bias Binding	**1 yd** (2) 16" strips cut into 2¼" strips on bias
Batting	**70" x 86"**

Sewing Setting Two Together

Row One

Measurements are for unfinished sizes.

1. Sew three Spider Web blocks with one Scalloped Fan.
2. Sew two 5½" x 8½" Spacers to Fan Baskets.
3. Trim Spacers to 16½". Sew together and press seam toward Spacers.
4. Sew blocks together with English Flower Garden.
5. Measure. Height should be approximately 16½" and Width approximately 48½".

Row Two

1. Sew two Scalloped Fans together with one Spider Web and one 8½" Solid Square. Swirl center.
2. Sew 1¼" Framing Border to Goose in the Pond and square to 16½".
3. Sew blocks together with Ocean Wave. Press seams to left.

Row Three

1. Sew 3" Framing Borders to both Posey blocks.
3. Sew one Scalloped Fan together with two Spider Webs and one Solid Square.
4. Sew three blocks together.

Row Four

1. Sew 7½" x 9½" Spacers to Arrows and Crow's Nest. Press seams toward Background.
2. Sew two 3" x 16½" Dividers between Arrows and Crow's Nest. Press seams toward Background.
3. Sew blocks together with Posey block.
4. Press seams to right.

Sewing Rows Together

1. Pin each row together and sew.
2. Press seams toward bottom.

Setting Three Teresa's Little Quilt

Pieced by Teresa Varnes
Quilted by Amie Potter

43" x 43"

In this third example, there are two rows that finish at 16" x 32", including two Spacers for Fan Basket. Two 8" Background Squares are included in the design.

Make these blocks following block instructions. Finished Size is the measurement of each individual block after it is sewn into a row.

Yardage Chart

Cut these pieces to complete your layout.

Background	**¼ yd**
Two Posies	(2) 8½" squares
Spacers	
Two Fan Baskets	(2) 5½" x 8½"
Blue Framing Border	**⅛ yd**
	(4) 1" strips
Dark Ice Cream Cone Border	**1 yd**
	(5) 6½" strips cut into
	(40) Rounded Cones
Light Ice Cream Cone Border	**1 yd**
	(4) 5" strips cut into
	(36) Flat Cones
	(1) 7" x 16" strip cut into
	(4) Corner Cones
Vine	**1" x 16" bias strip**
Flowers	**(1) 3" x 6"**
Leaves	**(1) 3½" x 20"**
Backing	**3 yds**
Batting	**50" x 50"**

Sewing Setting Three Together

Row One

Measurements are for unfinished sizes.

1. Sew two 5½" x 8½" Spacers to Fan Baskets. Sew Fan Baskets together and trim Spacers to 16½". Press seam toward Spacers.
2. Sew Dresden Plate block together with Fan Basket blocks. Press seams to left.
3. Measure. Width should be approximately 16½" and length approximately 32½".

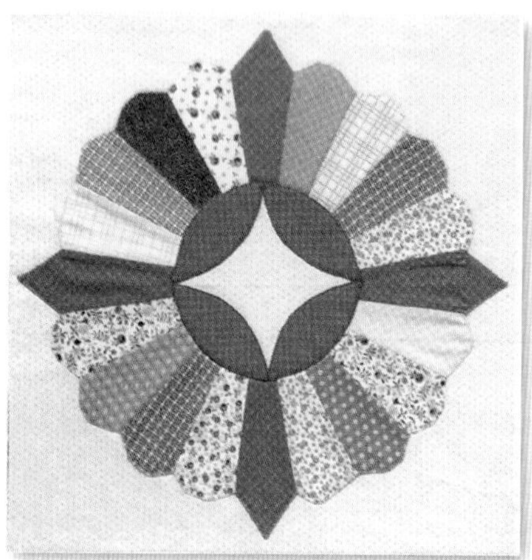
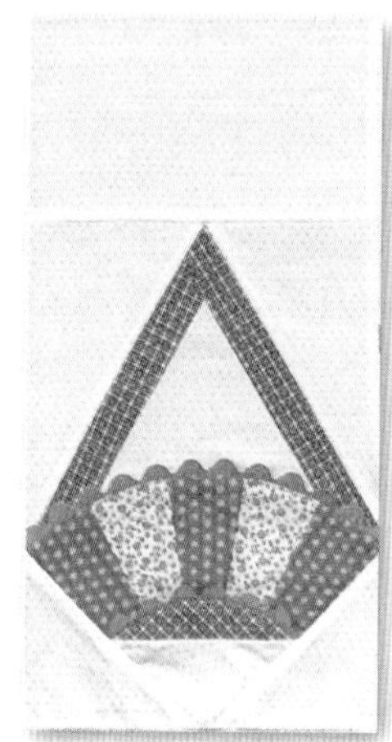
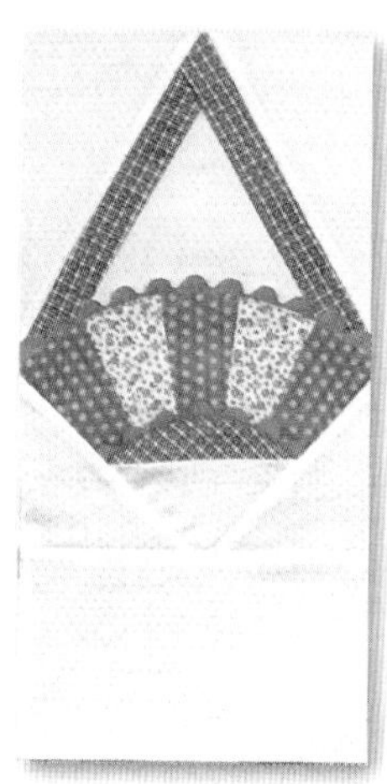

Row Two

1. Sew two 8½" Fans together with two 8½" Solid Squares. Swirl center.
2. Sew two Posey Flowers and eight Leaves following Posey instructions. Make a 16" Vine and sew it to Solid Squares following photograph. Stitch around Flowers and Leaves.
3. Sew Fans and Vine together with English Flower Garden block. Press seams to right.

Sewing Rows Together

1. Pin rows together and sew.
2. Press seams toward bottom.
3. Sew Framing Border to four sides.

Making Ice Cream Border

1. Find instructions for making Ice Cream Cone Border with Dresden Plate Table Runner beginning on page 32.
2. For each side, make nine pairs of Flat and Rounded Cones.
3. Add an extra Rounded Cone to right end of four sides.
4. Sew Four Corner Cones to both ends of two sides.
5. Complete with the Quick Turn Method.

Setting Four

Teresa Varnes *60" x 60"*

Use the illustrated lines for quilt construction. Sew blocks together in rows. Add rows to center, lock, and pin seams at each block..

Make these blocks.

One Dresden Plate
Two Ocean Waves left in quarters
Two sets of Spider Webs

Four Double Fans
  Two 6½" Circles
  Two Packages Rickrack

Making Double Fans

1. Cut wedges for eight Traditional Fans. Join together into pairs for four Double Fans.
2. Make (2) 6½" circles and cut in half. Sew rickrack to Fans and Half Circles.
3. Complete Fans on four 9" x 17" Background rectangles. Square Up to 8½" x 16½".

Additional Yardage for Finishing

Background	**3¾ yds**
Dresden Plate	(1) 16½" square
Ocean Waves	(4) 5" squares
Fan	(2) 8½" strips cut into (4) 8½" x 16½"
Side Triangles	(2) 13" squares Cut on both diagonals
Corners	(2) 13" squares Cut on one diagonal
Floral Border	(6) 7½" strips
Binding	**⅝ yd**
	(6) 3" strips
Vine and Leaves from Posey and English Flower Garden	**1 yd**
Vines	(1) 16" strip cut into (8) 1¼" bias strips
Thirty –Two Large Leaves Twenty –Four Small Leaves	Remainder of Fabric
Sixteen Posey Flowers	**¼ yd**
Sixteen Hexagon Flowers English Flower Garden	**¼ yd**
Backing	**4 yds**
Batting	**68" x 68"**

Finishing Your Quilt

Adding Borders

There are two Border selections to choose from:

- Straight Border
- Scalloped Border

You can custom size your quilt by changing Borders to any width. However, this may affect Backing and Batting yardages.

Adding Straight Borders

1. Cut Border strips according to your Yardage Chart.

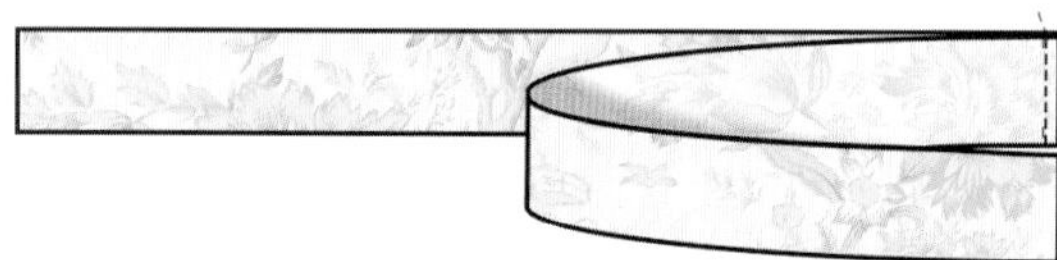

Lay first strip right side up. Lay second strip right sides to it. Backstitch, stitch, and backstitch again.

2. Trim selvages.
3. Assembly-line sew into long pieces.

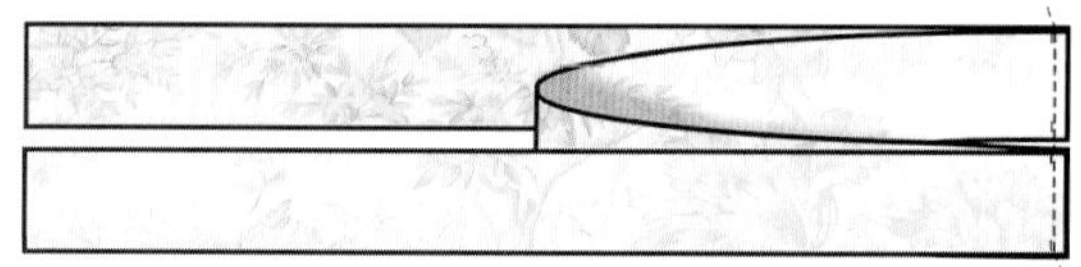

4. Cut Border pieces the average length of both sides.
5. Pin to sides. Sew from quilt side with Border on the bottom, so seams are sewn in direction they were pressed.
6. Open and press seams toward Border.
7. Measure the width and cut Border pieces for top and bottom. Pin and sew.
8. Press seams toward Border.

Marking Scallops

Use Quilt in a Day Scallop Ruler and follow detailed instructions included in packaging.

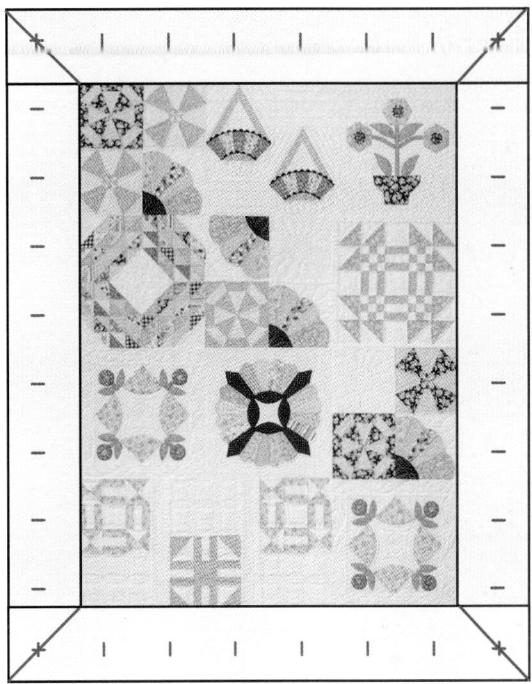

1. Measure sides of quilt. Subtract 4" from measurement.
2. Mark diagonal lines with hera marker or Frixion pen on four corners of quilt.
3. Refer to Chart on page 15 in ruler package. Chart tells you what size Scallop and how many to make.

Suggestion:	Top and Bottom
9 Scallops	7 Scallops
approximately	at
8¼" long	8¼" long

4. Mark size of Scallop on template with Glow Line tape.
5. Place mark on Scallop template on diagonal line, and solid straight line on template with outside edge of quilt.
6. Mark Scallops from end toward middle. Start on opposite side and mark toward middle. If necessary, make adjustment in very center Scallop. You may need to elongate or shorten center Scallop.

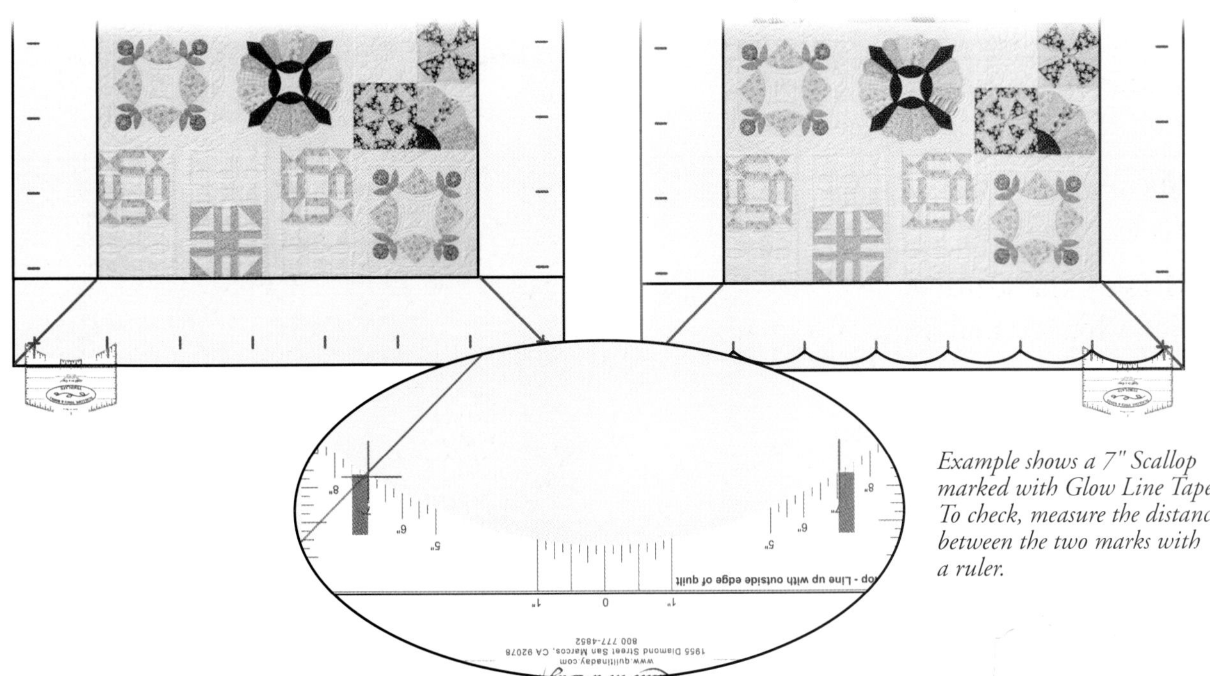

Example shows a 7" Scallop marked with Glow Line Tape. To check, measure the distance between the two marks with a ruler.

7. Round corners.
8. Mark from outside edges in toward center on all sides.
9. Use center scallop for an "adjustment", making it larger or smaller to fit.

10. As a permanent guide, topstitch on line with a long stitch length as 3.5 on computerized machine.
11. Layer quilt top with backing and batting. Quilt as desired out to Scallop lines.
12. After quilt is quilted, Scallops may be trimmed ⅛" away from permanent guide line before adding Bias Binding or after adding Bias Binding.

Layering Your Quilt

1. If necessary, piece Backing.
2. Spread out Backing on a large table or floor area, right side down. Clamp fabric to edge of table with quilt clips, or tape Backing to floor. Do not stretch Backing.
3. Layer Batting on Backing and pat flat.
4. With quilt right side up, center on Backing and Batting. Smooth until all layers are flat. Clamp or tape outside edges.

Safety Pinning

1. Place pin covers on 1" safety pins. Safety pin through all layers three to five inches apart. Pin away from where you plan to quilt.
2. Catch tip of pin in grooves on pinning tool, and close pins.
3. Use pinning tool to open pins when removing them. Store pins opened.

Machine Quilting

Quilting "In the Ditch" with Walking Foot

1. Thread your machine with matching or contrasting thread. Match bobbin thread to Backing.
2. Attach walking foot, and lengthen stitch to 8 to 10 stitches per inch or 3.0 on computerized machines.
3. Roll quilt from one long side to center. Place hands on quilt in triangular shape, and spread seams open. "Stitch in the ditch" along seam lines, and anchor blocks and border.
4. Roll quilt in opposite direction, and stitch in ditch along seam lines.

Quilting Blocks with Darning Foot

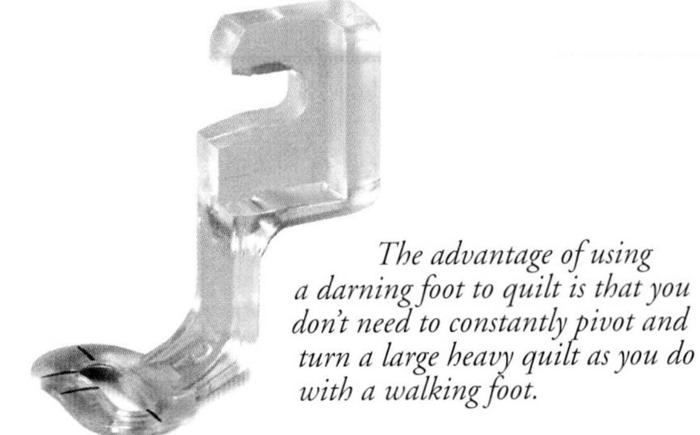

The advantage of using a darning foot to quilt is that you don't need to constantly pivot and turn a large heavy quilt as you do with a walking foot.

1. Attach darning foot to sewing machine. Drop feed dogs or cover feed dogs with a plate. No stitch length is required as you control the length by your sewing speed. Use a fine needle and invisible or regular thread in the top and regular thread to match the Backing in the bobbin. Loosen top tension if using invisible thread. Use needle down position.
2. Plan how to stitch, covering as many seams continuously as possible.
3. Place hands flat on block. Bring bobbin thread up on seam line.
4. Lock stitch and clip thread tails. Free motion stitch in the ditch around block. Keep top of block at top. Sew sideways and back and forth without turning quilt.

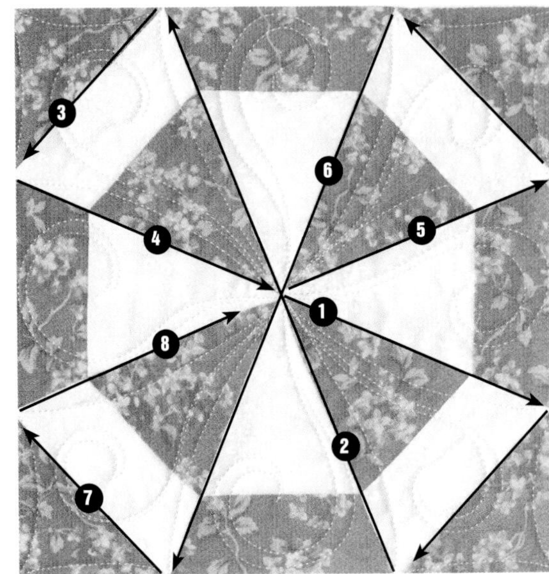

5. If desired, quilt ¼" away from seams.
6. Fill in Background area by stitching "pebbles"
7. Lock stitches and cut threads.

Marking for Free Motion Quilting

1. Select an appropriate stencil.
2. Center on area to be quilted, and trace lines with disappearing marker. An alternative method is lightly spraying fabric with water, and dusting talc powder into lines of stencil.
3. Attach darning foot to sewing machine. Drop feed dogs or cover feed dogs with a plate. No stitch length is required as you control the length. Use a fine needle and regular thread in the top and regular thread to match the Backing in the bobbin.
4. Place hands flat on sides of marking. Bring bobbin thread up on line. Lock stitch and clip thread tails.
5. Free motion stitch around design. Lock stitches and cut threads.

Pieced by Teresa Varnes
Quilted by Merry Jo Rembold
59" x 73"

Crow's Nest: Treat this block as a 25 patch and quilt a double continuous curve, going around the block twice to get the double effect.

Ocean Waves: The triangles are all continuous curve, which is just an arc from point to point. The center and corner triangles (use seams as registration line) are a curl with 2-3 feathers following, then a curl going the opposite direction toward center, followed by feathers to fill out the block.

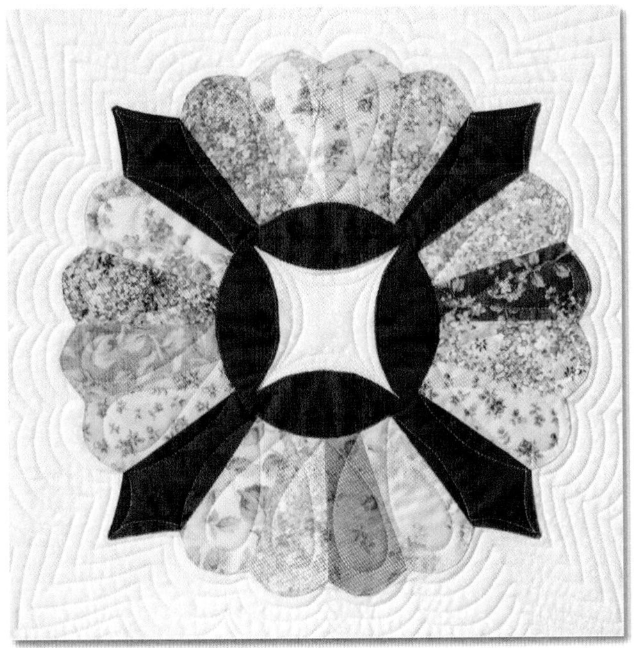

Dresden Plate: The center is CC which is a little exaggerated like a swag to fill up the space. The plate is a loop from the inside corner up to the top and back down to the other corner. In the brown points are CC'd to each point. The background is echo quilted, about ¼" apart.

Goose in the Pond: This block is created with a 9-patch pattern and was treated the same as the 25-patch block using a double continuous curve. There are rulers that can be used to get consistent arcs.

Making Straight Binding

1. Place walking foot attachment on sewing machine and regular thread on top and in bobbin to match Binding.
2. Square off selvage edges, and sew 3" Binding strips together lengthwise. Fold and press in half with wrong sides together.

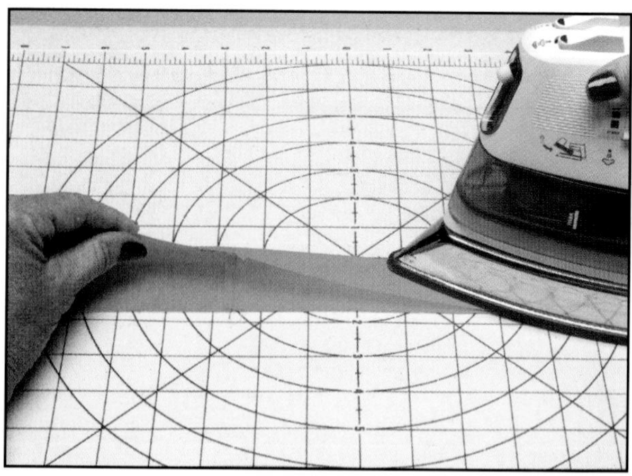

3. Line up raw edges of folded Binding with raw edges of quilt in middle of one side. Begin stitching 4" from end of Binding. Sew with 10 stitches per inch, or 3.0 to 3.5. Sew ⅜" from edge, or width of walking foot.

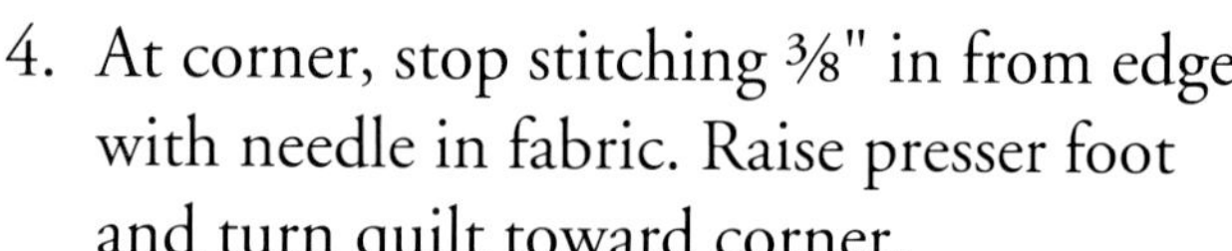

4. At corner, stop stitching ⅜" in from edge with needle in fabric. Raise presser foot and turn quilt toward corner.

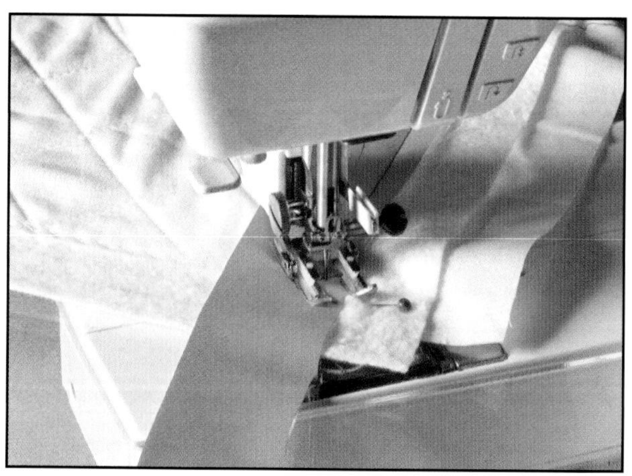

5. Put foot back down. Stitch diagonally off edge of Binding.
6. Raise foot, and pull quilt forward slightly. Turn quilt to next side.

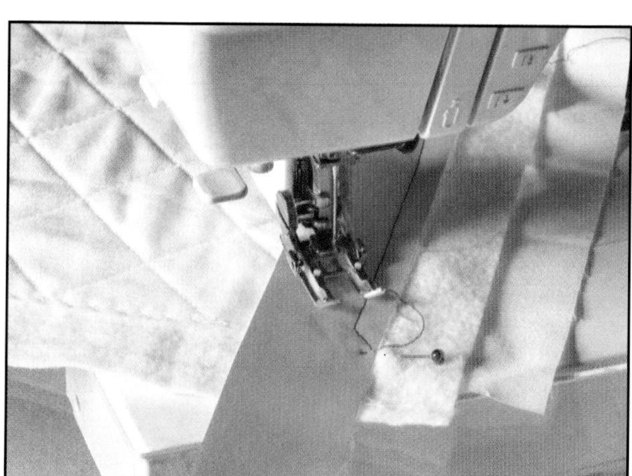

7. Fold Binding strip straight up on diagonal. Fingerpress diagonal fold.

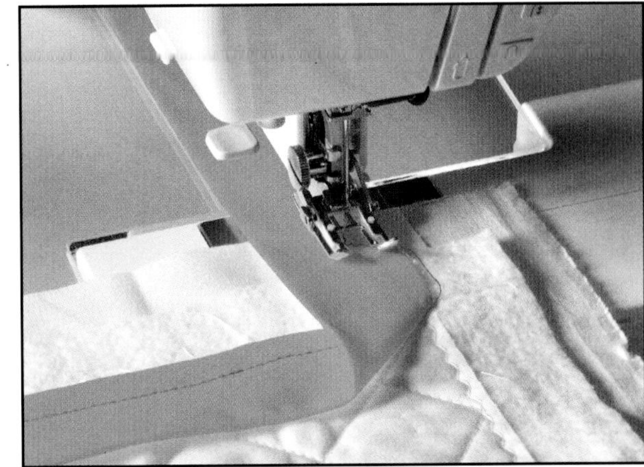

8. Fold Binding strip straight down with diagonal fold underneath. Line up top of fold with raw edge of Binding underneath.
9. Begin sewing from edge.
10. Continue stitching and mitering corners around outside of quilt.

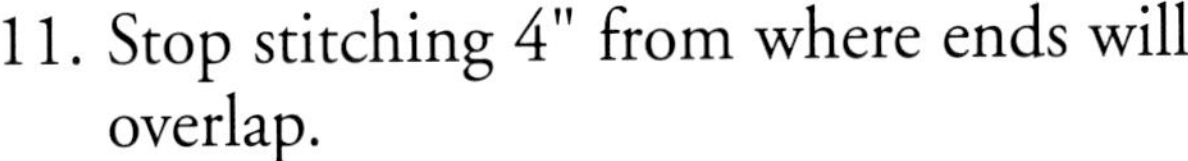

11. Stop stitching 4" from where ends will overlap.
12. Line up two ends of Binding. Trim excess with ½" overlap.

13. Open out folded ends and pin right sides together. Sew a ¼" seam.
14. Continue stitching Binding in place.
15. Trim Batting and Backing up to ⅛ from raw edges of Binding.

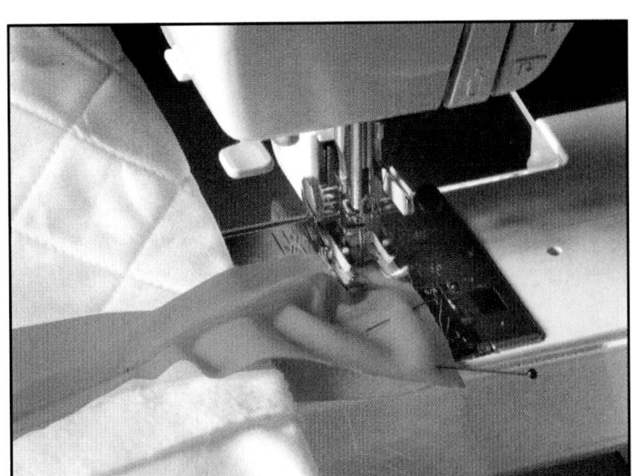

16. Fold back Binding.

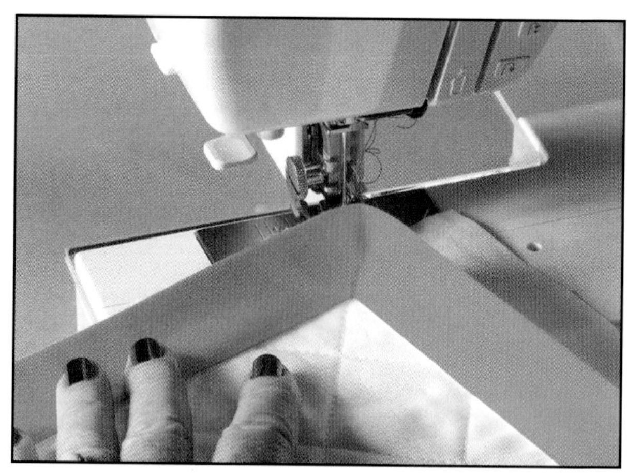

17. Pull Binding to back side of quilt. Pin in place so that folded edge on Binding covers stitching line. Tuck in excess fabric at each miter on diagonal.

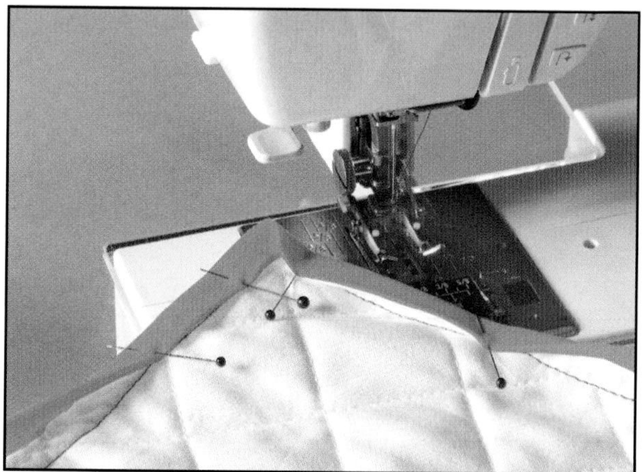

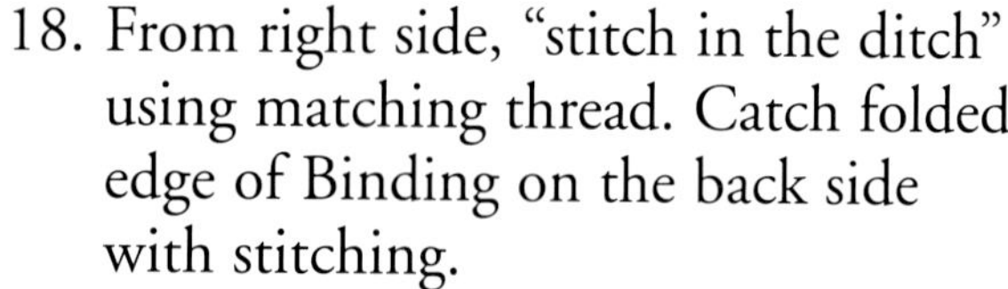

18. From right side, "stitch in the ditch" using matching thread. Catch folded edge of Binding on the back side with stitching.

    Optional: Hand stitch Binding in place.

19. Hand stitch miter.

20. Sew identification label on Back.
    Use extra block. Sign name, date, city, state, and any other pertinent information on Background space with permanent marking pen, or machine lettering. Turn raw edges under ¼". Pin to back side of quilt, and hand stitch in place around outside edge.

Making Bias Binding for Scalloped Borders

1. Cut Binding fabric into 16" selvage to selvage strips.

2. Line up 45° line on 6" x 24" ruler with left edge of 16" strip.

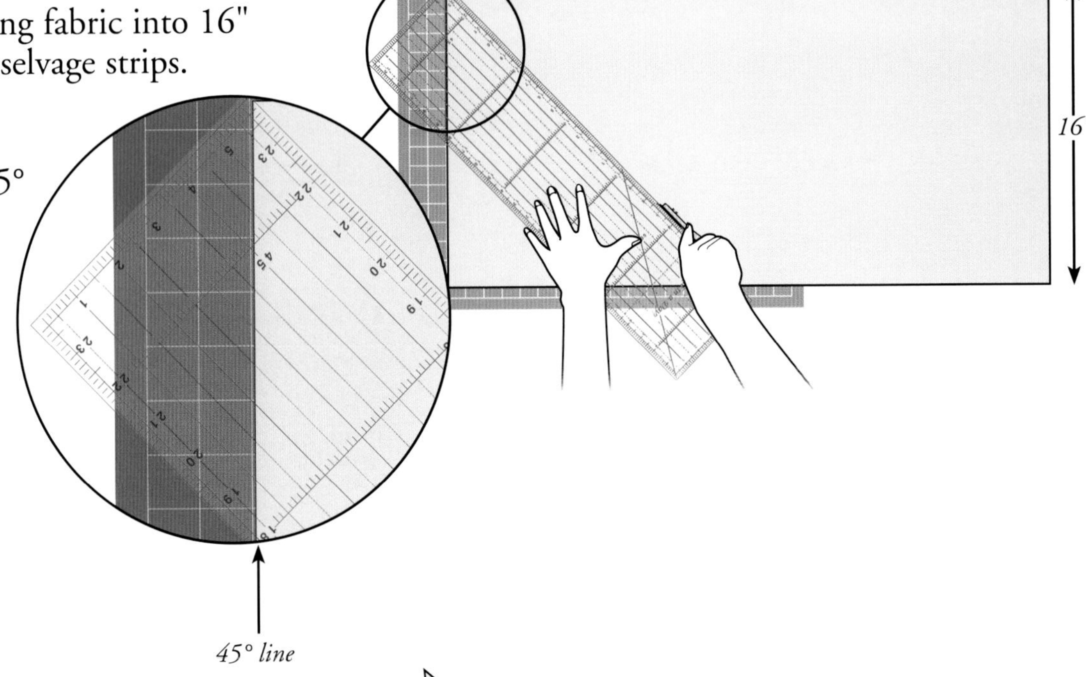

3. Cut on diagonal. Fabric from triangle to left of ruler can be cut into bias strips as well.

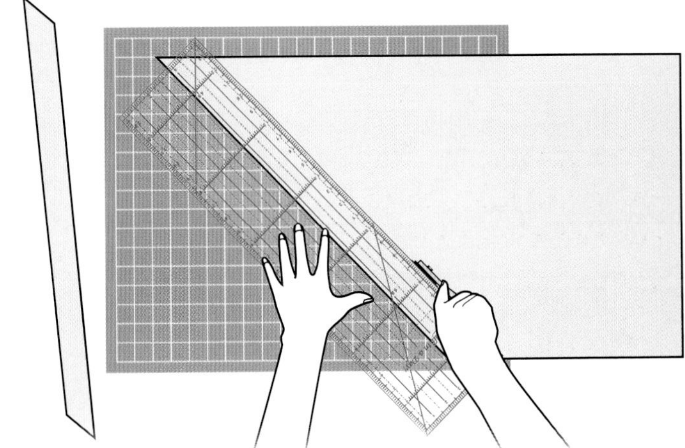

4. Move ruler over 2¼" from diagonal cut. Cut again.

5. Cut 16" strip into 2¼" bias strips.

6. Piece bias strips together on angle to outside measurements of your quilt.

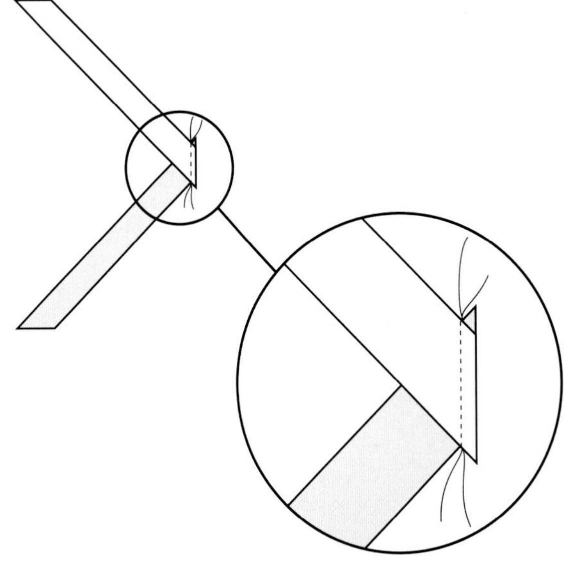

7. Press diagonal seams open.
8. Press bias strip in half lengthwise wrong sides together.

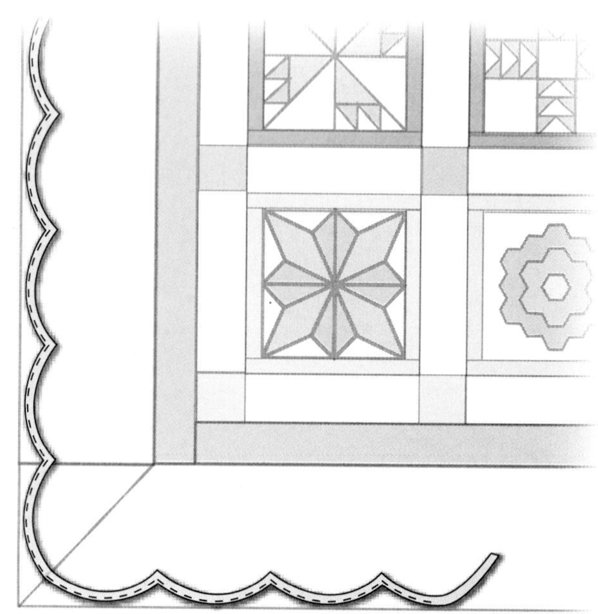

9. Line up raw edge of Binding with marked scallop line. Leave 3" of Binding loose. Begin stitching scant ¼" seam in middle of scallop.

10 Stitch to point between two scallops. Stop with needle in fabric.

11. Raise presser foot, pivot and continue stitching around quilt, easing binding around curves.

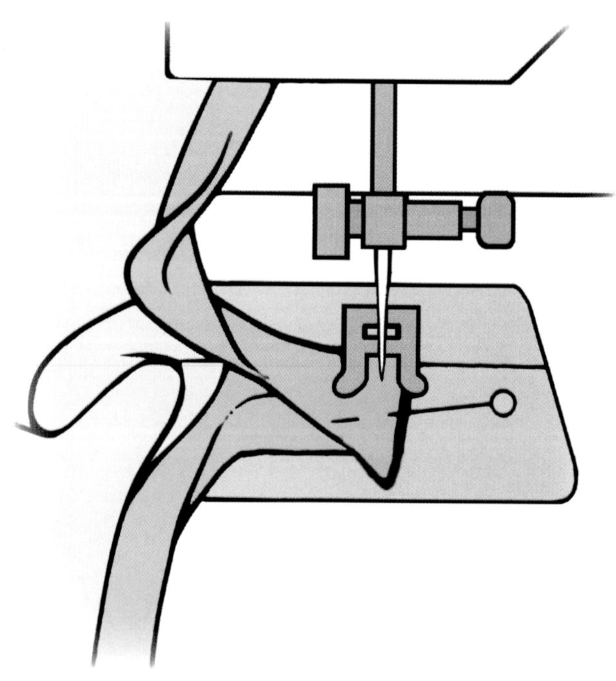

12. Stop stitching 4" from where ends will overlap.
13. Line up the two ends of Binding. Trim the excess with a ½" overlap.
14. Open up folded ends and pin right sides together. Sew a ¼" seam.
15. Continue stitching Binding in place.
16. Trim quilt top even with Binding. Clip between scallops to seam.
17. Turn Binding to back side. Pull folded edge over stitching line. Inside corners will automatically fold in place. Hand stitch folded edge.

Student Gallery

Pieced by Sue Bouchard
Quilted by Amie Potter

42" x 52"

Sue achieved a minimalistic look for her Fan Basket quilt by using only three fabric colors. Her strategic use of gray and black nine patches, lattice, corner fans and binding are perfect accents to her quilt.

Autumn Days
Pieced by Nancy Sandoval
Quilted by Kathy Marsh
48" x 64"

To accomplish the "floating" appearance for her blocks, Nancy selected a tangerine background fabric and deep, bold color for emphasis. The touches of yellow and white further add to the power of her eye-catching quilt.

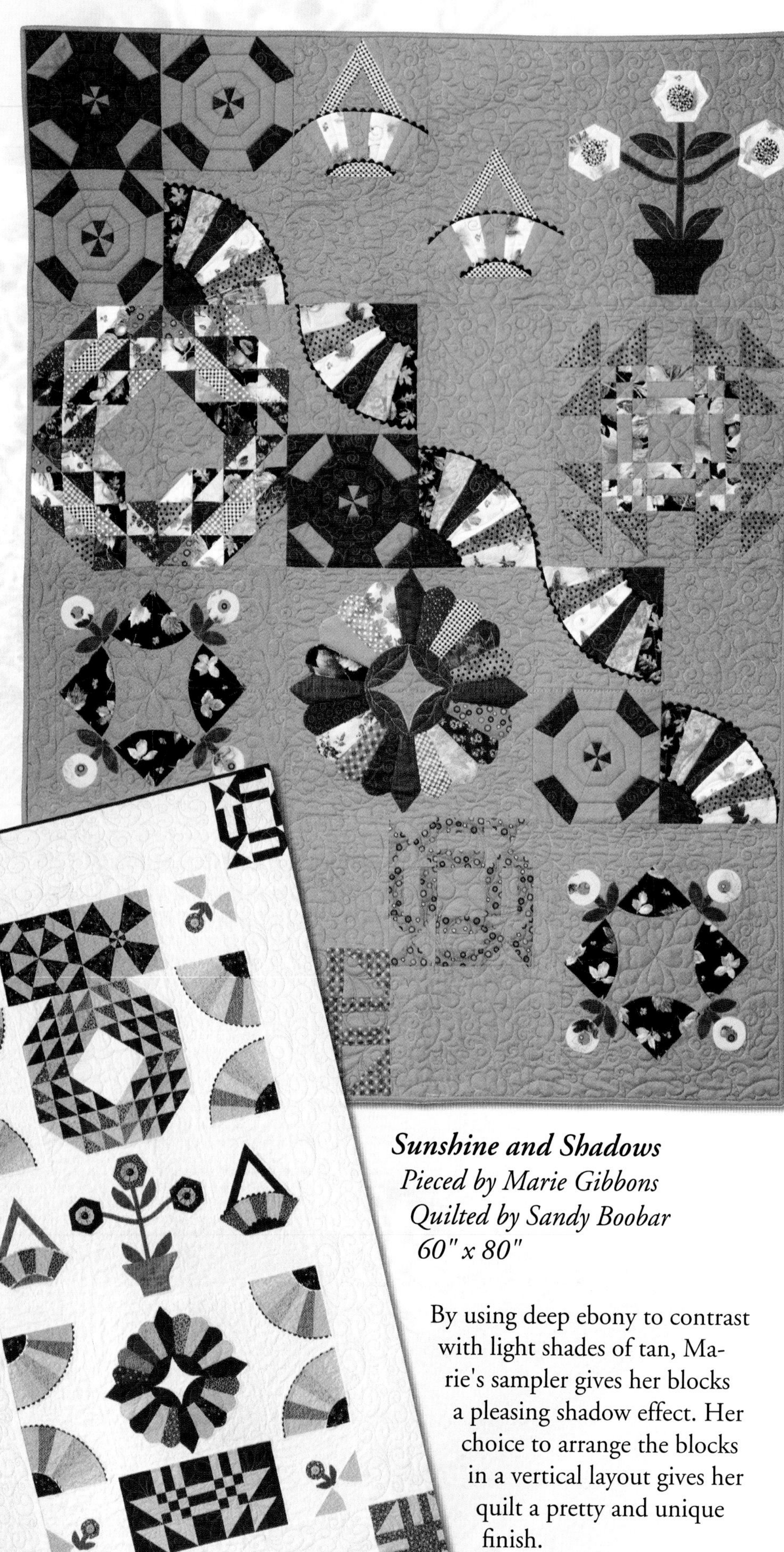

Sunshine and Shadows
Pieced by Marie Gibbons
Quilted by Sandy Boobar
60" x 80"

By using deep ebony to contrast with light shades of tan, Marie's sampler gives her blocks a pleasing shadow effect. Her choice to arrange the blocks in a vertical layout gives her quilt a pretty and unique finish.

Heirloom Sampler *64" x 82"*
Pieced by Juliana Scoggings
Quilted by Julia Gray

This stunning Sampler will be a family treasure for generations to come! Juliana chose to feature the Dresden Plate block for her center and surrounded it with Ocean Waves. She added pretty Fans, Fan Baskets and Posey blocks and framed them with a narrow border. Notice her clever use of the Arrow block in the border for a striking finish.

Stained Glass
Pieced and Quilted by Dori Firman
44" x 70"

Reminiscent of a stained glass window, Dori's distinguished Sampler attracts attention. On her creamy ivory background fabric, she featured her collection of blocks in deep rich tones, arranged in precise order for perfect symmetry. Her fabrics are neckties from a resale shop.

Sampler
Pieced by Teresa Varnes
Quilted by Judy Jackson
20" x 58"

Teresa used her blocks to make this pretty tablerunner that can double as a wallhanging. Her choice of dark red background features her blocks beautifully.

Classic Sampler 60" x 74"
Pieced by Rani Ramakrishnan
Quilted by Dani Fish

Rani selected the traditional setting for her blocks to very pleasing results. Notice her English Garden block. She extended the stems and grew her secondary flowers horizontally. She finished with a scalloped border and used green binding to accent.

Don't Be Blue *45" x 62"*
Pieced by Barbara Heldman
Quilted by Karen Ebbesmeyer

Using blue and white, Barbara achieved just the right balance of positive/negative appeal. She alternated her feature fabric between the two colors for striking effect.

Patterns

Fans

Making Templates

Photo copy patterns. Rough cut around patterns.Glue patterns to template plastic. Cut on lines.

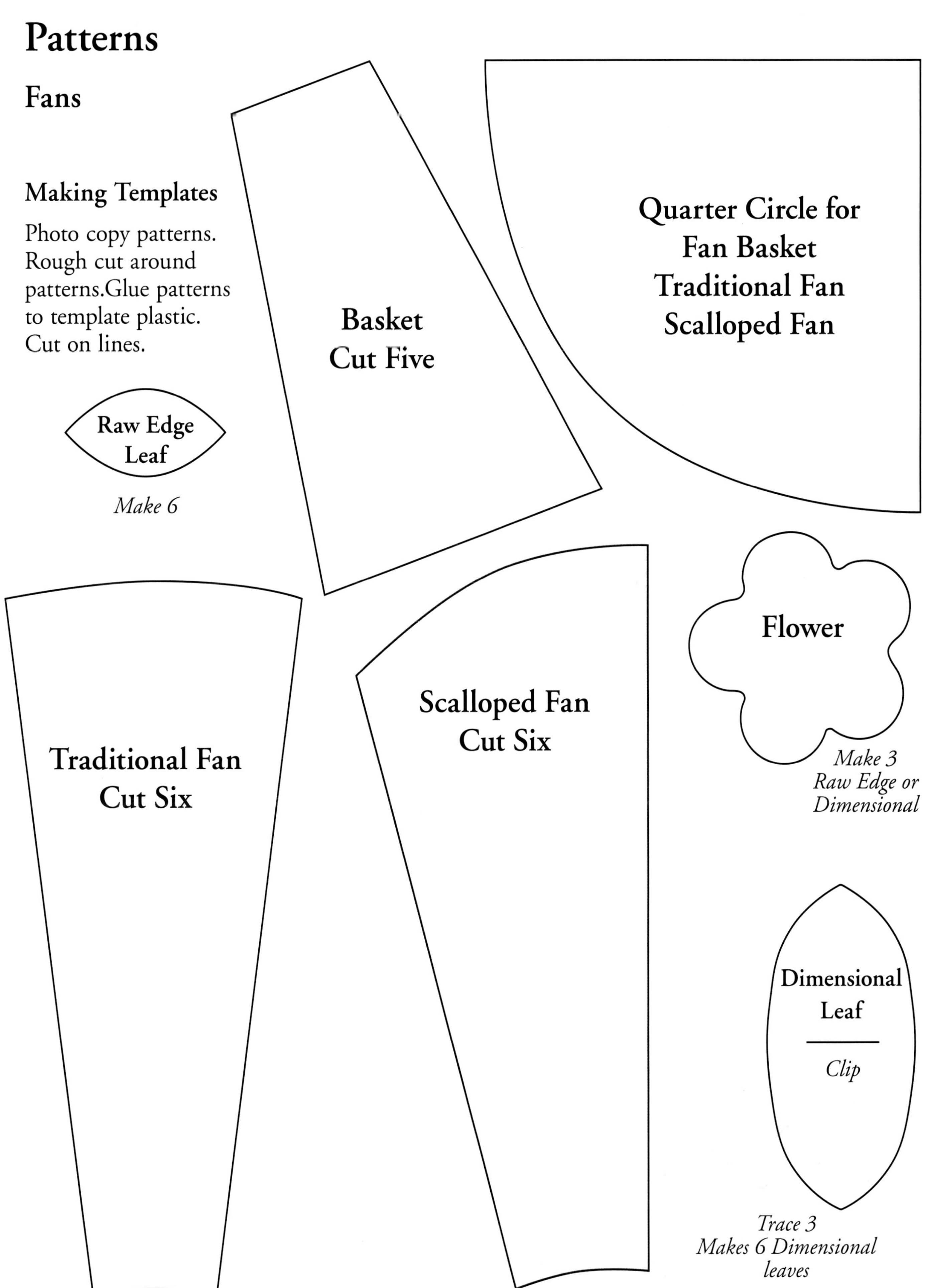

English Flower Garden Templates

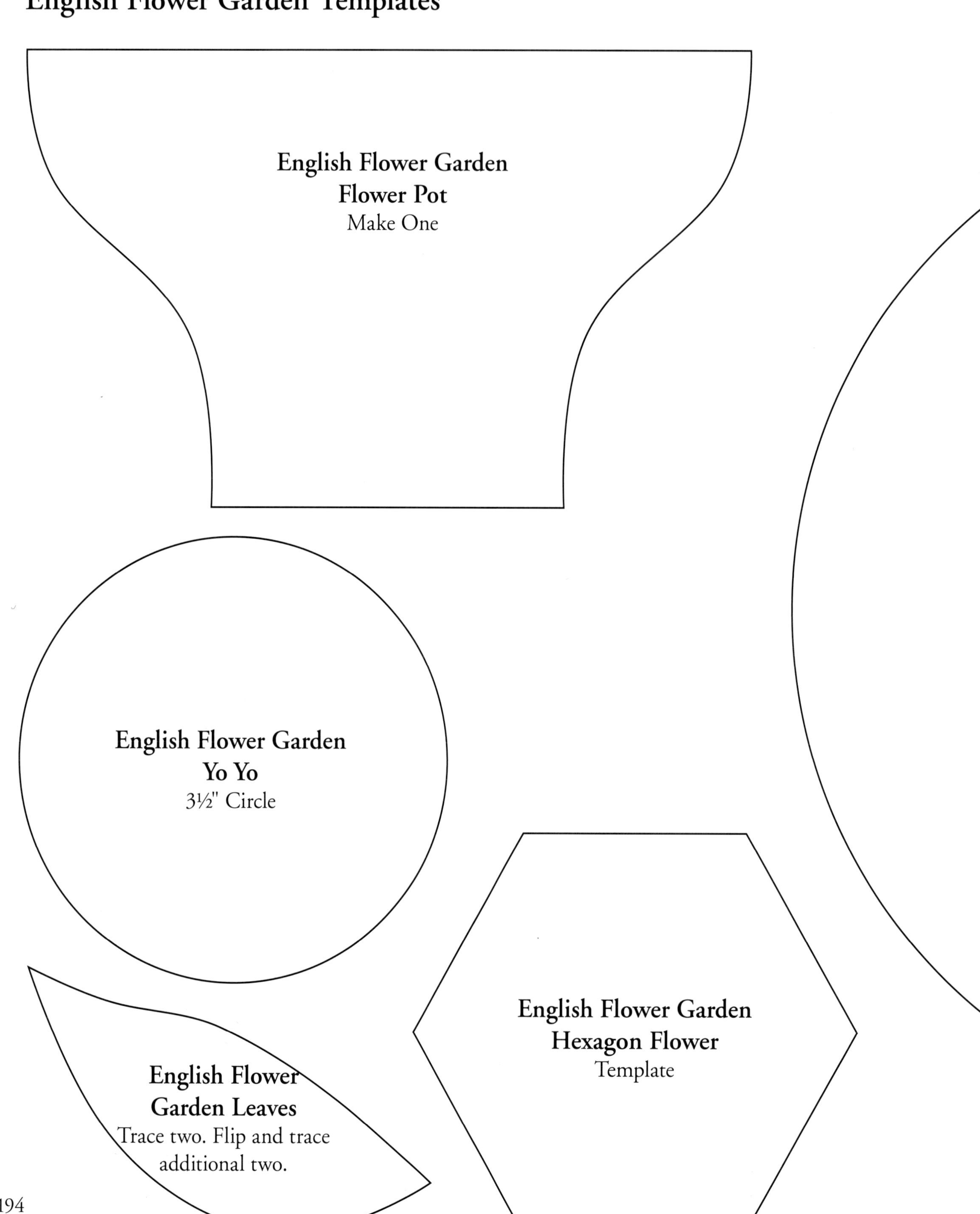

Posey Templates

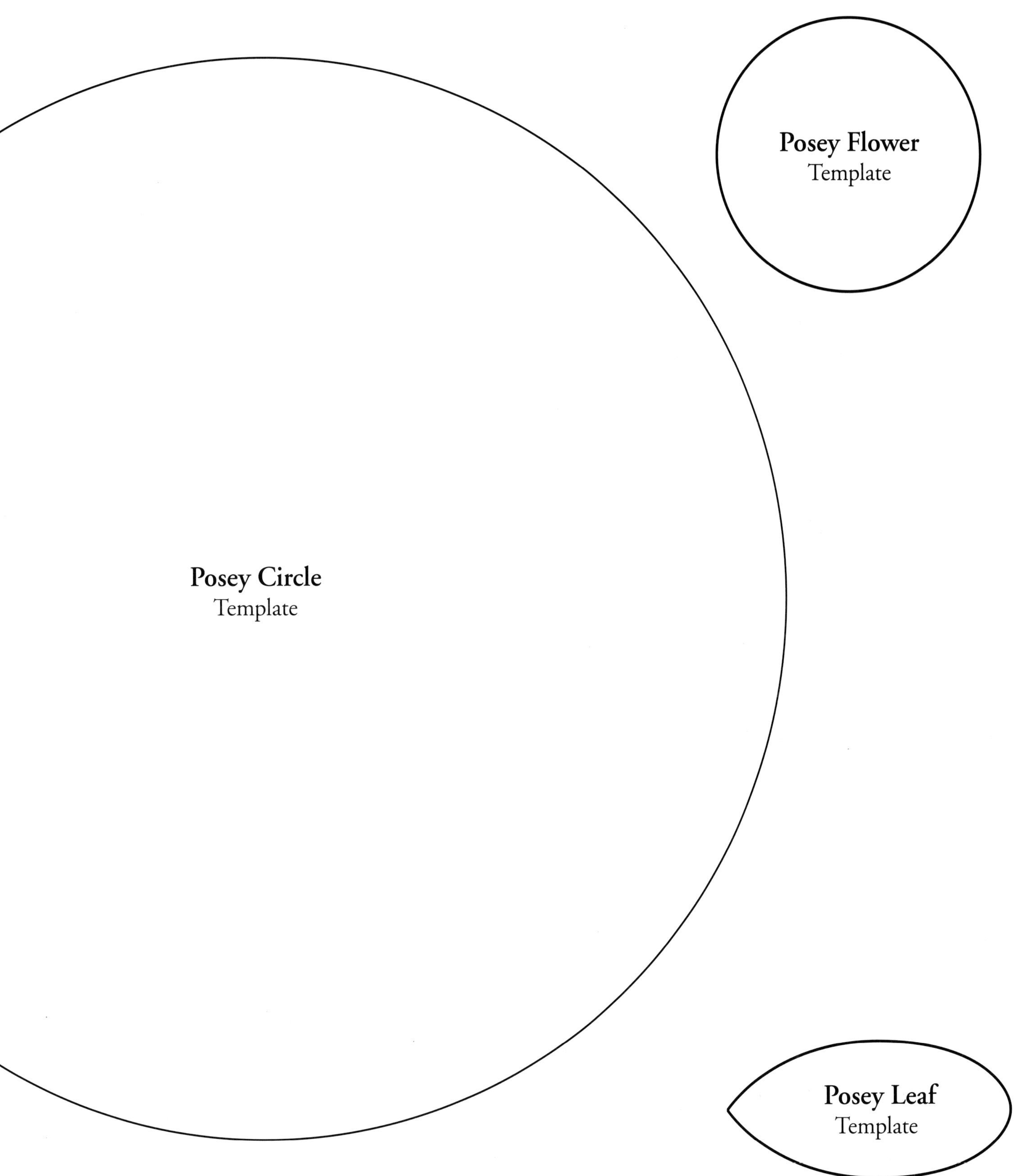

Ice Cream Cone Border

Making Templates

1. Photo copy patterns.
2. Rough cut around patterns.
3. Glue patterns to template plastic.
4. Cut on lines.

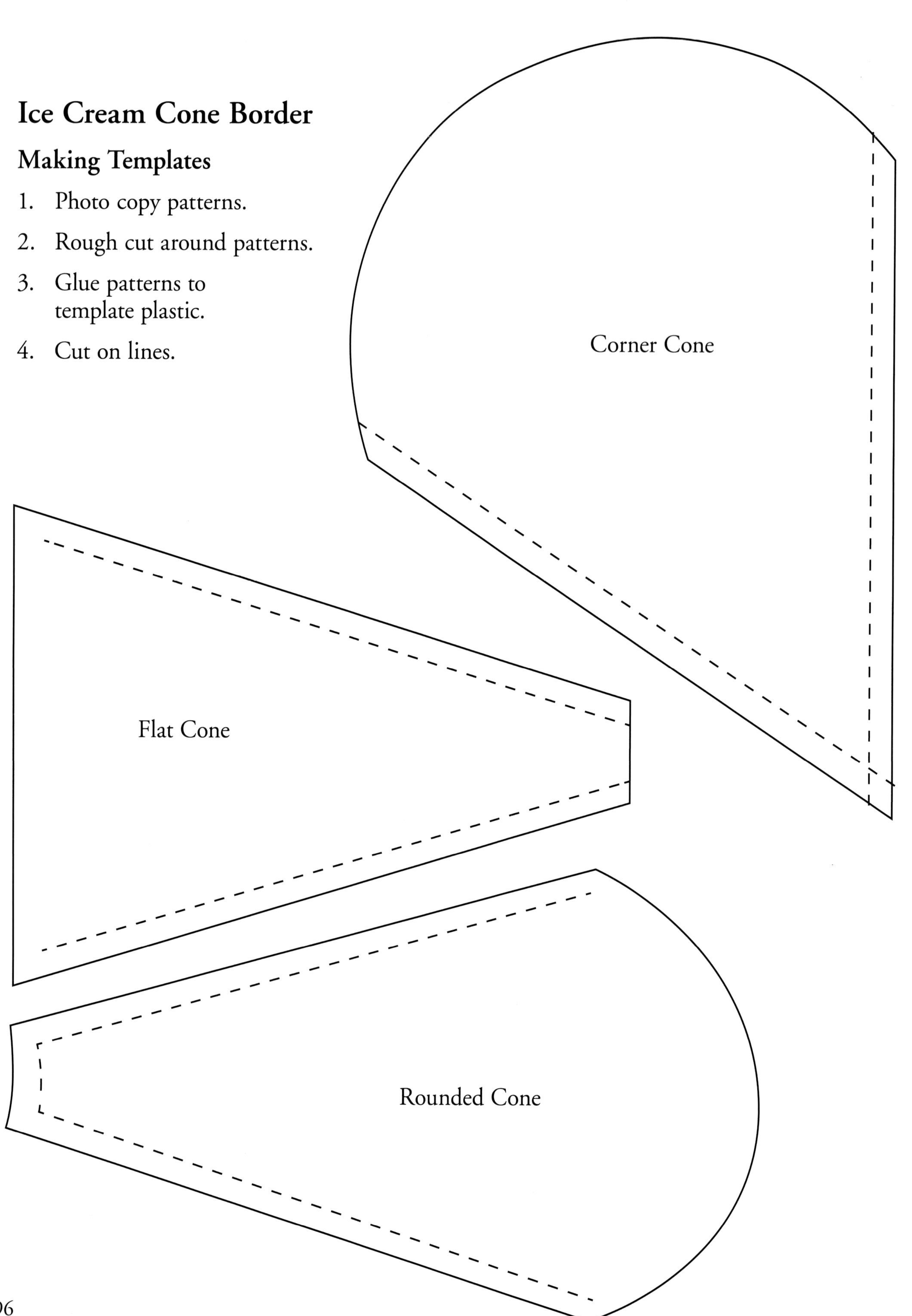

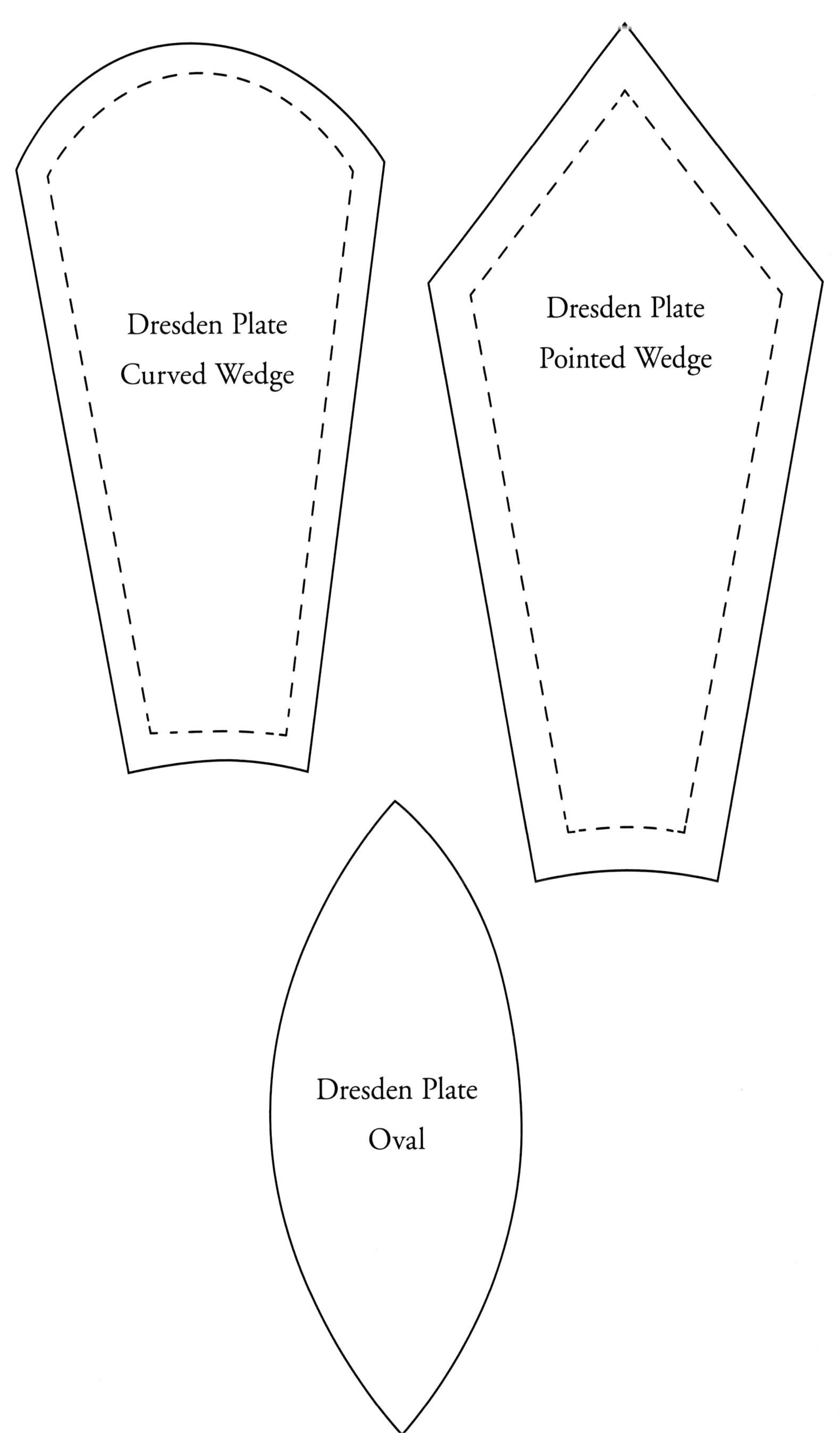
Dresden Plate
Curved Wedge
Dresden Plate
Pointed Wedge
Dresden Plate
Oval

Index

Confetti Seas
Pieced by Eleanor Burns
Quilted by Merry Jo Rembold
48" x 48"

Notice how the bright red pinwheels give movement, like the rolling seas to Eleanor's Ocean Waves quilt. For her color palette, she mixed her bright, cheerful colors for dazzling effects.

Visit Our Website

Watch Eleanor Online Free on our Media Theatre!
View *Quilts from El's Attic* Block Party taped monthly in 2014 with a live audience in the Quilt in a Day Studio. You can also watch many of our previous television series free on our Media Theater. www.quiltinaday.com/theater/library.html.

Facebook

Join the Fun on Facebook!
Download free patterns, participate in our contests and giveaways, and join in on the conversation on our Facebook Page. Be sure to share your finished blocks from El's Attic quilt!

Order Information

Quilt in a Day books offer a wide range of techniques and are directed toward a variety of skill levels. If you do not have a quilt shop in your area, you may write or call for a complete catalog and current price list of all books and patterns published by Quilt in a Day®, Inc.

Quilt in a Day®, Inc. • 1955 Diamond Street • San Marcos, CA 92078
1 800 777-4852 • Fax: (760) 591-4424 • www.quiltinaday.com

Purple Passion *42" x 45"*
Pieced by Patricia Knoechel
Quilted by Amie Potter

Patricia loves purple in all shades and her delightful wallhanging is proof! She embellished her quilt with a lace doily for her English Flower Garden and added ribbon bows to her Fan Baskets. Her creamy scalloped border framed with purple binding complete her display with charm.